SCHENECTADY'S
GOLDEN
ERA

(BETWEEN 1880 AND 1930)

By

LARRY HART

Old Dorp Books
195 Droms Road
Scotia, N.Y. 12302

First Printing...1974
Second Printing...................................1975
Third Printing 1976
Fourth Printing 1995

ISBN = 0-932035-02-7

This Book Dedicated to the Memory of

William B. Efner Sr.
City Historian 1946-1962

When a Feller Needs a Friend   :   :   :   :   :   :   : By BRIGGS

CONTENTS

PREFACE

$\mathcal{S}$chenectady has a long and unique history which goes back to the period of the French and Indian Wars in America, but what is presented here is a nostalgic glance back to the years between 1880 and 1930 and some of the events, big and small, which took place in the community during that time.

Schenectady celebrated its tercentenary in 1961, recalling the settlement of the small fur-trading outpost by Arendt Van Curler and 14 other patentees in 1661. In 1948, a Dutch kermis highlighted the sesquicentennial observance of its becoming a city in 1798.

Historians may disagree, as indeed they are so inclined when assessing periods of human endeavor, which era of Schenectady's history was most meaningful in terms of impact on its total growth structure. Some may argue that the stubbornness of the Dutch settlers in rebuilding and persevering after the terrible French-Indian massacre of 1690 put Old Dorp on the map to stay. Others may insist the construction of the Erie Canal by 1825 and advent of the railroads in the 1830s transformed Schenectady from a "sleepy little Dutch town" into a mercantile center almost overnight

For our own part, we remain convinced that the 50-year period we have chosen for this segment of Schenectady's history is the one which, up to the present day, most influenced its development as a second class city. The span from 1880 to 1930 was kind to Schenectady. It saw the growth of new industry and an almost unbelievable surge in population (in 1910, the city's census figure of 72,826 had more than quintupled that of 1880).

Social and physical characteristics of the one-time predominantly Dutch and English settlement changed drastically as attractive employment opportunities drew other nationalities to the city and its environs. Many were "fresh from the Old Country" as whole families of Irish, Italian, German, Jews, Scotch, Polish and Scandinavians gravitated straight from the New York port of immigration up to Schenectady, which had since become known as the Electric City. Ethnic communities sprang up within the city and, especially after the electric streetcar routes were expanded, out in the suburbs which in time were incorporated with the city. Some of these exist yet today — such as the Italians in the First and Second Wards, the Poles in the Ninth Ward, Germans on upper Albany Street, Scandinavians in Scotia and the Irish in the 12th and 14th Wards — although not nearly so prevalent as at the turn of this century.

Schenectady today is typical of America's "melting pot." Almost every nationality of the world is represented, succeeding generations now generally integrated in both neighborhood and family structure but with a continuing pride in their old world stock. Witness some of these social organizations which organized here nearly a century ago and flourish yet today: The Ancient Order of Hibernians, Sons of Italy, United Scottish Organizations, Jewish Community Center, Schenectady Turn Verein, Hungarian Benevolent Society, Polish National Alliance, etc. Naturally, in the ensuing years, Schenectady has been blessed by the contributions of its citizens of varied ethnic background in terms of public service and civic enterprise.

As we approach a 70-year span from 1930, there is a tendency to declare it a disaster from the point of view that so much was lost from the vitality engendered by the previous half century within Schenectady and its environs.

Of course, the Depression Thirties did little to enhance the beginning of this new era but changes were inevitable, just as surely as there is a new dawning — and sometimes a rainy day after a sunny one.

The stories which will follow tell of many grand happenings in Schenectady between 1880 and 1930; and those who remember some of these happenings are only too aware that "the old order changeth, yielding place to new." Gone are the trolley cars which blossomed forth in 1890 and enjoyed a fantastic popularity until they were phased out in the 1930s by buses and motor cars. Big and beautiful hotels, such as the Mohawk, Edison and the Van Curler, prospered with the splendor of that era — only to fall victim in recent years to auto-oriented motels. Likewise, the big movie houses and neighborhood theaters provided in-town entertainment which amazed its patrons through the gamut of the "flickers" to the "talkies" and now only the Proctors Theatre is left as theater-goers now frequent the drive-in movies and suburban cinemas. What of the recreation parks which made their mark after the turn of this century on a public which once found them exhilarating? All gone by the 1930s, closed and then torn down for lack of patronage.

Changing times also have taken a toll of the railroads, which passenger business in recent years has dipped to all-time lows. The repercussion of this has been keenly felt in Schenectady, first with the closing in the 1960s of the American Locomotive Co. which began locomotive manufactory in 1848 and then the razing of the railroad station that had been opened with much fanfare in 1908 adjacent to the Edison Hotel.

The first Great Western Gateway Bridge was among the last monumental contributions of the 1880-1930 period as it was opened to the public in December, 1925, and dedicated the following June with a week-long celebration. It, too, is gone, replaced by a new Western Gateway that was opened to the public exactly 48 years later on Dec. 19, 1973.

Throughout the first half of this century, Schenectady was called "The city that lights and hauls the world" because of the output of the General Electric Co. and American Locomotive Co. With the demise of ALCO, it has lost that title officially, although the phrase was rarely used anyway after World War II. However, as GE continues a strong influence in the industrial world, Schenectady still is referred to as "The Electric City" — in addition to the affectionate term "Old Dorp, from the Dutch word for "community" or "village."

If the foregoing paints a picture gloomy and desperate for the City of Schenectady — especially in contrast to the brightness of the era at the dawn of this century — it may be well to keep in mind that it takes only a few bold strokes of the artist's brush to change the whole concept.

Schenectady has suffered the growing pains of a different age along with most cities across the length and breadth of America. It has undergone extreme changes in social behavior and custom which could not help but alter the course of many things once thought permanent by older generations. Who would have imagined 50 years ago, for example, that the total population of the five towns would some day outstrip that of the city in Schenectady County as it did by the 1970 census? The trend to suburban living has caused all sorts of hardships to the urban mercantile trade, public transportation and the city budget itself.

But now, as we present in the following pages a potpourri of stories representing Schenectady's pivotal growth span between 1880 and 1930, may we hasten to point out that there is every reason to believe that another, and perhaps greater, period of redevelopment is on Schenectady's horizon. This city, like many others in the United States today, is finding ways to cope with the metamorphic structure of an age-old phenomenon called progress. The finished product may not be the one many of us grew up with, but who can say it will not be better in many respects?

– Larry Hart
December 10, 1995

PART ONE
Growing Pains

A view of the Schenectady Gas Works, probably in the 1880s, shows the round brick gas holder which stored manufactured gas primarily for illumination at that time. It was located on present Broadway nearly opposite the market square. The gas company purchased its property from James Fuller, a Schenectady lawyer, whose home can be seen in left background at the end of Lafayette Street.

1—Gas Industry Comes of Age

The use of manufactured gas for the purpose of illuminating streets and homes became increasingly popular in this country prior to the Civil War. True, only prosperous commercial establishments and sumptuous homes could afford the luxury of gas fixtures at first; but the old kerosene lamps, with their hand-painted globes or smudgy chimneys, were being relegated to attic storage in the average household before the beginning of the 20th century as the brilliant gas mantle became a practical convenience.

The technology of manufacturing coal gas in large quantities was still in its infancy when out-of-town capital became interested in Schenectady as a gas prospect. That was 1851, the same year that John Ellis organized the Schenectady Locomotive Works below College Hill. The city's population was only 9,000, but Robert Clements and John Eaton, who came here from New York as representatives of a gas firm, envisioned it as "a community which is ready to bloom."

The Schenectady Gas Works began operations in a plant built along South Center Street (now Broadway, opposite the market square) on property purchased from James Fuller. It consisted of several brick buildings, including a gas manufactory, storeroom and office, a stable and a round brick structure used as a gas supply tank capable of storing 20,000 cubic feet of gas.

Up to 1890, gas was used for illuminating purposes only. In that year three gas ranges were installed in Schenectady homes, the beginning of another new household convenience which gradually replace the old-fashioned coal and wood ranges. Gas customers in 1894 numbered a meagre 403; but by 1900 there were 1,511 and by 1930 more than 30,000!

There was a new awakening in Schenectady after 1890. Up until then, it had remained a quiet canal town with unchanging streets and buildings, the locomotive works or "big shop" being its main industry. But then, almost with lightning swiftness, the city was caught up in a maelstrom of activity that carried it into a new century with modern ideas. All of a sudden there seemed no end to the industrial development and technical improvements in the area.

With Schenectady as its headquarters, the General Electric Co. drew men of wide professional reknown who also took part in the city's civic life. Many of these same men — foremost of them being Thomas A. Edison and Charles P. Steinmetz—fostered projects such as electrification of the city streets, pushed plans for more schools and annexation of outlying wards to the city.

GE became so profound an influence upon Schenectady's business life, in fact, that between 1892 and 1904 the company actually controlled the interests of a number of corporations. J.P. Ord, a vice president in GE's Schenectady plant, was president of the Schenectady Railway Co.

The railway officials in turn supervised operations of the Mohawk Gas Co. and the Schenectady Illuminating Co. (the latter having first been organized as the Westinghouse Illuminating Co. in 1886, the city's first electric light company).

Thus for 12 years there existed a situation which today would be decried by antitrust advocates. Still the business flourished and citizens marveled at the initiative and ambitious plans of them all.

Trolley cars and extensive belt lines sprang from nowhere, brilliant arc lamps brightened the gloom of night along main streets, gas stoves were being installed in homes and cost of service was getting cheaper (gas in 1854 cost $4 per 1,000 cubic feet; by 1920 it was $1.50). No one could complain. The question was — what else is new?

GE's direct influence over the railway firm ended in July, 1904, when New York Central and Delaware & Hudson Railroads purchased the trolley lines. This was done to ease the effect of the competition of the electric cars on the Troy, Albany and Ballston routes.

After the railway company's interests were divorced from both the gas and electric companies, the two became separate entities but moved their offices to the second and third floors of the newly-built Parker Building in 1906. Several years later they consolidated into the Schenectady Illuminating Co. and in 1922 became part of the Adirondack Power and Light Corp., still later to be merged into the present Niagara Mohawk Power Corp.

In 1903, the Mohawk Gas Co. built a new plant on Villa Road (the site still occupied on Broadway opposite the former Mica Insulator works). It still maintained the old plant opposite the market square as a service center until the 1930's.

The company began construction of a new gas storage holder early in 1903. It was to be the smallest of the three huge steel towers on Broadway. The Seneca Street gas holder was erected in 1934, removed in 1961.

The first metal tank, completed in July, 1904, replaced the original round brick storage holder in the first plant. It was capable of storing an unbelieveable 800,000 cubic feet of manufactured coal gas — 40 times that of the brick holder built in 1851! The reason that the first metal tank was built, according to a gas company official in 1904, was that "the demand for gas is such that it has been necessary to pump the supply direct into the system as soon as it is manufactured."

There is an interesting sidelight to the story of the construction of that first metal tank on Broadway, the smallest of the three opposite Mica. As it neared completion in the spring of 1904, two GE photographers (one is believed to have been Otis Lawyer) arranged with the construction crew to build a makeshift platform midway up a section of steel girder that had been used to lift metal plating to the top of the structure.

The vertical boom was secured in two places at the south rim of the 125-feet high tank so that from a distance it looked like two matchsticks tied together. The steelworkers thought the two photographers were crazy, but up they went anyway, crawling another 50 feet up the swaying metal girder with camera and tripod until they reached the platform.

So it was that on a spring afternoon of 1904, the first aerial photograph of the sprawling GE works was taken. The picture was published—14 columns wide — in a special edition of the Evening Star on Wednesday, May 11, 1904. There was also a picture of the two men atop the tank, captioned "Photographer's Daring Feat in Making This Great

Picture Possible."

In September, 1960, wrecking crews moved in to reduce to rubble the old brick "round house" to make room for the Ten Eyck Apartments on the east side of Broadway. Along with the other old buildings in that block, the 109-year-old structure had become expendable.

The three metal gas holders on Broadway near Weaver Street were demolished in the late 1950s. They were no longer needed because of the adequacy of natural gas transmission facilities.

2—The Industrial Reawakening

*S*chenectady was never the same again after Tom Edison came to town. That was back in the summer of 1886 when he decided to move his dynamo manufacturing plant out of New York City, away from the high rent gouging of the big metropolis and the frequent interference of labor and political bosses.

The noted inventor, now drawn into the business of manufactory in order to market his products, had set up the Edison Machine Works on New York's Goerck Street in 1880 but was dissatisfied with its troublesome operations. So, in the spring of 1886, he dispatched three agents — one to Pennsylvania, one to New Jersey and another to upstate New York — to scout for a suitable site to move the factory. A combination of circumstances served to favor the ultimate choice of Schenectady, which in turn would prove a boon to the city's fortunes.

A man named Harry M. Livor was the agent who was sent upstate. He had not been impressed by what he had seen until he happened to look out the coach window of a train which chugged along the Broadway hill overlooking Schenectady's "big flat" along the Mohawk River. There in the distance he saw two lonely, deserted factory buildings in the middle of a large tract of land.

These were the two buildings which had been intended to make up the plant of the McQueen Locomotive Works, started in 1885 when Walter McQueen, plant superintendent of the Schenectady Locomotive Works, had a falling out with his boss, company president Charles G. Ellis. McQueen had obtained local capital to start the new factory and the two brick buildings were completed except for the roofs when his principal financial backer died, halting the project. By the time Edison's man passed through the area, McQueen had patched up his differences with Ellis and was back on the job at the other end of town.

Livor couldn't wait to get back to New York to report to his superior that he was certain he had found just the spot that Edison was looking for — a place with room to grow and in a city well endowed with transportation facilities.

Without a doubt, there were few among the approximate 15,000 residents of Schenectady at the time who might suppose that the community had anything bigger in its industrial future than as a place where locomotives were built. The Schenectady Locomotive Works down at the north end of town was the one large scale factory which employed several thousand people and was known as the "big shop." Several small plants continued to manufacture brooms and brushes from the broom corn which grew in abundance along the river flats on either side, there were a few smithies and a machine shop in operation and the few mills which produced knitted goods, muslin and cotton ware about rounded out the city's industry. Electricity was still a marvelous but unknown scientific phenomenon at the time and there was little thought of it influencing Schenectady's tranquil life style on the day that Livor was hurrying back to New York City to tell Thomas Alva Edison, inventor of the incandescent lamp, that he was certain he had found a spot for Edison's electric machine works.

Edison subsequently sent one of his top officials, Samuel Insull, to inspect the buildings and to inquire about the selling price.

The first mention of a possible sell of the property appeared in a newspaper May 23, 1886. The story said merely that "officials of the McQueen Locomotive Works said this morning that there was hardly a doubt the works would be sold shortly in such a way that the owners and the city would be the benefactors." They added that George Place of New York City was in Schenectady the previous day and made an offer which could not be accepted. Place, it was stated, came as "a representative of New York capitalists."

The McQueen works had gone into receivership and an appraisal of the property placed its value at $45,000. The Edison firm had shown a real interest in the site and serious negotiations soon got underway. But a hitch developed which threatened the refusal of the machine works to move to Schenectady. Edison thought the asking price too high. He offered a final sale price of $37,500 and would not budge from that figure. Not a little drama emerged from those few weeks preceding the deadline imposed by Edison as several leading businessmen of Schenectady stepped in to end the impasse and have the New York firm settle in the city.

Eighty-two Schenectady citizens and businesses contributed to a civic fund started to raise the necessary $7,500 by June 2, 1886. Edward Cohen described the final effort to reach the goal before midnight of the zero hour. At that time, Cohen worked for Jonathan Levi & Co., wholesale grocers. Both Cohen and Levi were perhaps the hardest workers among the merchants on State Street. Cohen told it this way:

"It was a very hot summer afternoon in 1886. I was in my shirt sleeves. It was so warm I went out in front of the store to get some air. The Mohawk Bank was next to us. N.I. Schermerhorn, Charley Thompson, Sam Jackson and Bob Furman were standing in front of the bank and as Mr. Levi came out of the store, also in shirt sleeves, Colonel Furman turned to the group and said, 'We have all the money subscribed except the last $500 and we must get that today or we are stuck. Mr. DeRemer (lawyer John A. DeRemer, the receiver) is in New York waiting for a telegram from me.'

"Upon hearing this, Mr. Levi told Colonel Furman he would give $250 of the needed $500 and Furman said he would give $250 in addition to the amount he had already subscribed. The colonel told Mr. Levi that the Edison works would employ 100 by October and in three years another 1,000 workers. 'Why we will have another locomotive works at the other end of town,' he said."

It is interesting now to note some of the names of State Street merchants who subscribed to the fund to get the new industry in Schenectady. The largest donors were John DeRemer, Barney & Co., Jonathan Levi & Co., Colonel Furman, all $500, followed by subscriptions of $200, others $100 and $50. The largest number of subscribers were in the $25 bracket of which there were about 40, mostly the small shopkeepers on lower State Street from Ferry Street up to the canal.

The day was saved. DeRemer got the go-ahead signal from Schenectady and he soon passed the word on to Edison's associates. The sale of the McQueen works was formalized within two days.

On the early morning of Aug. 20, 1886, Edison arrived in Schenectady from New York and checked in for breakfast at Given's Hotel adjacent to the railroad depot. A few civic leaders and a reporter for the Schenectady Daily Union got word of the inventor's visit and talked briefly with him on the veranda of the hotel. Edison told them about his plans for the McQueen buildings and that he had come to "look over my ranch."

He went down Dock Street alongside the canal and inspected the two unfinished factory buildings just beyond the Westinghouse farm machinery works which lay to the south of the Washington Avenue canal bridge. The vacant structures looked quite desolate, situated in the middle of a large field, partially surrounded by a white picket fence.

One may wonder, in those moments when Edison inspected the property he had just purchased, whether he might have envisaged the kind of operation which in a few years would take place on that site. Likely not the sprawling GE plant which in another two decades would have spread across the vast river flat acreage and made Schenectady a world renowned Electric City. He may, however, have been looking ahead to more than a factory which built electric generators, rather to an experimental laboratory and power plant to meet the demands of the oncoming electrical age.

Those who later worked at the Schenectady plant became familiar with the sight of those two original factory buildings on the Central Avenue, not far past the main gate. They were Buildings 10 and 12. A bronze plaque was later placed at the front entrance to Building 10 which read: "In this building, and in the building to the right, Thomas Alva Edison established the Edison Machine Works in the year 1886. From this small beginning grew the Schenectady Works of the General Electric Company."

It was in June, 1971, that the company decided to tear down Building 12, which had been used in later years as a storage facility. In the late summer of 1986—ironically the 100th anniversary of the founding of GE — Building 10 was demolished. Many parts of its were salvaged, however, for possible use in construction of a historical display center.

It took awhile to get things organized at Edison's new plant in Schenectady. William B. "Pop" Turner, an expert millwright, was one of the first of Edison's men to arrive here. It was his job to get the two buildings finished and to supervise the setting up of the machinery that was brought up from the New York factory. Other men, such as Charles Batchelor, a former shop superintendent at Goerck Street, and John Kruesi, who had built the first model of Edison's phonograph and heard it "talk back" to its inventor, came to Schenectady to supervise the opening of the new plant. (Kruesi Avenue, leading into Electric Park on lower Broadway, was named after him).

Before the fall season of 1886 had gotten underway, the people of Schenectady were aware that a most progressive enterprise was taking shape down at the former McQueen site. Hiring was taking place and more and more families were moving into Schenectady and its environs.

The Edison Tube Company and the Edison Shafting Company were formally merged into the Edison Machine Works before the year was out which made the whole operation much higher than had been imagined when Edison purchased the Schenectady property. By the end of December that year, the Edison Machine Works was in full operation...and there was well in excess of the 100 employees predicted by Colonel Furman six months before.

In the next few years, there began a period of industrial amalgamation which saw the relatively small Edison Machine Works grow into a maturity that thrust it into worldwide renown. And as it took place, Thomas Edison retrenched into his one and only love, the scientific laboratory. He was less in command of the big factories and international marketing, but he had made an extraordinary impact on the growth of the electrical industry — perhaps not entirely of his own volition — and now was only too happy to return to Menlo Park and pay full attention to where his ingenuity might do the most good.

In 1889, the shops of Bergmann and Company, makers of lamp sockets, switchboards and wiring devices, were moved to Schenectady after a consolidation and the Schenectady works that year became the Edison General Electric Company.

The year 1892 was the hallmark in GE's history, the year when the competing firms of the Brush Company, Sprague Electric and the enterprising Thomson-Houston electrical plant at Lynn — holder of the valuable transformer patents which unlocked the whole field of alternating current — were consolidated with the Edison works and became the General Electric Company. Charles A. Coffin was chosen unanimously as president of the new company.

E.W. Rice Jr., a Thomson-Houston man, was made technical director, and it was through his insistence that GE in its first year as a consolidated company purchased the Yonkers firm of Rudolf Eickemeyer and thus enlisted the services of a young electrical engineer by the name of Charles P. Steinmetz.

In less than six years, the amazing development of the Edison works into a huge electrical industry vaulted the fortunes of Schenectady into a prominent niche of a new era. Big names, important industrialists moved in and out of the city as skilled and unskilled labor were hired in increasing numbers. For a locality that had heretofore known only one "big shop" and an unchanging tranquility, the emergence of General Electric in 1892 as an industrial giant fairly shook the Dutch town from its lethargy.

During the early growth of the company, the living quarters for workers, both shop and office, were wholly inadequate. Hotels for boarders were hastily built near the works and many residents opened their homes to boarders. A few of the early hotels were the Globe Hotel on Van Guysling Avenue, Wiencke's at Liberty and Center Streets, The Curtis House on Washington Avenue, Twoomey's Hotel on Broadway at Kruesi Avenue and the Gilmore House at 89-94 Washington Avenue, owned by Fred Auchenpaugh and his wife, Ruby. In later years, their son, Fred, told of the lunches his father fixed for GE workers and which were delivered each noon to the main gate in a horsedrawn wagon.

"We sold about 250 lunches each day," he said. "They were 25 cents and consisted of two slices of bread, a platter of meat, potatoes, a cup of vegetables, an apple or banana pie, hot coffee, milk or beer and a cotton napkin."

But then the expansion began, probably starting with the electrification of the trolley lines (by GE) in 1891 and the spreading out of its routes into outer parts of the city and gradually to other cities. GE took over control of the transportation company, as well as the city's illuminating company, by 1898. General Electric also fostered the plan to make available for its many executives an ideal residential area by esablishing the GE Realty corporation shortly before the turn of the century. Many wooded acres of land were purchased just above the Union College campus and homes which then cost between $30,000 and $50,000 were built on spacious lots. It is still known today as the "GE Realty Plot," that picturesque section of Schenectady bordered roughly by Wendell Avenue, Nott Street, Parkwood Boulevard and Union Street, now a qualified historic district.

The Edison Hotel was built by 1900 and the Mohawk Hotel by 1907. But in the meantime, the so-called suburbs of the city also mushroomed with new housing along the trolley routes. The incredulous on-rush of settlement in Schenectady, due mostly to the economic climate engendered by GE, resulted only a few years later in the city's incorporation of such sections as Bellevue, Woodlawn and Mont Pleasant into its taxable limits.

Men's clubs soon were formed. The Mohawk Club was chartered in 1886 and rented quarters on Liberty Street just east of Barney's store, moving into the present club headquarters at Church and Union Streets, the old Union Classical Institute, in 1903. The Mohawk Golf Club built a course and clubhouse on Lenox Road in 1898 and moved out to its present Troy Road site in 1904. For the test men of GE, the Edison Club was formed with club rooms on the third floor of the previous Gazette Building on State Street, a short time later building a new headquarters (still standing) at Washington Avenue and State Street and developing a golf course in Rexford. The GE Women's Club bought a fine residence at 32 Washington Avenue, giving it over to the Schenectady County Historical Society in 1959 where it is presently located.

Down at the GE plant, progression continued at the same dizzy pace. Dr. Willis Whitney established the GE Research Laboratory (today known as the Research and Development Center at the Knolls) beside the main gate in 1900. The names of noted scientists and laboratory specialists who worked there and brought fame to GE because of their work are almost too numerous to mention — but a few who come to mind are Dr. Whitney himself, Dr. William D. Coolidge, Dr. Irving Langmuir (Nobel Prize winner in 1940), Dr. C. Guy Suits, Dr. Katherine Blodgett, Dr. Vincent Schaefer and Dr. Ivar Giaever, who won the Nobel Prize for physics in 1973.

Dr. Charles P. Steinmetz and Dr. E.F.W. Alexanderson were outstanding contributors to electrical engineering patents credited to the parent company. Martin Rice inspired the formation of Radio Station WGY by 1922 which promoted the new slogan, "Schenectady, the city that lights, hauls and tells the world." The work of Dr. Walter R.G. Baker, vice president and general manager of the GE electronics division, formulated experiments in the television medium in the 1920s and when a GE television station was formed in 1939 it bore his initials, Station WRGB.

General Electric today has plants spread all over the U.S. and parts of the world, but its main plant continues to be the Schenectady works — which in 1886 started from two unfinished factory buildings that, but for the effort of a nucleus of citizens in raising the necessary $7,500 to meet the purchase price, might never have become a reality.

A 1923 portrait of George R. Lunn as he looked when he served as lieutenant governor in the Alfred E. Smith administration.

3—The Lunn Era in Schenectady

The period just before World War I was a period of direct importance to Schenectady. There already existed an ethnic mix of families and there was a rapidly expanding economy and population with such industries as General Electric, American Locomotive and the Schenectady Railway Co. booming.

With it came the municipal reform movement of the early 20th century and one of the most interesting figures to emerge from Schenectady's urban reform of that time was George R. Lunn.

He dominated Schenectady politics for the greater part of a decade with a flourish that the old town had never before seen and may never see again. He was elected mayor four times, twice as a Socialist and twice as a Democrat. Later he became a congressman and then lieutenant governor of the state, both as a Democrat.

Ask anyone who has been around Schenectady for 70 years or more what he thought of Mayor Lunn and you may be certain the response will not be without an emphatic opinion — one way or the other. There is no denying that George R. Lunn had a flamboyant nature in all that he did and said, but neither was he shy about becoming involved in a great many issues when it might have been much more comfortable to avoid them. In short, he set himself up as the "great crusader," which was enough in that pre-World War I era to win him many friends along with a host of scoffers.

Lunn was born on a Iowa farm in 1873 of Scandinavian lineage, worked his way through Belleview College, Nebraska, and then came east to study at Princeton University and Union Theological Seminary. He was ordained in the Presbyterian ministry in 1901.

Shortly after, he became associate pastor of the Lafayette Avenue Presbyterian Church in Brooklyn, then met and married a wealthy Brooklyn girl, Mabel Healy, daughter of a man known as the "Leather King of the World." It was about this time, in 1905, that he received the call to come to Schenectady as pastor of the First Reformed Church.

When the Lunns came here, the family had three children — George Richard Jr., Mabel and Betty. Born later at the Union Street parsonage were Raymond and Eleanor (later to become Mrs. Carroll "Pink" Gardner). Mabel, Betty and Raymond are now deceased.

The new minister of the influential Dutch church was a striking looking man, of medium build and wavy brown hair which turned prematurely gray in a few years to give him an even more dignified look. But it was his gift of oratory, his ability to capture human emotions with colorful phraseology which won him attentative audiences. He was, as many were to discover, a strong-willed man who did not accept the premise of defeat easily, rather taking swift and drastic action to win his cause.

In the beginning, his sermons in the big church at Union and Church Streets expressed concern with social questions. Late in 1908, however, disgusted with growing corruption in city government, Dr. Lunn became increasingly specific in his weekly sermons, citing various scandals and officials involved.

The church consistory, composed of many community leaders,

took umbrage at Lunn's charges and requested his resignation. Although urged by the congregation to remain, the young pastor submitted his resignation at the end of 1909. This, in effect, began what was to become known as the "Lunn Era in Schenectady," a period which stamped Lunn as a man of controversy, a man of action.

After leaving the First Reformed Church, he took two very important steps which launched his political career: He formed his own church and he founded a newspaper.

Dr. Lunn and a nucleus of supporters who left the Dutch church organized a non-denominational church called the Peoples' Church. For a time, they rented, of all places, the Mohawk Theater which was a burlesque house, for Sunday morning services (this building later became the Hudson Theater, used mainly for stock company shows in the 1920s and 1930s).

Within a few months, the trustees of the Jay Street Congregational Church approached Lunn with the idea of merging into the United Peoples' Church and he and his followers agreed. Then began a brief period of bickering and dissatisfaction as former members of the Jay Street church claimed they were being "ousted" from their own church. They charged that Dr. Lunn used dictatorial methods in installing his own people in responsible church positions and in denying them free use of the building. This led to court tests and, in the end, resulted in the formation of the Pilgrim Congregational Church on upper State Street.

In later years, the old Congregational church building opposite the present Jay Street parking lot of the post office became the home of the Trinity Presbyterian Church. In the late 1950s, this congregation built a new church on Swaggertown Road known as the United Trinity Presbyterian Church and the former United Peoples' Church building was torn down to be replaced by a two-story brick-faced commercial building.

Also, in the spring of 1910, Dr. Lunn founded the weekly newspaper, "The Citizen," backed by the local Socialist party. He was now publisher and managing editor of a news organ which at the outset had as its chief aim the promotion of socialistic ideals and to do battle with the local newspapers which did not treat those ideals kindly.

So, shortly after leaving the First Reformed Church, Dr. Lunn had a pulpit and a newspaper to use as sounding boards for his attacks on local government, cries against discrimination of the working class families and tirades against what he termed "wasteful and corrupt" political machines.

His sermons in the United Peoples' Church were really political talks advocating reforms. His editorials in "The Citizen" hammered on issues such as exorbitant rates of the Mohawk Gas Co., the high price and poor quality of street paving in Schenectady, the lack of recreational areas, increased interurban fares on the street cars and the excessive cost of repairs and construction at the Schenectady High School.

By now, Lunn was becoming well known in the Electric City. His church services were packed with non-member followers who saw him as the workingman's friend fighting City Hall graft which kept their paychecks low and taxes high. There were also legions of hecklers who hooted the pastor from the galleries during his hard-bitten sermons.

Dr. Lunn was a registered Republican, but naturally he was shunned by the two major parties as a mayoral candidate. After all, he had spared neither Republican nor Democratic officials in his sermons and editorials of the past year. What was more natural than that the local Socialists would ask him to be their candidate for the 1911 mayoral contest? They did, and he readily accepted.

On Nov. 7, 1911, Lunn was elected by a wide margin along with eight new Socialist aldermen. The city's Common Council was then comprised of 13 members, so the new mayor had a clear working majority to put his vaunted reform program into action.

Dr. Lunn came on the American political scene at a time which, for a man of his reformative leaning, was extremely opportune. There was a clamor for social and governmental reform in this country within the first decade of the 20th century. The Progressives, the Populists and the Socialists worked independently for such innovations as social security, a shorter work week, no child labor, initiative and referendum, income and inheritance tax, and government relief for the unemployed.

It was the Socialist Party's shining hour and it glowed especially bright in the national election of 1912 when it polled nearly one million popular votes for its perennial candidate, Eugene Debs. Woodrow Wilson reaped the benefits of the reform movement, which served to split the Republicans.

So when Dr. Lunn entered politics in 1911 as a Socialist mayoral candidate, he cast himself on a rising wave of popularity.

Realistically, Lunn was elected not so much as a Socialist as a reformer. He said he wanted economic, not radical, socialism to set things right in the city. "Socialism is progressivism," was his favorite slogan during his first political campaign and he stressed a thorough but peaceful return of the government to the people.

In commenting on the Socialist Party's victory in Schenectady, the Utica Globe described the new mayor as "by birth an insurgent, by temperament a fighter." Others called him a "renegade." The dictionary defines "renegade" as "one who deserts a faith, cause, principle or party for another." In retrospect, Lunn may have fit that description in a political sense only by the fact that he later left the Socialists to become a Democrat — but he could not be accused of deserting a faith, cause or principle once he had applied himself to them.

Lunn took over as Schenectady's first and only Socialist mayor on Jan. 1, 1912. He moved right into the mayor's office which in those days was located on the south front end of the city annex (which formerly housed the Ellis Hospital) next to the old City Hall on Jay Street. His administrative assistant for the first few months was none other than Walter Lippmann, then 22 years old and a Harvard graduate, later to become noted as a brilliant editor and political analyst. Lippmann was attracted to the Socialist Party ideals and he jumped at the opportunity to work within a new Socialist administration. He soon went on to New York City and greater things, however.

Lunn said he would be a full-time mayor and he kept his promise. As a matter of fact, his administration set out to accomplish the impossible — to try to do everything that had been promised by the Socialists in the 1911 campaign.

While the Republicans, Democrats and Progressives watched with wary eye and some envy, the Lunn administration accomplished the following during 1912 and 1913:

Improved the city water system.

Arranged better and cheaper paving on the city streets through a more rigid method of bid-letting.

Established the system of free trash collection in Schenectady.

Developed the market square off Broadway for the early morning marketing of farm produce.

Reassessed the real property in Schenectady, with the result that the downtown business district was upped by some $2 million while the working class homes were lowered collectively by about $300,000.

Established a program of consumer protection, which included the inspection of meat and dairy products.

Set up free maternity clinics and children's free dental clinics in the city schools.

Began a survey of the existing schools to ascertain the scope of the shortage of classroom space.

Organized a park commission for a survey of feasible park sites for public recreational facilities.

Reorganized the city welfare system which included the construction of public baths and lodging houses and operation of a municipal farm to provide free food for the needy.

Lunn, as a man of action, got into an awful lot of controversy and conflicts with leading citizenry and the courts. For example, he did not like it a bit when the laying of a new sewer line on Front Street was delayed in 1912 by a saloon keeper who threatened a law suit if the city cut down a fair-sized maple tree in front of his establishment. Lunn took matters into his own hands, going to the site of contention and chopping down the tree. Litigation which followed lasted three years and ended in the mayor paying a $300 fine.

He was dissatisfied with the postal service, noting "It is rather obvious that the Post Office is incapable of delivering the mail." Early in his administration, he got the city police to help with the postal operation until extra postal help was hired.

Mayor Lunn complained about the fact that the blue collar worker and his family were denied, among other things, band concerts where they could spend enjoyable evenings or afternoons for family recreation without spending a lot of money. He pointed out that the more affluent families had their country clubs and other private organizations but "for the poor, there is nothing but their front porch or backyards."

He tried to obtain use of the state armory for the concerts, but the state authorities said it was impossible. So, for a time, Lunn arranged for the leasing of the Mohawk Theater (where he once conducted church services) on Sunday afternoons, the cost to be paid from proceeds of marriage license fees at City Hall. In the end however, Lunn got his way. He pushed through a resolution in the Socialist-controlled Common Council for construction of a new and larger bandstand in Crescent Park, the cost of which was $17,000. Then there was no further need to rent halls.

Against the objections of most of the city clergy and many civic leaders, Lunn also permitted the movie theaters and baseball parks to open on Sundays the first it had ever been done.

He founded his own company, Lunn Associates, for the purpose of selling coal, ice, baked goods and groceries to the working class families at wholesale cost. However, he was to fail in this venture even though afterwards he proclaimed a moral victory for "showing up some demagogues for what they are."

It was suspected that some political leaders (not of Lunn's party) encouraged a local merchant to bring suit against Lunn and his company because they were doing business on city property — in the basement of the annex. In the trial that ensued in county court, and which went against Lunn, the mayor went a bit overboard in protesting the lawsuit and in downgrading his opposition. On the way out of the new courthouse that day, a friend warned the mayor that if he continued in that vein he might be held in contempt of court.

"That is impossible," Lunn said. "If anything, I am concealing my contempt for the court!"

During the initial campaign for more schools in the city school system (in which one of the slogans was "A seat for every pupil"), Lunn observed publicly, "What we need are more school books and less prayer books."

He was soon taken to task for this statement by a prominent churchman who declared that what the city needed most was the word of God.

"That may be very well, sir, but if you walked down the street clothed only in the word of God, I'd be forced to arrest you on the spot," Lunn shot back.

At first, Lunn tried the open door policy at the mayor's office but he soon found that he couldn't get much work done with a constant parade of well-wishers, office seekers and salesmen. Within a few months, he had an electrician install a buzzer system so that his secretary in the outer office might screen his callers and buzz him only if they had legitimate business to discuss.

There were frequent Socialist gatherings, often up at Crescent Park but sometimes on Clinton Street in back of City Hall. It is said that Lunn attended the meetings at every opportunity, to speak to the people and sound them out on city problems his administration might have missed. On one occasion, he ended a grandiose address with the question, "And now. my good friends, is there anything that is troubling you . . . anything you might be in need of that we can provide?"

A voice came loud and clear from the back of the crowd, "What we need is a saloon on every corner!"

Mayor Lunn involved himself in labor strikes anywhere in the area. He and some associates were jailed for a time up in Little Falls when they persisted in addressing the picketers on company property.

During the 1913 strike at the General Electric plant in Schenectady, Lunn worked long and laboriously trying to find grounds for a peaceful settlement. In time, he was successful, but not before he issued a stern warning to company officials not to bring in armed strikebreakers — a charge that may or may not have been called for. He was called a "publicity seeker" for this action.

During the strike at the American Locomotive Co., Lunn made innumerable visits to the company and to the picket lines. One early morning, as he was crossing the swing bridge over the canal at Nott Street, a company guard mistook Lunn for an unruly striker and threatened to throw him into the canal. Luckily, an Alco official come by and recognized the mayor — and an embarrassing situation was avoided.

It was mentioned earlier that Lunn was clever at colorful phrases.

During his 1911 campaign, he told the voters that "the Republicans will skin you up and the Democrats will skin you down."

In that same campaign, he called Charles Beckwith, Schenectady businessman and staunch Democrat, "King Charles I, King of the Paving Trust."

Toward the end of Lunn's first administration, in 1913, the Democrats, Republicans and Progressives formed a fusion ticket with J. Teller Schoolcraft in a successful attempt to oust the Socialist mayor. Lunn called this a "Succotash Ticket."

He was elected again in 1915 on the Socialist ticket but near the end of that term, he switched to the Democratic Party and in 1917 was elected Congressman. He had become disenchanted with the Socialists, mainly over the war issue. He favored the new draft system as the most equitable way of mobilizing an army for World War I. The Socialists were not only opposed to the draft but advocated draftees not to report and to resist the war effort.

When he split with the Socialists in 1917, his erstwhile party members pulled a Lunnism by referring to his new followers as "Lunnatics."

It was while Dr. Lunn was serving as a Congressman during World War I that he endeared, himself to the patriotic constituents of that period. He had broken with the Socialists who by now were reviled as anti-American because of the party's stand against the draft and any compulsory war service. The Socialists were called traitors to themselves, their country and even to Russia, although those few who were still in office around the country maintained they were fighting only for the freedom of the individual citizen and an utter disdain for war. Dr. Lunn, now a Democrat, disavowed any allegiance to war-time Socialist principles and said that while he. too, abhorred bloodshed, this was no time to preach abstinence of one's duty to his country.

In March, 1918, his pastorate at the United People's Church was filled by the Rev. B.G. Newton, who came from Granville. Dr. Lunn, it was announced at the time, would be expected to "preach at the church whenever he can arrange to do so."

That same month, much publicity was given the fact that a $2 million army warehouse facility would be built in Rotterdam and would employ several hundred people at the outset. It was constructed by authority of the quartermaster general of the U.S. Army, but in Schenectady the people were reminded that Congressman Lunn — as an influential member of the House Military Affairs Committee — was chiefly responsible for location of the depot in Schenectady County.

He served one term in Congress, then returned to Schenectady and was elected mayor — the third time — as a Democrat in 1919. He was reelected in 1921 by a comfortable margin, now having the support not only of many middle class families but also of prominent politicians.

In 1922. while he was serving out the first year of his fourth term as Schenectady mayor, Lunn was tapped by the state Democrats as the running mate for Alfred E. Smith, Democrat, who was trying a comeback against Republican Governor Nathan Miller that year. Lunn even had the backing of Charles F. Murphy, Tammany Hall leader, although some years before, Lunn had assailed Tammany domination of New York State politics and referred to that faction as "a slimy reptile." The Smith-Lunn team was elected.

While lieutenant governor, Lunn was a strong advocate of the state's development of its natural resources.

In 1925, Lunn was appointed state public service commissioner, a post he held (with subsequent re-appointment by Governors Roosevelt and Lehman) until his retirement in 1942.

He often told his friends, after taking the state position, that he missed the hurlyburly excitement of politics. He drove to his Albany office each weekday (once being involved in a near-fatal crash into the steel abutments of the railroad overpass on Central Avenue on the outskirts of Albany on Jan. 13, 1931) and returned home without being too much involved in local politics except for an occasional guest speech. He complained he was "out of touch with the people." It is not generally known that in 1928, Lunn narrowly missed being nominated for governor by the Democrats — nosed out by none other than Franklin D. Roosevelt. The ex-Schenectady mayor was embittered toward Roosevelt when, after it was agreed to have a wide open state convention, it developed that FDR had indeed lined up delegates to support his nomination.

However, this rancor later left him as Lunn saw the President practice his ideas on a national scale in the New Deal program.

After his retirement as public service commissioner, Lunn moved to California to enjoy a life of leisure. He had since remarried, his first wife having died several years before. He died Nov. 27, 1948, at Delmar, Calif., at the age of 75.

One year after leaving his job with the first Lunn administration, Walter Lippmann came out with his first book, "Preface to Politics," in which he dealt with the changing focus of politics and the reform movement. He did not refer specifically to the Schenectady administration, but there were frequent accounts of the trials and aspirations of a newly won Socialist majority in a city government which might well have been the result of Lippmann's brief tenure with Lunn's first term as mayor.

Perhaps Lippmann had his former boss in mind when he wrote of a typical reformist politician:

"Many people said he tried to be all things to all men, that his speeches and many of his actions were attempts to corral votes. That would be a left-handed way of stating the truth. A more generous interpretation would be to say he had tried to be inclusive, to attach a hundred sectional agitations to a reform program. "

Surely no one can deny that some exciting times emanated from that period of our city's history more than 80 years ago, when the

Socialists sought to justify their election. They were not always right and did not always succeed in their endeavors . . . but it was a refreshing time of action, quite devoid of the sort of "stand pat" politics that is rampant today in governments of all levels.

4—Steinmetz—The Electrical Genius

Schenectady was stunned the morning of Friday, Oct. 26, 1923. Word of the death of Dr. Charles. P. Steinmetz spread like wildfire around the sprawling GE plant, then overflowed into most areas of the city by mid-morning.

The gentle doctor had died peacefully in his fine brick home on Wendell Avenue shortly before 8, just as breakfast was about to be brought up to his second floor bedroom. Although he had been not feeling well for the two weeks following a train trip to the west coast, he had obeyed his physician's orders not to return to his GE laboratory until stronger and was not thought to be in even near critical condition from a heart ailment which had plagued him in recent years.

But now the news struck like a shock wave, set off by the telephone call which Joseph LeRoy Hayden, adopted son and laboratory partner of Steinmetz, dutifully made to the company plant minutes after Dr. H.P. Groesbeck made a last visit to his patient and friend of many years. He listed the cause of death as "acute dilation of the heart, following chronic myocarditis of many years standing, which is a weakening of the heart."

"Steiny dead . . . you don't mean it !" was the general reaction to the sad tidings. In a rush came fleeting but vivid mind pictures of the diminutive, hunchbacked Steinmetz riding his bike down Union Street, sitting intently behind the motorman of a GE-bound trolley car, greeting some visiting dignitaries down at the plant, being driven in his Detroit electric out to his summer camp along the Mohawk just west of Scotia, lecturing before a local group, contentedly puffing on his Blackstone panatela while he strolled the tree-lined grounds of his home in the GE realty section . . . these and many more recollections were stirred by the realization that, after 30 years, this most unusual personality would no longer be a part of the Schenectady scene.

Who was this man Steinmetz, who had such an impact on the industrial and civic life of Schenectady at the turn of the century?

Reams of copy have been written about him and his accomplishments; stories which grew out of his eccentricities, his brilliance and his humaneness were told and retold during his three decades in Schenectady and for generations after. Old timers, those who remember him whether by personal or casual acquaintance, delight in keeping those stories alive – even though some have stretched the truth.

When he came to Schenectady in late 1893 from the Lynn plant, from which the newly organized General Electric Co. had transferred him specifically to set up an electrical engineering laboratory here, there were few among the citizenry who could be aware that a rare jewel had just been placed in their midst. Several top GE officials knew, including E.W. Rice Jr., a future company president, who two years earlier had advised the purchase of Rudolf Eickemeyer's small machine shop business in Yonkers just so the company might have the services of a German immigrant by the anglicized name of Charles Proteus Steinmetz. They had knowledge of his uncanny talent in mathematical calculation and that he had already astounded the staid American Institute of Electrical Engineers with his Hysterisis Theory.

His Schenectady arrival coincided with the fourth anniversary of his entry into the U.S., having fled his native Germany as a young graduate of the University of Breslau for fear of political persecution by the Bismarck regime because of his socialistic ideals. If there had been such a poll that day in June, 1889, Steinmetz probably would have been voted "the one least likely to succeed" among all the aliens who had just disembarked from the French ship LaChampagne.

He was barely five feet tall, with a large head that seemed to have been forced upon a neckless and twisted torso. He knew only a word or two of English and had no money. Little wonder he was nearly deported before he reached the mainland – and would have been had not a friend intervened just in time and vouched for his ability to earn a livelihood.

So here he was, four years later in Schenectady, still the misshapen mite of a man and yet under vastly different circumstances. He was assured a top job with an industry that showed promise. His persistence in learning the English language quickly had paid off, earning him lecture engagements before the AIEE and other technical groups. At 28, he was ready to make his mark in the new and exciting world of electricity. . . and in the esteem of the citizens of the Electric City.

His experiments with "man-made lightning" in the early 1920s vaulted Steinmetz into worldwide public recognition and scientific acclaim. He was dubbed "The Modern Jove" and "Electrical Wizard." Those who knew him, however, said he took more pride in developing the alternate current system of electricity and in establishing an engineering department at GE that was second to none in this country by World War I. As for the publicity, he took it as a compliment and a boost for the electrical engineering field.

"This can be good for us, like a fisherman's shiny new lure," the mathematical genius said one day to a beaming GE official as they discussed a feature magazine article which told of recent technological accomplishments by Steinmetz and his department. "Now we wait to see what great young talent it brings in."

It was because of Steinmetz' reputation abroad, for example, that GE came into the services of Ernst F.W. Alexanderson, who later made his own mark in the field of radio and television.

Alexanderson, educated in his native Sweden and in Germany, came to the U.S. in 1901 before the ink was entirely dry on his sheepskin. He had read Steinmetz treatises on various electrical subjects and made up his mind to meet and talk with the author.

The young engineer was hired by GE in 1902 upon the recommendation of Steinmentz, who was impressed with Alexanderson's grasp of problems in the infant world of electricity. It paid big dividends to the industry, GE in particular, as Alexanderson reeled off a number of inventions that were patented by the company – a total of 321, to be exact, before his retirement in 1948. These included the first high frequency alternator for long distance radio transmission and the color television receiver.

Incidentally it was Alexanderson who in 1927 gave the first home demonstration of television in Schenectady, using high frequency neon lamps and a perforated scanning disc. He gave the first public demonstration of television in May, 1930 at Proctor's Theater in Schenectady.

By now, 1915, Steinmetz' engineering section had become known as "the Supreme Court of GE" and, indeed, aspiring mathematicians and electrical engineers were being drawn to it in the magnetism of worldwide renown. Any new electrical theories being developed anywhere in GE plants were first put to the test of utmost scrutiny by Steinmetz and his assistants – and only if they passed that test were they given the go-ahead sign.

The doctor's theory of sizing up the capabilities of his charges was perhaps best summed up in his statement: "If a young man goes at his work as a means to an end, like getting a raise in salary or making a million dollars, I am not much interested in him. I am interested, however, if he seems to do his work for the work's sake, for the satisfaction he gets out of it."

When he first came to Schenectady, he rented a room on Washington Avenue, then leased the big Charles Ellis house at Liberty Street alongside the Erie Canal crossing. By 1901, he moved into a wood frame house on Wendell Avenue which would become his laboratory in another three years when his three-story Elizabethan style brick home was completed (an addition, linking the main house with the laboratory, was built in 1911.)

Soon after he had taken over the large house, he adopted his "family." J. LeRoy Hayden, a newly married lab assistant, became his legally adopted son and the three children born to the Haydens – Joseph, Marjorie and William — became his foster grandchildren. To all of them, including Mr. and Mrs. Hayden, he was "Daddy" Steinmetz.

It was not a case of Steinmetz becoming a famous man by virtue of his reputation at the GE works and becoming engrossed in his profession. His hobbies were many and varied: horticulture, photography, boating, bicycling, reading, chess, gardening, motoring, lecturing, philately, nature study and Indian lore, among others. He loved to be around people, especially children, and would keep a visitor waiting (as he did Henry Ford one evening at the Wendell Avenue home) while he finished his bedtime story to the Hayden children.

Steinmetz never "sat" down. Because of his deformity, he would kneel on a chair or stool. When GE set up his office in Room 445 of the then new Building 2, he was provided with an expensive yellow leather desk chair. He never asked to have it removed but neither did he use it, preferring to stand at his desk to look over parper work before going back to the laboratory.

He really didn't smoke as many cigars as people thought, even though he was rarely seen without a stogie clamped between his teeth. The cigar often would be unlit as he pondered a problem or was deep in conversation. His favorite was the Blackstone light panatela, which was ordered six boxes at a time from a Boston firm.

He became very much involved in community affairs, especially after he had journeyed mysteriously down to Yonkers one day in 1894 – exactly five years after he had come to America. He returned home a full-fledged U.S. citizen, his face flushed with the excitement of the occasion.

Union College was anxious to engage him as a lecturer on electrical engineering and, with a special arrangement by General Electric, Steinmetz was able to fit this additional assignment into his schedule as a professor of electrical engineering – a post which he regarded highly and managed to keep until the early 1920s when the pressure of other duties forced him to become an occasional rather than a regular instructor.

His concern for educational opportunities for all children led him to seek election to the Schenectady Board of Education in 1910. Not only was he named to office but in a short time became board president. He at once set out to campaign for more schools ("a seat for every pupil" was his slogan), better playgrounds, free textbooks and lunch programs.

There was, of course, opposition to some of his demands but they were lessened considerably by the election of a Socialist mayor, Dr. George R. Lunn, and a Socialist majority on the Common Council in 1911. The city had more control over the city school budget and building projects in those days so naturally, Steinmetz, himself a Socialist, was delighted over the turn of events. He had every reason to expect more cooperation and help from the city administration in pushing for expanded school facilities – and he was right.

The lunch program and free textbooks soon were implemented, but the new buildings and the playgrounds were to be stalled for a few more years.

Mayor Lunn thought so highly of Steinmetz, he persuaded him to run for alderman in the 1915 election. Again, Steinmetz not only was elected but was made council president, which he held simultaneously with the school board presidency. Lunn assigned Steinmetz to the committee studying city parks development, which included the "vest pocket" neighborhood parks Steinmetz had so often advocated. In Lunn's absence from the city, Steinmetz was acting mayor.

As with most public figures, the stories about Steinmetz were legend . . . and many of them were untrue.

One said he refused to work in the GE lab unless he was permitted to smoke cigars in violation of the company rule. "No cigars, no Steinmetz," was his supposed ultimatum. An associate, still alive today, refutes the story, stating there never was any confrontation between Steinmetz and General Electric on the cigar issue. The company, on its own initiative, simply waived the no smoking rule in Steinmetz' case and he continued puffing his cigar as though unaware there was an issue at stake.

Then there was the tale that Steinmetz never was given a salary by GE, that he had a "blank check" privilege. His private secretary, Miss Celia Rhein, said he was paid a salary and, in addition, the company maintained laboratories for him at his home and at the plant. Whatever he needed at these labs in the way of equipment or supplies, the company provided without question. All of his findings were available for GE patent.

Another story had him tagged as an atheist. People often wrote him about this so Steinmetz prepared a form letter in which he set forth his religious beliefs.

He was confirmed in the Lutheran Church in his native Germany, but shortly after coming to America he joined the Unitarian Church. However, he avowed no individual should be deprived of his right to think for himself, even in religion.

"No man really becomes a fool until he stops asking questions," he said.

He was an active member of All Souls Unitarian Church here and often lectured in laymen's classes. The Hayden family, too, attended the same church.

Soon after moving from Liberty Street into his Wendell Avenue home, Steinmetz bought a 1907 Stanley Steamer but promptly drove it over a neighbor's lawn and shrubbery as he lost control. He had two battery-powered cars after that, including the celebrated Detroit Electric, but never trusted himself to drive. Either LeRoy Hayden or a lab worker drove while a serene Steinmetz lay across the back seat, smoking a cigar.

Often he would prefer to take the trolley to work and return. He boarded the workmen's streetcar at Rugby Road and Wendell Avenue which took him straight down to the main gate. A Schenectady Railway Co. motorman later recalled that Steinmetz always observed the no smoking rule on the company cars – but would never fail to light up once he alighted.

He wrote a great deal, explaining his experiments and deductions. He was a master at mathematics, his mind grasping the results of complicated equations and formulae before his pen could set down the figures. His writings were in a shorthand known only to himself and his secretaries. He devised the system about 1903 after he studied all available shorthand systems and found none of them to his liking. His publisher, McGraw Hill, was at first interested in the Steinmetz shorthand but later turned it down as "impractical for the average person."

Perhaps, most of all, he loved the frequent excursions up to his summer camp on Viele Creek (about opposite the Scotia Naval depot) which overlooked the Mohawk River and the Rotterdam hills. Much of his technical work was done here, either while he was drifting alone in a canoe or knelt cross-legged before the rough plank table on the porch.

He called it Camp Mohawk and invited one and all to visit and partake of his cooking and enjoy a glass of white wine or Jamaica rum. He particularly was fond of a veal loaf and a dish which he called "cuddle muddle," a kind of stew, cooked over an alcohol stove.

Steinmetz' whimsical nature was revealed in this eye witness story concerning the camp. When he had the porch addition built on stilts, precariously close to the creek, he wondered about its stability. One weekend he invited a large party of guests and had a German band serenade on the new porch deck. Naturally, the guests gathered around and the porch was full of people most of the evening. The next morning, the wily mathematician was heard to remark: "With all those people and with all that weight, I think the porch has been proved sturdy enough."

It was this camp, when struck by lightning, that began Steinmetz' investigations leading to the construction of the first machine to produce artificial lightning. The camp was dismantled in 1930 and rebuilt as a memorial at Henry Ford's collection of Americana at Dearborn, Michigan.

The late Emil J. Remscheid, formerly Scotia, especially remembered Steinmetz in connection with Camp Mohawk. He was still an undergraduate, working summers in the GE Engineering Laboratory, when he came to know Steinmetz as more than a patient, understanding department head. It was in the early 1920s and he had been invited on many occasions to join the camp festivities mostly on weekends. He personally chauffeured his host in the Detroit Electric a number of times (including the time when Steinmetz discovered the camp had been lightning-struck and excitedly dispatched Remscheid back to Wendell Avenue to get the camera) to the Glenville site.

Remscheid had other things besides his memories of Steinmetz. He had copies of the doctor's shorthand, a cigar box bearing Steinmetz' likeness (the GE wizard endorsed the brand as a favor for a local cigar maker, a brand known as Luzon Cigars, although he never smoked them) and a diary for the year 1923 – the year of Steinmetz' death. It was perhaps grimly prophetic that Steinmetz, upon leaving the camp for the last time in August of that year, finished the entry with, "Getting ready to go home."

Recollections of Steinmetz also have been shared by Miss Rhein, his Building 2 office secretary from 1917 until his death. When she was first assigned to his office in a secretary pool, she arrived there early on the appointed morning with some trepidation.

Miss Rhein had heard about Steinmetz being a "big man" by reputation long before she was given the assignment. Therefore, she recalls, she fully expected to see "a large man, six feet tall with broad shoulders" walk into the office. Instead, in came Steinmetz, small of stature and stooped with a spinal deformity. He looked at her a bit quizzically, introduced himself and said good morning.

One of the first things he told her was this: "All I want is good work. Never sacrifice accuracy for speed."

Miss Rhein recalls he was neat in his attire. He favored the color gray for his suits and sometimes wore a turtleneck sweater instead of a shirt and tie. His hair was cut in semi-brush style and his beard trimmed carefully. His black shoes, obviously polished when he put them on, often had traces of dried mud on them – the result of his having strolled through his greenhouse before coming to work.

He always said "What's new?" when he came in the door each morning, the same opening he invariably used to begin a conference in his office as he passed around a box of cigars. LeRoy Hayden also had a desk in Steinmetz' office. The floor was never waxed by cleaning personnel on strict orders because of the danger of Steinmetz slipping.

Often, in the margin of a letter he wanted answered, Steinmetz would write this instruction to his secretary: "Nice letter. Not too long. Not too short."

One of her fondest memories of Steinmetz is the quotation which he particularly liked and had framed and hung on one wall of the office. It read:

"The man who once most wisely said,
"Be sure you're right, then go ahead,
"Might well have added this, to wit:
"Be sure you're wrong before you quit."

Another Schenectadian with fond personal memories of Steinmetz was the late Nicholas (Nick) Dinardo. He was Steinmetz' barber from 1907 until 1922, the year he suspended his trade to take a job with the State Department of Engineering as an assistant on a "sweep boat" in connection with the building of the Great Western Gateway Bridge.

"He was a wonderful man," Nick recalled. "Sometimes he would want to talk a lot and I talk right along with him. . . but other times, he just sit in the chair with his eyes closed and then I leave him alone."

Nick remembered that Steinmetz' hair was dark at first with just a sparse amount of gray hairs in his whiskers. By 1920, the whiskers were totally gray and the head generously flecked with white. Steinmetz always wanted his hair quite short, but not in the typical German brush cut. "A little round on top," Nick said.

When he first started cutting Steinmetz' hair, Nick was a young apprentice working in a ground floor shop of the old Edison Hotel facing Wall Street later, he opened his own shop in the basement floor of the Mohawk Hotel.

Many boxes of Steinmetz' glass plate negatives exist today, a testimony to his scientific mind and expertise in all that he undertook. There are pin-sharp views of the river valley both in winter and summer, of circus parades and picnics. comparative shots of the effect of vari-colored light on growing plants and countless pictures of "the family."

Once he organized the Glenville Flying Club, when aviation became a serious topic following the successful flights of the Wright Brothers in 1903. Nothing much came of the experiments of these members as They sought to imitate the birds with "man-made wings" in the Glenville hills. However, Steinmetz managed to fool a lot of people for some time as he made a composite photograph – combining one with the aviator still on the ground but with wings spread and another of the sky just above the treetop fringe – the result of which was proof positive that a Glenville Flying Club airman had soared fearlessly over the wooded hill.

The golden age of electricity possibly was the 30-year period in which Steinmetz was with General Electric — from 1893 to 1923. The industry saw an astounding stride forward and the electrical profession was thrust in the forefront of modern science. Much of this development was due in no little part by the work of Steinmetz.

He was on top of all new theories and often looked ahead at what the future might hold for man and his environment. Many of his predictions, made in dissertations either before an audience or in magazines, were amazingly prophetic. He foresaw the use of air conditioning and electric ranges in homes, electric refrigerators and a form of television — as early as 1917.

Steinmetz was vitally concerned about air pollution and the excess use of coal and gasoline. He said the electric car was the auto of the future because "it runs cleanly and quietly and burns only rechargeable fuel."

In 1915, he wrote an article on energy of the future, warning: "Oil and natural gas will long have vanished, indeed they may be the first to go. Wind and tide and wave power may be used as far as possible . . . There is only one other source of energy left, and that is the energy of sunlight, but this is the greatest of all energies."

So this was the man whose death on that chill autumn morning brought grief to a city which had come to know him as a fellow citizen and friend. Eulogies were given throughout the day, and probably the most meaningful of them all was this statement released to the wire services by the man who brought the electrical industry to Schenectady, Thomas A. Edison:

"I regret very much to learn of the death of Charles P. Steinmetz. The world has lost one of the greatest practical mathematicians and the electrical industry will miss one of its shining lights."

Thousands came to mourn between 4 and 8 p.m. on Oct. 28, 1923, the Sunday following his death. A long and continuous stream of automobiles deposited men, women and children before the Wendell Avenue house. Trolley cars brought more and still others came on foot.

The body of Steinmetz lay in state in the living room of the big home, a room almost filled with flowers. They surrounded a dark mahogany casket in which the small form had been placed, clad as was his wont in life, in a familiar suit of gray.

On Monday, the day of the funeral, the public schools and Union College were closed as a tribute to Steinmetz. The city and county offices closed their doors at noon. At 2 p.m., the hour of the funeral, the huge GE plant here was silent for five minutes and the city trolleys stopped for two minutes.

The service inside the house was private and simple, attended only by the immediate family and a few personal friends. Rev. Ernest Caldecott, pastor of the Unitarian Church, officiated.

Thirty minutes later, the long funeral procession moved slowly over town to the Brandywine Avenue gate of Vale Cemetery and turned into the grounds to the family plot opposite the end of Columbia Street. Hundreds of people surrounded the roped-off area to witness the final rites of the 58-year-old electrical genius.

The house on Wendell Avenue was torn down in 1944 and a small stone monument at the end of the grassy plot now marks the spot where it stood. There had been much discussion at the time, and continues even now, that the structure should have been preserved as a memorial to Steinmetz.

That, however, seems besides the point. The legacy which this unpretentious man — a giant in his own right — left to the city and the realm of science is in itself a lasting tribute to his memory.

Radio in its earlier days was not just for the older folks, as this Gazette advertisement of July 18, 1923, attests. It was the ultimate thrill for young and old alike to assemble their own receiving sets and then tune in to the few radio stations that were broadcasting.

5–A Matter of Mystery

THE EARLY DAYS OF RADIO

*B*ack in the days before the magic picture box was introduced into the American home, when conversation was an accepted part of family life, radio was all we had and we were loyal to it. Many will recall this antiquated period, and doubtless just as many wish it offered the programming it once did.

Looking back on those days, it seems that radio's prime function was to provide entertainment on Sunday nights. By then family activities had concluded, the Sunday paper had been read and the dinner dishes were cleared away.

We're thinking back to the 1930s. Radio was not long out of its pioneering stage even then, but when the folks would tell of the head phones and "cat whisker" crystal sets, it seemed incredulous that they could have put up with such hardship. And before that no-radio. Just as a youngster today wonders how anyone got along without television.

Radio made as much of an impact on American life as the gramaphone had done before the turn of the century. In 1924, three million sets were purchased, compared with 60,000 only two years before. Most of the new sets were equipped with loudspeakers, but many earphones were still in use about 1930.

With the beginning of all-day programs in 1925 (the first network, NBC, began in 1926) the age was a cornucopia of long-dreamed-of marvels: the automobile, the airplane and now the radio.

Radio also lightened the burden of the Adirondack Power and Light Corp. (forerunner to Niagara Mohawk) in the public relations field. Since 1910, the power company had arranged to flash election results (and some heavyweight fights too) by a preannounced signal. . .such as, in the 1920 presidential elections, one blink of the lights for Harding and two blinks for Cox, whichever candidate won. The signal was repeated at one minute intervals for about 10 minutes. There were many residents who stayed up far into the night on some occasions, waiting to catch the signal.

In November, 1925, the public utility issued an official announcement that it had decided to discontinue the practice of "signaling news" to its customers. Officials of the company gave as the reason surges on the electric equipment caused by the throwing on and off of the current were too great to be safely borne and sensitive equipment was jeopardized. Actually, the real reason was that the extra service was no longer necessary. Radio had arrived.

About this time, many fans were purchasing build-it-yourself kits, featuring the new superheterodyne circuit – which was considered a great step forward in radio, making possible marked increases in sensitivity and volume. However, it was during the 1930s that the big veneered consoles – some in combination with phonographs – found their way into many American homes.

The Sunday programs were something special. In the late afternoon we never missed "Moonshine and Honeysuckle," a half-hour series dealing with life in the Ozarks with characters named Clem and Gypsy Carter in the cast. Then came the Blue Coal thriller of "The Shadow," which included Lamont Cranston's weekly warning that "the weed of crime bears bitter fruit. . .the Shadow knows."

Comedy was an important part of a Sunday evening, too. Eddie Cantor sang of potatoes and tomatoes being cheaper so "now's the time to fall in love." Fred Allen was superb as the inquiring citizen of Allen's Alley in "The Salad Bowl Review." Graham McNamee was the foil for Ed Wynn, "The Perfect Fool." Later on in the Thirties, Jack Benny called Dennis Day "a stupid kid" and Phil Harris spoke disparagingly to Frankie the guitar player and Sam Spade asked Effie the secretary who took the bottle from his desk drawer.

For a time, Jack Pearl as "Baron Munchausen" and Edgar Bergen with Charlie McCarthy also shared popular Sunday night spots. When there got to be an excess of talent, some of the shows were shifted to prime time on week nights.

Between 9 and 10 on Sunday nights, a lot of schoolchildren duti-fully did their homework while the parents listened to the musical pro-grams, "The Studebaker Champions" and "Manhattan Merry-go-round." Then they might be allowed to stay up long enough to listen to Phillip Lord's production of "Seth Parker." The setting was imaginary, as was all radio fare, but listeners could visualize the gathering of friends at the Parker household for a Sunday social evening. It was partly religious, always with some hymn-singing and a prayer. The Captain usually told a thrilling account of a sea-faring adventure and boxed the compass right around to "Nor' Nor' East" in his booming voice. Cephas was a dull-witted but kindly character beloved by his neighbors. The show always ended with the guests singing a hymn as they left, their voices trailing off in the distance as Ma and Seth Parker listened at the doorway.

Sunday was the big radio day back then, but that is not to say the family totally ignored it the rest of the week. There were those favorite weekday programs such as "Uncle Abe and David" and "The Goldbergs" (as if a real radio buff could miss that episode, which usually began with Gertrude Berg as Molly Goldberg throwing open her tenement window and shouting, "Yoo hoo, Mrs. Bloom!")

Weekdays always started with the setting-up exercises, set to music, from 6:45 to 7:15 a.m. Then breakfast was eaten while listening to "Jake and Lena." After the kids were off to school and Dad went on his way to work, Mother could then settle down to her housework with sooth-ing morning programs like "Cheerio," a pleasant sort of format complete with poetry, music and bird-chirping. The housewife also had her 15-minute dramas to follow each day. They were the progenitor of the clas-sification, "soap box opera," simply because most of them were sponsored by a soap company. The titles spoke for themselves: "John's Other Wife," "Ma Perkins," "Mary Marlin," "Pepper Young's Family," "Love of Life," "The Guiding Light," "Bob and Betty" etc.

Radio had its big moments with sports fans. Every June, there was a heavyweight championship fight, usually from Madison Square Garden. One did not need a picture before his eyes, with Clem McCarthy at the ringside mike, to visualize Maxie Baer toppling the giant Primo Carnera

29

or Joe Louis keeping the crown by evening the score with Max Schmeling.

Then the World Series every October. What a thrill it was for baseball fans not accustomed to seeing their diamond heroes play (much less hear broadcasts) during the season and now to hear the radio account of the series set-to. Those who lived far from big league parks always followed the league races in the newspapers each day since the big networks did not begin airing play-by-play seasonal games until the early 1940s.

The Rose Bowl game, which in those days was the only post-season football game and the only "bowl" in existence, called for a gathering of sports fans on New Year's afternoon. The old Atwater Kent, standing upright in a corner of the living room with the soft greenish glow from its dial, was a friend indeed as all attention was glued on every detail of the big game being broadcast all the way from the west coast.

It was a harrowing and limited existence, growing up without television, but we managed to live through it all.

STATION WGY. . . ON THE AIR

Radio was still a toddling infant and very few people hereabouts had bought their first crystal set when Station WGY entered the field over 50 years ago.

At exactly 7:47 p.m. on Feb. 20, 1922, a young man named Kolin Hager stepped up to a microphone in a fourth floor room of the IGE Building and said: "This is Station WGY – W, the first letter in wireless, G, the first letter in General Electric, and Y, the last letter in Schenectady."

So on that Monday evening, with few people in the room except for the par participants, the station performed its first broadcast, lasting a full 63 minutes. It is not certain how many people listened to that program . . . only that those who did sat close to a homemade receiver, sliding coils of wire in and out, periodically shifting a "cat whisker" to a new spot on a chunk of galena in the hope of getting a louder signal in the earphones clamped to their ears.

There were no tried and true ground rules for these WGY pioneers to follow when they set up the broadcasting station. Announcers who soon joined Hager — such as A. O. Coggeshall, William Fay, Carl Jester, Edward Smith and Robert Weidaw — were known by initials alone, because announcers frequently "doubled in brass" as soloists, musicians and even actors in the dramatizations to follow. It was discovered that visiting personalities developed "mike fright," which was solved in those early days by covering the bulky microphone with a lampshade.

Acoustics was to become a problem, licked by the installation of heavy drapery around the studio and carpeting on the floor.

A native Schenectadian who took part in WGY's first broadcast and who remembered it well was the late Edward A. Rice of 601 Bedford Road. In fact, he was the very first "live" musician to perform on that station, playing a violin solo, "Romance," to open the program. His brother, the late Earl Rice, played a piano solo.

Was there an aura of excitement in the studio that first night?

"I don't recall that there was," said the veteran violinist. "We were all concerned with doing our very best. Afterward, though, when we realized we were sort of pioneers of radio, I guess then we got a little puffed up about the whole thing."

Rice recalled that his "fiddle" sounded like a "wet sponge" in that broadcast because of the monks' cloth that shrouded the studio.

His association with the radio station soon became permanent, as he was made musical director (a position he held for 35 years) and music program arranger. Many in this area will recall the Rice String Quartet, the Rice Ensemble and his popular musical offering of the live radio days, "Voices Down the Wind."

WGY was a pioneer in studio sound effects because it inaugurated full length dramas with the WGY Players, the early shows being fed to the early stations of KDKA of Pittsburgh, WJZ in New York and WRC in Washington, D.C.

In those days there were no recorded sounds of moving trains, whistles, bells, splashing water. In a 1924 presentation of "Pierre of the Plains," the WGY Players put realism into a scene in which two men were supposedly fighting amid dry leaves – simply by piling crumpled paper on the floor beneath the mike and having the principals grunt and groan while stomping amid the debris.

There were other sound gimmicks which seemed quite authentic over the air: A spectacle case was snapped shut for a gun shot, crackling cellophane was a raging forest fire, a hand fluttering through a half-filled tub of water for a swimmer, two pairs of roller skates moving back and forth over long pieces of metal placed on a studio table for the sound of a moving train. These devices were used for many years.

When Station WGY's license was issued on Feb. 4, 1922, it called for an output of 1,500 watts — a lot of power in those days. On May 8, 1926, the U.S. Department of Commerce authorized WGY to use 50,000 watts for regular operation, because by this time radio had become extremely popular as home entertainment. With its new power, and considering the airwaves were comparatively uncluttered at the time, WGY's signal reached out to many distant lands.

A few years after its initial broadcast the WGY studios and offices were moved to the lower floor of the IGE Building. On July 9, 1938, WGY's brand new studio building was dedicated at Washington Avenue and Rice Road (since torn down for the traffic complex in that area).

On the technical side the radio station served as the experimental laboratory where Dr. E. F. W. Alexanderson, Dr. W. R. G. Baker and other radio pioneers worked out equipment and techniques that later became standard in the industry. Also, as early as 1926, these men began experiments with the new medium of television. By World War II, WGY had a sister station — WRGB television station, which operated from the former Edison Club building at Washington Avenue and State Street alongside the Western Gateway Bridge.

In 1957 both WGY and WRGB moved to its present and imposing structure at 1400 Balltown Road. Also sharing the studios was WGFM, the frequency modulation station. Station WGY moved to Albany in 1994.

Today, 70-odd years since its inception, Station WGY has the distinction of being the oldest in the state. Two others, WJX and WDT of New

York had received their operating licenses a few months previous but they have since suspended operations. In fact, because of the high mortality among earlier broadcast licenses, WGY today stands as one of the 10 oldest broadcasting stations in the world.

6—The Banks. . .and How They Grew

$\mathcal{I}$t wasn't until 1807—146 years after the founding of Schenectady and nine years after it became incorporated as a city—that Schenectady got its first bona fide banking institution as the Mohawk Bank was chartered and opened for business in the same building now located at 10 North Church St.

How, one might ask, did the community get along all that time without a bank to handle its transactions and keep its collective wealth intact? A perfectly good question, at that, and the marvel is that the people of the new world colonies managed at all to keep any semblance of order to a monetary system that was grossly complicated in its shortcomings.

During the pioneer days of the late 17th century, traders dealt with Indian wampum, furs, copper and brass kettles, iron axes, knives, rum and cloth. Farmers traded produce for their household goods and grist mill services. The only "sound money" in circulation up through the Revolutionary War consisted of metallic coins—mostly British, French, and Spanish. During the Revolution, literally carloads of paper money were issued by the states and Congress, and the country was flooded with notes "not worth a continental" as the saying went.

There were issues of notes by individuals or by an association of subscribers who agreed to take out their share of the notes and to accept them in trade as the equivalent of money; but almost every bank note in circulation became subject to depreciation with the result that there was a widespread loss of confidence in paper money.

Probably the first crude attempt at banking in Schenectady was the construction in 1753 of an oak chest with a lock to hold the money of the community. This was in the care of the Collector, also called the Town Commandant or Magistrate. There was not, however, the facility for transacting a banking business and it virtually left everyone to be his own banker.

In 1791, two years after the inauguration of George Washington, a plan for a United States bank devised by Alexander Hamilton and approved by Congress was established in Philadelphia—and the way was paved for a safe and sane banking system in America.

Generally speaking, the most prominent currency used in Schenectady during the 18th century was that of the English. The "pound" referred to in early Schenectady history was the "York pound," worth about $2.50. In May of 1802, however, the currency in Schenectady was changed from pounds to dollars as the influence of the U.S. bank and its accreditation in principal cities of the new nation put local banking on a sounder footing than had ever before been possible.

Still, the city's first bank was not established until 1807 when the Mohawk Bank was chartered. It was founded by James C. Duane, who had already put Duanesburg on the map; his son-in-law, General William North, who also was George Washington's aide-de-camp; Lewis Farquharson, the prominent Scottish merchant; Henry Jr., John and Joseph C. Yates; James Murdock, the opponent of Thomas Jefferson, and Dr. Eliphalet Nott, Union College president.

The bank's first customers were the merchants, farmers and millers of Schenectady as well as the owners of the many stagecoach lines which were popular at the time. The early bank even financed the construction of Theodore Burr's suspension bridge connecting Schenectady with Scotia in 1808.

About 1820, the Mohawk Bank had outgrown its original quarters and moved into the new building at the northwest corner of Union and North Church Streets. It was designed by the famous colonial architect, Philip Hooker, who drew up the plans for many of Albany's first public buildings. The same building was used later by the Union Classical Institute and today is the home of the Mohawk Club. In later years the center of trade had gradually moved eastward on State Street due mainly to the building of the Erie Canal and the Mohawk and Hudson Railroad, so in 1857 the Mohawk Bank moved to its present location at 216 State St. This was the once familiar brownstone building, the facade of which was topped by a bronze Indian in a canoe. In 1956, the bank purchased the old Jonathan Levi building adjacent to the east and remodeled the interior and the whole front of the new facility. When it was removed, the paddling Indian was turned over to the Schenectady County Historical Society where it is now on exhibit in the society gardens.

Just as the Mohawk Bank was the city's first bank, it also became its only national bank for many years when in 1865 it officially became the Mohawk National Bank. Eventually, in the 1970's, Mohawk National became a Northstar Bank but now belongs to the Fleet chain.

The Schenectady Bank was established on the north side of State Street near Church Street in 1832, and two years later the Schenectady Savings Bank was chartered and conducted its business in the Schenectady Bank headquarters next to what was the Daniel Campbell mansion of the 18th century."

The two banks were closely allied for years after. In fact, by 1875 they moved "up town" to the Levi building opposite Wall Street and both banks had side-by-side operation with even a hallway between.

However, since 1905 Schenectadians had been accustomed to seeing the Schenectady Savings Bank where, as that institution has long proclaimed, "Clinton crosses State." The savings bank purchased a three-story brick structure at that southeast corner, now the 500 block, which had once been the Columbian Hotel and later the private residence of William Van Vranken. The building was razed in 1904 and by the following year the Schenectady Savings Bank moved into its permanent home.

In 1927, the bank purchased the Wallace Armer Building to the east at 502 State St. and enlarged its quarters both along State and Clinton. By 1955, the bank embarked on another expansion program, this time perhaps more ambitious than ever. It completely remodeled, enlarged and air-conditioned its facilities into a modern structure little resembling the 1905 model. In the past few years, it purchased the United Scottish Organization building (formerly the Daily Union building) and the former Union-Star building southward on Clinton Street for future expansion. Both of these structures were torn down in 1971. It was during the 1955 remodeling that a new time-temperature apparatus was installed on the front of the bank. This replaced the once familiar four-sided clock on the corner of the bank by which downtown shoppers had checked their watches for about 35 years.

By the late 1980's, the Schenectady Savings Bank changed its name to Northeast Savings, then to Shaumut and possibly to Fleet. This time it acquired more State Street property to the east, which recently housed Roth's Restaurant, and built a marble faced addition which complemented the existing building. It was opened to the public early in 1974.

We mentioned the Schenectady Bank, which had been founded in 1832 and moved up to the Levi building in 1875. It was on June 9, 1902 that the Schenectady Trust Co. was formed through the purchase of the assets of the Schenectady Bank and the new institution remained on the premises opposite Wall Street—where it is yet today. S. M. Hamill of the General Electric Co. was named its first president and there was a staff of 11 persons.

Schenectady Trust later purchased the property to the west which had formerly housed the savings bank. In 1919, it had built the imposing structure which is there today at 316-318 State St. The interior was modernized, however, after 1947 when Schenectady Trust Co. absorbed the Union National Bank which had been in business in a brick building next to the Gazette building since 1891.

The Schenectady Trust Co. again enlarged its interior in 1973 and not long after acquired the former Jonathan Levi Products building at the rear of the bank, enlarging it and renovating its interior as an office and computer center. It also became Trustco Bank with Schenectady's main office still at 320 State Street. It had purchased the small building to the west and also bought the lot to the rear of the bank which had once been the Olney Redmond gas station, thus providing a customers' parking lot with access to Erie Boulevard. Trustco, of which Robert A. McCormick is current president, maintains 12 other banking offices throughout the area.

The year 1889 saw the organization of the Schenectady Building Loan and Savings Association which opened for business at 118 Wall St. with Joseph Insull as its first president. The objective of this institution was "to provide a means for the regular, safe and profitable investment of the savings of its members, and by these savings accumulate a fund for the purpose of making loans to shareholders whereby they may be enabled to purchase real estate, to build or provide for themselves dwelling houses, to remove encumbrances therefrom and to accumulate a fund to be returned to members who do not obtain advances." An unusual and lofty plan but we must remember those were unusual times after the settling of the Edison Machine Works in this city. Workers and their families were flocking to Schenectady and good housing for a time was at a premium. The new bank was catering to those who longed to own their own home.

In 1938, Schenectady Building Loan and Savings Association moved into its new home at 267 State St. In that same year it changed its name to Schenectady Savings and Loan Association.

GIVENS HOTEL.

SCHENECTADY, N. Y.

Guests are hereby notified that the Proprietor will not be responsible for Valuables, Money, Jewelry, Etc., un
deposited in the Safe at the Office.

F. MITCHELL, Pro

Date.	Name.	Residence.	Time.	Room.
Friday Aug 20 86				
Thomas A Edison	New York City.	B		
J. H. Col	Albany M			
A. A. Buckle		D		

(1) The distinctive signature of Thomas A. Edison on the Givens Hotel register when he first came to Schenectady on Aug. 20, 1886. (2) The two McQueen buildings as they looked when Edison bought them in 1886. (3) Col. Robert Furman, one of the men responsible for Edison's move to Schenectady. (4) Part of the "lunch hour brigade" in 1902, when children brought hot meals to their working parents at GE.

*(1) GE main gate in 1910, with Bldg. 2's roof line being raised in center backround.
(2) Henry Ford, left, and Ge President Gerard Swope pose 1926 in front of Bldg. 10, one of GE's first factory buildings. It was demolished in 1986, while Bldg.12 had been torn down in 1971.*

(1) Walkout of GE employees Nov. 25, 1913. (2) Striking employees walking from plant along Dock Street. (3) Pay day on Nov. 28, 1913, during strike. Line stretches along Dock Street from State Street (foreground). Erie Canal in background.

(1) The old Givens Hotel, center, where Edison first checked in. Note railroad tracks at ground level on State Street. (2) Aviatrix Amelia Earhart at WGY mike on March 23, 1929. (3) Round-the-world flier Wiley Post, left, with Dr. William D. Coolidge, director of GE Research Laboratory, in 1933.

W.G.Y.   2/20/22.   1.5 K.W.

PM
7:47   Announcement WGY
7:48   Xylophone Record
7:51   Announcement of Program
7:52   Violin Solo Edward Rice Romance
7:59   Announcement "Carry me Back" Shannon Four
8:05   Shannon Four   Rosary
8:09   "The Shepherd Boy" Piano Solo Earl Rice
8:13   W.G.Y. Scotch Songs Mrs. Brownell "My Laddie"
8:18   "Comin thru the Rye" —
8:23   Shannon Four   "Annie Laurie"
8:29   "Spanish Dance" Earle Rice
8:35   Shannon Four "Little Tommy went a fishing"
8:39   "Song of India" Violin Solo Ed Rice
8:43   "Ave Maria"   Edward Rice WGY
8:50   Signing Off.

(1) Program listing for Station WGY's first broadcast, Feb. 22, 1922. (2) Young Joe Hayden, early radio buff, in photograph made by "Daddy" Steinmetz at Wendell Avenue home Sept. 19, 1921. Steinmetz titled photo, "Joe and his radio station."

(1) Mayor George R. Lunn at his City Hall Annex desk, 1912. (2) Mayor Lunn at Schenectady railroad station, 1912, on return from Socialist convention in Rochester. (3) Women Socialists at 1912 Crescent Park gathering. (4) Speakers on old bandstand during 1912 Socialist meeting in the park.

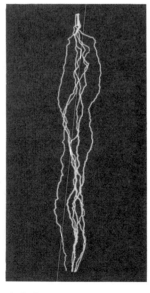

(1) Thomas Alva Edison, founder of GE, in his Menlo Park laboratory, 1916. (2) Dr. Charles P. Steinmetz in 1923, the year of his death. (3) Edison and Steinmetz during Edison's 1922 Schenectady visit. (4) Photo by Steinmetz titled "Static Spark."

(1) Steinmetz' Wendell Avenue home and conservatory. (2) The renowned "fake" photograph by Steinmetz which he titled, "Flying Ship in Mid-air (!)" (3) The cactus garden at Wendell Avenue.

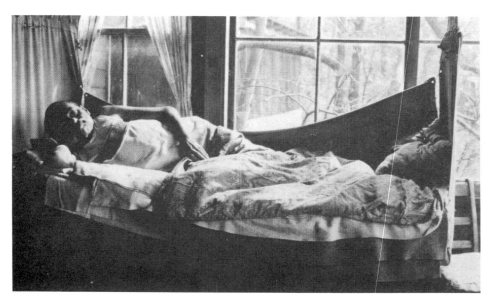

(1) At his favorite spot at Camp Mohawk. Steinmetz labeled this one, "I working at camp in cold weather, Sept. 22, 1921." (2) Resting on front porch cot that same weekend.

(1) Lt. Gov. George R. Lunn, right, and Ernst J. Berg, left, arriving at Wendell Avenue home for Steinmetz funeral Oct. 29, 1923. (2) Pallbearers carrying casket from front of home. (3) Crowd at Vale cemetery for final rites.

In 1959, it purchased the old Van Horne Hall property adjacent to the west and built a spectacular louvered front building extending from 251-263 State Street, complete with chimes. In recent years it is known as Schenectady Federal Savings that today stands at 261 State St. The former bank building next door was taken over by Citizens Trust Co. for its trust division offices.

The Citizens Trust Co. was organized in 1906 by William G. Schermerhorn who became its first president. It opened its doors for business on the ground floor of the Parker Building, still the tallest building in Schenectady as when it was built in 1906. A few years later, Citizens Trust purchased its present property next to the Parker Building (now Phillips Building) and opposite Jay Street and erected the fine bank edifice at that site.

In 1965, Citizens Trust was bought out on a merger by National Commercial Bank of Albany and so became known as the National Commercial Bank and Trust Company or sometimes, as "the Bank." It has since become part of the Key Bank of New York corporation, so now its Schenectady office has become Key Bank. Lester W. Herzog, of the Albany office, is president of the bank which has 60 branches strung along northeastern New York from Hudson up to the Canadian border. The First Commercial Bank, Inc. is the holding company.

Meanwhile, modeled along lines established by Arthur J. Morris, a young Norfolk, Va., attorney, the Morris Plan Co. of Schenectady was organized in 1916. Mr. Morris' idea was to found a bank that would specialize in individual borrowing and put it on the same basis as commercial credit in the business world. The first president was James P. Hamilton and the first offices were located at 512 State St. in the Schenectady Railway Co. terminal building. Four years later the bank leased premises at 131 Wall St.

In 1925, the Morris Plan Bank moved to 224 State St., which offices were enlarged and modernized shortly after it changed its name in the 1940s to the Industrial Bank of Schenectady. On April 1, 1965, the bank merged with the Industrial Bank of Commerce in Albany and once again the name was changed, this time to the Community State Bank with Clarence Visscher of Albany as president. Besides the lower State Street office, Community State Bank also has branch offices on upper State Street and Hamburg Street locally. In 1925, the Morris Plan Bank moved to 224 State Street, which offices were enlarged and modernized shortly after its name change in the late 1940's to the Industrial Bank of Commerce in Albany. Once again the name was changed, this time to the Community State Bank. Later it was taken over by the Key Bank chain but the original bank no longer exists. Incidentally, Mr. Morris, the man who founded the Morris Plan, died in November 1973, in his Virginia home at the age of 92.

Across the river in Scotia the Glenville Bank was founded to accommodate the banking requirements of that growing community. Frank Higgins was the first president. The bank opened for business on Dec. 3, 1923 in temporary quarters at 126 Mohawk Ave. and in 1926 it moved into its present main office location at 201 Mohawk Ave., corner of Ten Broeck St. The new bank building was officially opened for business on Jan. 28, 1926.

Like most area banks the growth was slowed with the coming of the depression, but the Scotia bank was never in danger of closing. In fact, to indicate to customers that plenty of money was available when the bank opened after the holiday declared by President Roosevelt, large piles of it were placed by each teller's window. An expected run on the bank never materialized and as the country moved out of the depression, the village bank continued its rapid growth. When Mr. Higgins died in 1936, J. H. Buhrmaster was elected president. On his death in 1952, Mr. Buhrmaster was succeeded in the presidency by his son, Kenneth E. Buhrmaster, a position he held until 1966 when Kenneth Lindsay became president and Mr. Buhrmaster became chairman of the board.

When the Scotia bank became a national bank in 1952, it changed its name to Glenville National Bank. However, with the thought of moving a branch bank into Niskayuna, the bank had petitioned to change its name to First National Bank of Scotia, a name it adopted in 1954 and continues until the present time.

Through the years, the Scotia bank enlarged its home headquarters, introducing for the first time in this area the drive-in teller concept so that customers could transact business without stepping from their cars. First National of Scotia now has five branch banks in the area. Louis H. Buhrmaster, son of Kenneth L. Buhrmaster, became president in 1969 following the retirement of Mr. Lindsay. Kenneth E. Buhrmaster is still board chairman.

The banking crisis which struck the nation after the 1929 crash was hard on the local banks—but all but one remained solvent after the Mar. 12, 1933 radio broadcast by President Franklin D. Roosevelt who said only sound banks would be opened after the bank holiday. All but one Schenectady bank were allowed to open on March 14. The one Schenectady bank to fail was the Capitol Trust Co., which had been located since 1925 in the ground floor of the Bucci Building at the northwest corner of State and Wall Streets. It was not able to guarantee payment to note holders and depositors. However, even though it failed, this much credit must be given the bank and its officers—Capitol Trust did manage to pay back about 95 per cent of its holdings over a period of a year and a half even though it was declared insolvent. Several other banking institutions of Schenectady helped during the crisis.

The above-mentioned banking institutions are those with long association with Schenectady and its suburbs. Of course, in recent years there have been several other "out-of-town" banks which have established branch offices in this area. In fact, Albany Savings Bank moved into downtown Schenectady in 1973 when it opened a modern, striking building on the State Street block bordered by Clinton and Barrett Streets, a site once occupied by the Lorraine Block, the old "Illuminating Co." building and the Barcli Theater.

With so many banks and varieties of banking services now available to Schenectadians, we might once again go back to the question asked at the beginning of this piece: How did the community get along at that time without a bank to handle its transactions and keep its collective wealth intact? How, indeed. Just ask any banker in town and he probably would shake his head in disbelief.

Lower State Street, corner of Church Street (at left), showing Simon C. Groot's dry-goods store at extreme right. He was also president of the new Schenectady Bank, next door to the left. Daniel Campbell's home of the mid-1700s is at left on corner, which building still stands.

The community of Rexford is shown beyond the aqueduct in this view of the early 1900s. At left background can be seen the old Grandview Hotel built by Jacob Ruppert in 1901 and which inspired the development of a recreation park in that vicinity.

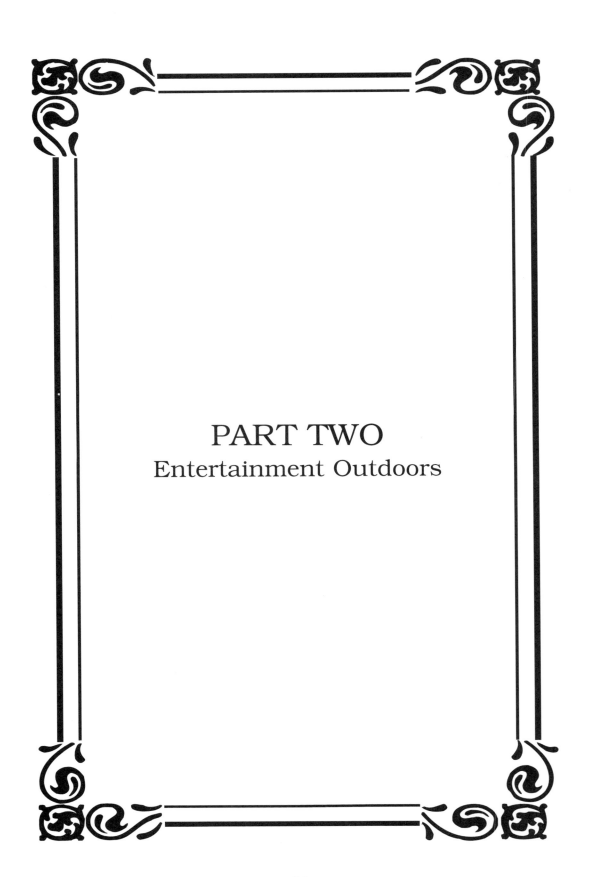

PART TWO
Entertainment Outdoors

7—The Park on the Palisades

It has been well over a half century since wrecking crews moved into the big amusement park in Rexford to begin dismantling the web-like contour of the roller coaster and the many wood-framed buildings which once formed a midway of family fun.

There are many who still recall the happy times and the excitement of boarding a trolley car in Schenectady which would take them out Aqueduct Road and over the steel bridge to Rexford and the park. Holidays meant something special for the whole family. On Labor Day weekend of 1908, for example, an estimated 10 to 14 thousand persons thronged Luna Park for a day of thrill rides, free attractions, ice cream cones, a picnic in the park grove, concession stand prizes. . .Lasting until ticket-takers closed their booths at 11 p.m.

All this, of course, was before the automobile widened the scope of family activity, before the depression of the 1930's slimmed the family paycheck.

It was first Collonade Park, Palisades Park, Luna Park, then Dolle's Park and, finally, Rexford Park until its dying day on April 3, 1935, when workmen began demolition of the buildings and roller coaster trusses. Down they came, and with them went an era of public entertainment that was robust, gay and exciting. It is certain that natives of this area who can hark back at least 39 years will have memories of Rexford Park (as most people referred to it, no matter what the owners named it). For three decades, Rexford Park was the place to go for weekend or holiday fun.

The park changed ownership a number of times from the day it was started about 1901 when Jacob Ruppert, New York City brewer, built the Grandview Hotel against the hill which faced Aqueduct across the Mohawk.

Improvements were made each time a new management took over. When the first roller coaster became "tame," a higher dip was built. Later on, in the mid-1920s, the original structure began to rot, so a bigger and more daring roller coaster replaced it in another part of the park.

It cost only a nickel to ride the open summer trolleys out Van Vranken Avenue at half-hour intervals and across the bridge to Alplaus, where the "Park Specials" would veer to the right for Rexford Park.

Back in 1908, there were not as many rides and booths as there were even a decade later . . . but there were more free attractions, such as the daredevil tank artists, the latest in "flickers," band concerts and public skill contests. Many a lucky man returned home on the trolley with a greased pig squealing in a crate propped on his lap—or maybe it was a rooster or a turkey that struggled to get out of a burlap bag.

The ladies, in ankle-length dresses, strolled up the concession avenues with their husbands or beaus, pausing at the Japanese Bazaar where they could win a set of china on the Pull-a-String gimmick, or the shooting gallery where masculine skill was displayed at "three shots for five cents."

Children flocked to the Penny Arcade, the aeroplane ride, the House of Mirrors, the boat slide and the merry-go-round. This four-sided building stood in the center of the park with entrances at all corners. It housed perhaps the most ornate carousel in the country. About 100 wooden animals glistened with bright enamel and imported glass jewels; the center piece was well built and heavy with a profusion of plate glass mirrors, gilt and hand-painted scenes. Four organs ground out such tunes as "Put On Your Old Gray Bonnet" and "Little Annie Rooney."

A man named Serafino ran the hot dog and lemonade stand. He was the park electrician in emergencies and had a habit of sticking a finger in a light socket to test for current.

Benny Simmonds, the park cop, stood for no unnecessary roughhousing and more than one young gay blade had his evening at the park cut short by this burly watchman. Once he stopped a fight by grasping the two belligerents by their coat collars and knocking their heads together. They left on the next trolley by his orders.

The amusement parks prospered until after the 1920s, when business began to decline. Some said it was because they had degenerated from family parks into rowdy and boisterous carnivals. The automobile was blamed by others, who claimed it took families farther from home to other types of amusement or for "rides in the country." It might have been the depression after the Crash of '29, motion pictures, radio, baseball parks or simply a change in family habits.

It was the same story with other area parks which offered family fun and thrills for two generations—Mid-City Park in Menands, Forest Park at Ballston Lake and Mohawk Mills Park in Amsterdam. Of course the renowned Sacandaga Park near Northville went out of business in 1928 for a different reason, the building of Conklingville dam and the reservoir. The parks gradually lost patronage and then the rides and booths were removed so that all that remained for a year or so were the pavilions used for public dances or clambakes.

Anyway, the last proprietor of Rexford Park—the Riverside Operating Company of New York — decided after the 1933 season that it was time to quit and pulled out its equipment. For the remaining two years of its life, Rexford Park was used for socials and clambakes.

The several acres of former park land of the Cyrus W. Rexford estate (to the left of the north end of Rexford Bridge) for the most part lie deserted and overgrown with brush and trees. There are still some of the pine trees which grew throughout the life of the old park.

A half mile to the west, at the foot of Snyder Road in Alplaus, a few limestone block piers remain as evidence of the crossing of what was once the longest trolley bridge in the world when it was built in 1902 expressly for the Saratoga run. The span was dismantled in 1942 when the country was in need of steel for the war effort.

On a summer's night, the gentle breezes which blow in from the river through the lofty pines in the old Rexford Park area often create strange far-off sounds . . . as though in the distance, if one listens real hard, can be heard the downward rush of a roller coaster, shrieks of excitement, the laughter of a happy crowd.

8—Central Park

$\mathscr{I}$t might be said that the actual beginning of Central Park was in 1912 when the Mayor George R. Lunn began his first term as Schenectady's "reform mayor" and avowed that one of the first things he intended to do was to see that the city had a park system .

Establishing a park system within city limits was set by Dr. Lunn as an early goal in his reform movement because, as he publicly stated, the "common man needs more relaxation from work. . . and there is little place around here where he can find it." The mayor pointed out that there were country clubs and golf courses for the affluent, but no large parks that were easily accessible to the blue collar worker and his family.

Mayor Lunn's request for a bond issue of $800,000 was brought before the newly organized council but failed to pass the necessary two-thirds approval as the minority questioned the advisability of immediate action. When it became clear that no agreement could be reached, after months of heated debate on the subject, a nonpartisan Commission of Parks was created by the mayor early in 1913. Appointed to this group were John R. Parker, Joseph H. Clement Jr. and Isaac L. Hotaling, who were each to receive $180 for their services.

Several months of study by the new commission showed that a rational beginning of a park system would require at least $300,000—and this figure, more acceptable to the council, was authorized.

The commissioner, assisted by planners, had conducted a survey of open land still within city limits which might be adaptable to park use. The survey report recommended that the city consider purchasing land in three areas — the old Cotton Factory Hollow which was then a wooded vale between the 7th and 9th Wards, the river front along the rear of Front Street and, lastly, the upper reaches of rolling hills and trees above McClellan Street.

Strangely enough, the site which was to become known as Central Park and would in a short time be developed as the city's principal park was least thought of by the commission as a desirable location. But it must be remembered that the city by 1913 was growing fast both in population and industry and the commission no doubt was fearful that the building boom would take away the vale in a short time and was aware that an alarming rate of "dumping" was taking place along the river front. On the other hand, the uptown site was still relatively free from builders' encroachment and was not centrally located, although it could be easily reached by streetcar via the "belt" lines or Albany interurbans.

At any rate, the parks commission set about to make land purchases on behalf of the city which were all ratified by the aldermen. In 1913, the Cotton Factory Hollow site of some 40 acres was bought from Charles Scott for $49,000. Shortly after, the Mohawk River frontage was purchased from landowners in that vicinity.

On April 10, 1914, the commission made the following purchase awards for what was to form the nucleus of the future Central Park: $59,850 to Henry S. DeForest for 62 acres; $46,850 to Edward D. Cutler for 42 acres; $23,500 to the Furman estate for lands just east of McClellan Street; and $8,750 to Chadwick-McDonald Realty for 16 lots, together with damages occasioned by the closing of streets. This initial park land purchase amounted to $138,950.

All of this left about $60,000 available from the original council appropriation for development of the park sites. The city hired Charles W. Leavitt, a landscaper of considerable reputation in the northeast U.S., to survey the three proposed park locations and advise the Commission of Parks on how best to proceed with development on a priority basis.

The upshot of this was that Leavitt, as it was reported, needed little time to commerce complete his survey and to make recommendations that (1) the uptown park be considered as the prime park goal, (2) put in access roads around a natural bowl which, because its marshy center was fed by a creek, could be made into an attractive lake, and (3) to eventually consider buying more land to the east towards Consaul Road before developers built new roads.

Apparently, the park commission and the aldermen followed his recommendations because an additional $100,000 appropriation was approved primarily to begin the development of what was to become Central Park.

By the fall of 1914, gangs of workmen from the city's engineering department, under the direction of City Engineer Thomas Wooley, had moved in and cleared timber for access roads and creation of a man-made lake.

Harold "Doc" Clowe, who started work with the engineering department in 1912, recalls the initial efforts to build the park. There were beautiful woods throughout, although quite dense with undergrowth in some sections. The area on Robinson Street hill was still farmland,with apple orchards and pasture lands for grazing cows.

When it came time to excavate for the park lake, it was found that the hollow was marshy and the soil that was being moved was on the mucky side. An agreement was struck between the city and Clarence F. Robinson, who owned 25 acres of land atop the hill in the vicinity of the present Central Park Junior High School, for an exchange of top soil. The park workers drew out the yellow blow sand from Robinson's hill known in those days as "huckleberry hill," and deposited the wet, dark soil along the ridge of what is today Bradley Boulevard.

Mr. Robinson settled in the area in 1880 with his new bride, the former Fannie Hadsel. It was considered part of Niskayuna at that time. Miss Cora Robinson, a daughter, lived in the old homestead at 410 North Elm St. It was torn down several years ago.

Just down the hill towards McClellan Street (in the vicinity of St. Clare's Hospital) was a slate quarry. Many of the old slate sidewalks of Schenectady, of which few are left today, were quarried there.

By 1916, when Dr. Lunn again became mayor after a two-year absence, the lake was being used principally for skating in the winter but swimming was forbidden because of the still-mucky bottom (children were allowed to wade in the lagoon however). Rustic bridges were built over the creek near the Wright Avenue entrance and a park administration office was constructed in that area. On May 12 that year, Superintendent of Parks Daniel J. Sweeney ordered 12 new ornamental street lights installed on Bradley Street and Wright Avenue to glamorize the approaches to the park. Flower beds were planted by the park crew and a wood-frame casino was built.

Delivery of 100 park "settees" was received from Sing Sing Prison, whereupon the city installed 65 of them in Riverside Park, 23 in Central Park and 12 in Fairview Park in Bellevue.

It is interesting to note that the naming of Schenectady's new parks was done by popular vote of the people as the Gazette, in cooperation with the city, consented to conduct a poll to determine which names were suitable to park users. This poll lasted nearly two months in the summer of 1915 as the newspaper ran a tabulation of votes for suggested names almost daily.

Some of the more popular names submitted for Central Park were People's Park, DeForest Park, Van Curler Park, Pearson Park and Columbia Park. . . but Central Park, which had been its tentative name from the beginning, prevailed by a large margin.

Before it was named Pleasant Valley Park, the Cotton Factory Hollow site had suggested names as Sunny Brook Park and Cantuquo Glen Park (after the Indian who was the first signer of the deed conveying land to Arendt Van Curler in 1660).

Riverside Park (since renamed Rotundo Park) was most popular, winning over such entries as Peach Park and Mohawk Park.

Pleasant Valley Park never reached the potential envisaged in those earlier days. Instead, after a mill pond was drained and a road built through its length from Broadway to Strong Street, the city began to use its south side as a dump. Of course, today it forms part of the Thruway Spur as Interstate 890.

Shortly after development of Central and Riverside Parks, the city turned its attention to land between Bellevue's Second and 11th Streets along Campbell Avenue and built what became Hillhurst Park as an adjunct to the tiny Fairview Park.

Central Park, however, soon became "the" park and the city took the advice of Leavitt by increasing the park acreage from the original 120 to about 260 acres. In addition, 210 acres were acquired and developed into the Municipal Golf Course.

In its first stages of development, Central Park boasted of clay tennis courts, hiking and bridal paths, a few picnic tables and benches and, of course, skating, boating and fishing on Iroquois Lake. But improvements continued to be made.

The eight-foot, five-inch bronze statue of the Spanish-American War soldier, known as the Hiker Monument, was installed in the glen near Bradley Boulevard during Memorial Day services the morning of May 30, 1921. At about that time, a beautiful fountain was installed near the center of Iroquois Lake featuring ever changing colors in the arching water spouts above the heavy concrete base. The late Allen Bailey, a GE engineer, designed the lighting system. He later was called upon to design the intricate lighting arrangement for Radio City Music Hall.

In 1919, a memorial gate was constructed at the park entrance opposite Wright Avenue by the widow of Henry S. DeForest, who instructed builders that no expense was to be spared in order to make it an appropriate memorial to her late husband. It was constructed of tapestry brick with two main posts topped by ornamental lights. Plans for the gate were drawn by E. G. Atkinson, a Schenectady architect.

Incidentally, DeForest – a prominent Schenectady businessman who was twice mayor of Schenectady and an ex-congressman—had a run-in with the city shortly after he sold his 62 acres for future park development, the largest single piece of property in the original park. Because of DeForest's harsh retaliation to testimony given by city witness James Veeder that his property was worth only a fraction of what he received for it, DeForest was sued by the city for $100,000 for criminal slander. However, both sides cooled off quickly and the lawsuit was withdrawn.

The first superintendent of the bureau of parks was W. D. Goodale, who served only until 1916 when the job was taken over by Daniel Sweeney. Fay Marvin became park director in 1938 when the Department of Parks and Recreation was established, and he was soon followed by William M. Leonard who made a number of marked improvements and innovations.

William F. Eddy, who succeeded Leonard in 1948 and served until 1970, also promoted additional facilities for Central Park – including the popular rose garden adjacent to the DeForest Gate and which replaced the tennis courts that had been moved to another section of the park. Eddy thought the park needed more attractions for the small fry, so he set up Tiny Tot Land, the motorized "railroad," a bird pen and a wading pool.

The original casino burned and was soon reconstructed between 1932-33 with labor paid by the Works Progress Administration. Improvements to that building, including a locker room for skaters, have since been made. Speaking of ice skating, Central Park's Iroquois Lake was the scene of several North American Speed Skating Championships during the 1950s under Eddy's direction.

Some of the improvements made after 1920 were the new tennis courts, a baseball diamond which attracted large crowds to Twi-Light League games during the 1930s and early 1940s (later a "B" diamond was added), horseshoe pits, a platform shell known as "Music Haven" which is used for all types of performances, a lily pond, on shore controls for the fountain lighting system, a soccer field which was especially well used and attended by throngs of spectators years ago, and a pavilion to be used by picnickers in case of inclement weather.

Obviously, Central Park has come a long way since it was in the planning stage 80 years ago. The extent of its public popularity today must exceed even the wildest expectations of those who had a hand in its creation.

9—The Fairgrounds

For about two decades before the turn of this century, there was an area not far above the Hamilton Street hill known as the fair grounds and which enjoyed the distinction of being the focal point of major entertainment while it lasted.

It was bounded roughly by Schenectady Street, Duane Avenue, Craig and Stanley Streets and was established by action of the Schenectady County Board of Supervisors. When it was developed about 1880, a high board fence was erected around its perimeter and a few stables and barns were built next to the fences. A neat oval track was laid out and covered spectator stands were put up near the finish line opposite the fair grounds entrance from Hulett Street. This was the outer fringe of Schenectady's growing urban section in those days. Once past Summit Avenue and the bowery woods, there were few residential buildings to the southwest.

The county's "poorhouse farm plot" was adjacent to the southern edge of the fair grounds, bounded by Craig Street, Brandywine Avenue, Emmett Street and Duane Avenue. It was on this plot that the county built its almshouse in 1901, later to become the headquarters of the Schenectady Museum. Today it is the site of the Dr. Martin Luther King Jr. School, built in 1966.

The old fair grounds were used for a variety of events. For instance, the Retail Merchants Association got permission from the county board to promote a fair on Sept. 2 (Labor Day), 1889 for the purpose of raising money to assist the Free Dispensary Building Fund. The Schenectady Agricultural Society also had authorization to use the grounds annually for its county fair and farm exhibits — a one-week event not unlike the county fairs of today, featuring farm implement displays, food booths, horse races, wagon pulling contests and stage entertainment. The circuses which came to town from May through August also used the hill grounds.

Louis Hutchinson was hired as groundskeeper for many years. He was paid $125 annually to keep the buildings, track and fences in good repair. A county board commerce committee inspected the grounds regularly to see that its investment was protected.

Then, by 1890, it became apparent that the growth of the city was such that the fair grounds would have to go. There was a petition before the board that year for an extension of Hamilton Street through the fair grounds to Craig Street. On Dec. 30, 1891, the county board requested that the state legislature act to enable the county to lay out streets through the fair grounds and to divide the land into building lots. The sale of the county land, it was pointed out, would make it possible to obtain a new site and erect a much-needed almshouse.

The state act was passed in 1900, authorizing the county to sell its poorhouse farm and buildings, the fairgrounds and its buildings. The poorhouse farm lay easterly of Craig Street, formerly known as "Factory Street" or "Factory Avenue" which led down the hollow to Archibald Craig's Cotton Factory.

The sale of the fair grounds buildings went at public auction – the barns and stables to the rear of the grounds, the small building bordering the racetrack (known as the judges' or referees' stand), a refreshment stand and a building known as the music hall were sold to the highest bidder and were hauled away in sections.

The circuses which came to Schenectady had to find a new site after 1899. They went up to Rugby Road and McClellan Street at first, but as this area also became settled, the tent shows shifted to a field on McClellan Street between the Plaza and Grand Boulevard (now the site of Linton High School). By the 1930s, the circuses went to Anthony Street, Campbell Road extension and finally to Ford Avenue in Rotterdam when Ringling Brothers-Barnum & Bailey gave its last outdoor performance here in 1956.

The need for more housing in Schenectady was quite evident by 1900 when the fair grounds were sold for real estate development. 'The General Electric Co. was hiring almost frantically as business boomed and new factories were going up; but along with this, new businesses were also springing up and the city's population rose steadily.

One man in particular saw the importance of this need and did something about it.

Samuel Dickhoff, a German immigrant who once clerked for Jonathan Levi's wholesale grocery firm on lower State Street, recruited a number of prominent investors and organized the Union Reality Co. Its prime objective was to develop the upper regions of Schenectady in those parts of the 7th, 8th and 13th Wards which once formed the spacious fair grounds.

The company bought this acreage and developed it into streets and building lots. Houses were sold before they were actually built, there was that much demand in the real estate market.

Dickhoff's firm built most of the two-family houses which still stand in that area today. This included the south side of Emmett Street from Craig to Steuben. Stanley Street, Delamont Avenue, Lincoln Avenue, Grant Avenue and the north side of Duane Avenue.

The late Mrs. Dickhoff recalled that she and her husband lived at 819 State St. while the home building project was going on. The last of the houses was completed about 1916. "Many times after he had come home late from the office, Mr. Dickhoff would walk over Hulett Street to where the new houses were being built to check on the joker stoves that were kept burning to dry the plaster walls," Mrs. Dickhoff said.

Samuel Dickhoff, who died in April, 1940, was supposed to have become a resident of Amsterdam when he came to this country from Germany in 1885. However, he "stopped off" in Schenectady, liked the looks of it and decided to settle here. He became a U.S. citizen in 1893. He bought the four-story brick building at the southwest corner of State Street and Broadway in 1913, and it has since been known as the Dickhoff Building. It was sold at auction by his widow in 1966.

The section atop Schenectady's summit, which overlooks the city to the west above Veeder Avenue, has undergone vast changes in recent years. There was a time, from the Revolutionary War times until the 1880s, when it was commonly referred to as the Bowery Woods. Large trees, mostly pitch pine, towered above the crest of the hill. What is now known as Hamilton Hill was once called Paige Hill because of the extensive property holdings of the Paige family.

Many homes that were built just prior to the turn of this century in the Hamilton Street area above Schenectady Street have been razed. A low income housing project for that section has been in the works for several years, but to date has not been implemented.

The Schenectady County almshouse at Emmett and Craig Streets in the 1880s.

10—The Circus Fire

$\mathcal{F}$or a scant five minutes on a May afternoon in 1910, the lives of nearly 12,000 persons hung in the balance as the circus tent which enveloped them suddenly burst into flames and burned like a mammoth torch. And yet, miraculously – and partly because some cool heads prevailed at the time, not one person was killed and only a few were injured, none critically.

This was the celebrated Barnum & Bailey Circus fire in Schenectady, still remembered and talked about today by some people who were youngsters in that matinee throng of so long and by others whose elders had been among the lucky survivors. It probably generated more excitement and conversation than anything that had occurred in Old Dorp since the Erie Canal was dug through the city in the 1820s.

Schenectady's rapidly growing population (75,000 in 1910 as compared to but 20,000 in 1890) looked forward with great anticipation to the much-advertised visit by the Big Top on Saturday, May 21, 1910, perhaps more than it had in many previous years. The show was ballyhooed as "the greatest ever" on the strength of Barnum & Bailey's opening season's performance in New York's Madison Square Garden in March that year. Advance sale tickets for reserved seats for both scheduled performances were at an all-time high.

It had been publicized that the circus would, as usual arrive at the Edison Avenue freight yards about 4 a.m. and that the rolling stock would soon be at the circus grounds to set up tents and concessions. The customary parade was to leave the grounds, just off McClellan Street and Rugby Road in the area now occupied by Phoenix and Van Curler Avenues, at 10 a.m. The parade route would be down Rugby, over Union Avenue and down Union Street, over Church Street and up State Street to McClellan and back to the grounds. A matinee performance was scheduled for 2:30 p.m. and an evening show at 8.

As it turned out, bad luck dogged Barnum & Bailey on this day. One of its circus trains, containing a few advanced cars, rolled into Schenectady about 1 a.m. — but it would be nearly 10 hours before the main portion of the big traveling show finally reached the D&H yards here. The reason: a wind-fanned grass fire along the railroad tracks just outside of Rochester, where the circus had just played, prevented the circus train from leaving that city after the last performance.

Once in Schenectady, there was unforeseen difficulty in getting the heavy wagons to the grounds. The reason: Edison Avenue was being widened and resurfaced and the wagons frequently were mired axle-deep in soft dirt. Heavy planking and elephants brawn pulled them out with great difficulty.

Throngs of people lined the parade route for hours, many of the families unaware of the late arrival of the circus, until they were informed well after the noon hour that the free show was cancelled. There was some grumbling, but all were assured that the two performances were still to be given on time and, as an added bonus, the animal tent was to be opened an hour early for public exhibition.

Matinee shows always drew families with children and so, on this

Saturday afternoon, there were probably as many youngsters as adults roaming the circus grounds and filing into the main tent as show time drew near. By 2:30, nearly 6,000 persons already were under the Big Top, waiting impatiently for the "Grand Entry" to start the performance. About then the ringmaster announced through his huge megaphone that there would be "a slight delay of about 10 minutes" before the show began. Hawkers were having a field day, selling their wares to a hot and thirsty crowd – a capacity crowd at that.

No one was ever certain how the fire started, but there were two "eye witnesses" with different versions. One claimed he saw a boy playing with matches below the bleacher seats, while the other said he was positive a man lit a cigarette and carelessly tossed a hot match into the folds of the paraffin-impregnated canvas from a top row seat in the north bleacher section.

At any rate, it was exactly 2:45 (and the performers were lined up outside the Big Top ready to make their entrance) when a group of men and boys suddenly leaped from their seats and with coats and jackets tried to beat out some flames which seemed to appear from nowhere.

Someone called "Fire!" and for a split second that big audience sat stunned. A frantic exodus of wide-eyed humans, who only moments before were grousing about the late show start, was underway as soon as a sheet of bright-orange fire ignited the north wall of the tent and by now roared upward toward the scalloped fringes of the roof.

At the time of the outbreak of the fire, a few latecomers were still strolling about the midway when a group of perhaps 50 people rushed from the main entrance of the Big Top. Someone asked "What's the matter?" A woman who was dragging her small child by the arm, glanced around with fear-strained features and uttered one word, "Fire."

The pell-mell rush to safety (men, women and children were screaming, pushing, dropping below the bleachers and scrambling from beneath the tent) might have been disastrous if it were not for the heroic efforts of Police Chief James W. Rynex, who was at the circus, and the men he quickly pressed into service. Rynex rounded up the dozen uniformed policemen there on duty and about 20 civilians, and speedily organized a force which later was credited with calming the crowd and keeping them to an orderly but fast pace in exiting from the flaming tent.

In exactly four minutes after the first cry of fire, the entire assemblage was evacuated.

A quick assessment was made as to possible fatalities. There was none. As for injuries, one woman was taken to Physician's Hospital to have a broken left arm set – but she was the only hospital case. Others said they would have their physicians treat such things as abrasions, cuts and sprains. There were a few lost children, but they were found within minutes either with other adults on the grounds or sitting on porches of nearby homes.

Meanwhile, the circus hands worked at a feverish pitch to save what they could of company property. Once the crowd left the tent, gangs of workers dropped the high wire apparatus and the large center poles to the ground, ripped unburned canvas away from the conflagration and collapsed nearby tents that were in danger of catching fire from showering sparks.

Animal trainers herded uncaged creatures out of the animal tent to a distant lot away from the fire scene, while trumpeting elephants were put into action pushing the heavy animal cages to the perimeter of the circus grounds. There was a momentary fright among some of the people, now fringed at a safe distance about the burning tent to watch the activity, when the cry went up, "The lions are loose!"

One woman was indignant that police and others should be telling the people to take their time and not to worry when, at the same time, circus employees were hastily removing animals to nearby fields. A mounted patrolman immediately was dispatched to clear the street as far back as Rugby Road, turning back autos and pedestrians now converging on the scene.

Only three minutes after the fire started, someone turned in an alarm from Box 68 opposite the trolley car barn at McClellan Street and Eastern Parkway.

Fire department records show that the tapper bell sounded in Station 6 at Eastern and Wendell at 2:48 and, in less than two minutes, the horse-drawn steamer from that station pulled into the circus grounds. Next to arrive was Engine 4 from Station 4 at Avenue A and Nott Street, then a Westinghouse gasoline pumper from Brandywine Station 9 pulled by two black fire horses and, lastly, Truck 1 from the Central Fire Station opposite Crescent Park, only station with motor-driven equipment, having just that year become completely mechanized.

Deputy Chief August Derra was in charge of fire-fighting operations at first, but later Fire Chief Henry R. Yates took over – having driven from his Ballston Lake camp in a matter of minutes in his first chief's automobile, spurred by the certain knowledge that his young son, Edmond, was at the matinee show.

The entire top of the tent was soon consumed by billowing flames, but some of the side panels were saved by the quick action of the riggers as well as the big center poles which need only be repainted. The firemen's job was made easier by the fact that the circus gangs had already removed nearby tents and equipment which might have fed the fire.

Although the all-out was listed as 4:15, the actual blaze was over by 3:15. By now, scorched bleachers stood starkly in the midst of smoldering debris. Off to the north, drifting farther away was a pall of black smoke which earlier had been the chief cause of attracting hundreds of curious visitors to the circus grounds – that and, of course, the incessant clanging of fire engine bells.

The work of razing seats and fixtures began almost at once as circus gangs loaded damaged materials on wagons to be hauled to the freight yards.

Watching this loading operation was one of the circus officials who, surprisingly, seemed not the least disturbed over the day's misfortune. He was thankful that there had been no fatalities and was optimistic that the circus had not suffered any great set back. The circus carried a spare main tent, he said, and would give its regular performance Monday in Buffalo — right on schedule. The loss in this day's fire he put at about $10,000.

To show its gratitude to the Schenectady Fire Department for its quick and efficient response to the alarm of fire, the circus gave Chief Yates the pick of the fine draft horses which pulled the show wagons. The animal chosen was assigned to Fire Station 3 on Jay Street and soon broke in as a fire horse with the name – what else? – "Circus."

Circus officials gathered at the office wagon up at the circus grounds were besieged by requests (and demands) for refunds scarcely before the embers of the fire had been squelched. It must be remembered that all of those inside the tent at the time of the fire had paid their admission fee, many of them for reserved seats. What were the circus people to do?

"We can sympathize with those who paid money and didn't see a show," moaned one circus man. "But there are a lot of spectators here right now who didn't come to see the circus but to watch a fire. What can we do . . . we just can't open the pay wagon and return money to everyone who asks for refunds. As it is, we stand to lose a lot of money on this fire. It looks like everyone is a loser."

However, at the end of the season, Barnum & Bailey made a generous settlement to compensate for the show that was never given. It was reported that the circus returned to the City of Schenectady the sum of $12,000 (two dollars a head for those who had paid) and that the money was to be designated for the city's newly established parks fund.

Soon after the fire broke out, nearly every residence in the neighborhood was besieged by people seeking such things as smelling salts, ammonia, water, witch hazel, bandages, brush brooms and telephones. These houses were practically thrown open to the public.

In the mad rush to evacuate the premises, many persons left behind hats, shoes, parcels, parasols, jackets and other personal effects. The firemen and police managed to round up many of these items that were not damaged by the fire or trampling and took them down to the police station on Jay Street. Announcement was made in the newspapers that owners might reclaim their property after proper identification. Public Safety Commissioner James C. MacDonald handled this operation.

The morning worship service held the next day in St. George's Episcopal Church reflected the feeling of the whole community. Rev. Dr. B. W. Rogers Tayler, before delivering his sermon, told his congregation that it was "a matter of thanksgiving to Almighty God that a catastrophe which might have brought sorrow to every home in the city was averted by a succession of events which seemed indeed providential. I have no doubt that God's hand stayed the disaster."

Perhaps there were two reasons why area residents this Sunday were thankful for deliverance. Only last Wednesday May 1, 1910 the doomsday prophets had warned that the world would come to an end with appearance of Halley's Comet. A severe electrical storm the night before frightened many who thought the seers may have been right, but the comet came and went on cue without more than a promise that it would return 76 years later.

The author is made quite aware of the impression that the celebrated Barnum & Bailey circus fire of 1910 made on those who witnessed it. Even in later years, up to today, those who were small children at the time and are now past retirement age can recall vividly many details of that harrowing experience.

The circus fire story is one that the author relates frequently in his talks on Schenectady's history before local groups. Invariably, there are several persons in the audience who have firsthand knowledge of what transpired in that near disaster. They have been telling their children and grandchildren for years of the experience - how they went with their elders to the circus grounds supposedly to enjoy the show under the Big Top, but instead narrowly escaped with their lives.

The consensus is that the fire was started by the man who carelessly tossed a cigarette butt into the canvas folds, that it began at first as a "bright speck" in the roof section but quickly spread outward with frightening intensity despite efforts of both circus personnel and spectators to extinguish the blaze and, finally, that miraculously everyone managed to get out before the flaming canvas fell to the ring sections.

Some said they slid down poles, others jumped from the back of the bleachers into the outstretched arms of adults below, while still others remember hanging briefly from the bleacher seats and having their fingers stepped on before dropping to the ground. Many went out the way they had entered, but there were quite a few who escaped by scrambling underneath the wall canvas to the outside.

(1) The celebrated boat slide at Rexford Park. The launches were pulled up via pulley at left and were released down ramp at right, hitting the pool below with a delightful spray. (2) The first roller coaster at Rexford. A second, and more daring coaster, was erected in the mid-twenties.

(1) It was Dolle's Park during the World War I era when Fred Dolle took over its management. (2) The ice cream parlor at Rexford. (3) The trolley stop at Rexford. The merry-go-round is in right foreground (4) Waiting at the trolley stop. (5) A general view of Rexford Park's midway in 1915. It was called Luna Park then.

(1) A State League baseball game in progress in the late 1890's on Island Park, located on the Mohawk's Van Slyck Island. (2) The 1919 World Series was going on here when crowds gathered in front of the Gazette Building to watch play action board. Traffic was often slowed to a standstill.

(1) The fire had just started at the circus grounds in Schenectady when W.J. Schuster made this shot on May 21, 1910. (2) Fear stricken circus goers were running from the blazing main tent of Barnum & Bailey in this remarkable on-the-spot photo by Schuster who later cleaned up with his postcard views.

(1) A circus parade coming out of old Center Street now Broadway into State Street about 1890. (2) Here come the elephants! Youngsters along the curb on lower Union Street excitedly scan the paraders for the main attraction in 1916 circus parade.

(1) The county almshouse at Steuben Street shortly after it was built in 1903. (2) The Hiker Monument at Central Park, dedicated May 30, 1921. (3) Samuel Dickhoff, the man whose real estate promotions developed that portion of Hamilton Hill where the fairgrounds were located.

(1) This was what the Central Park site looked like in the summer 1914, before work formally began on its development. View is from what is now Bradley Boulevard looking toward the gully which became Iroquois Lake. (2) A summer scene about 1928 on Iroquois Lake. (2) A summer about 1928 on Iroquois Lake in Central Park.

(1) The entrance to Forest Park on Ballston Lake, a facility set up and operated for many years by Schenectady Railway Co. (2) The Forest Park launch, Comanche, taking on passengers at the Ballston Lake pier in the summer of 1914.

11—The Island Park

The area has been changed so drastically since its existence that Island Park, a place where baseball was once played on the banks of the Binnekill, almost seems a figment of a hazy memory. And yet, there really was such a park, one that was a popular showplace for local and, occasionally, big-time baseball talent.

It was located on what used to be called Van Slyck Island, which was the large Mohawk River island opposite State Street on the Schenectady side. Part of it was taken over by the eastern approach of the first Western Gateway Bridge after 1923 and, since the recent construction of the second bridge, part of the Binnekill has been filled in so that Van Slyck is no longer an island. Many years have elapsed since the old ball park was last used, but doubtless there are a few people around who can remember the top-notch games that were once played there.

It was known first as Island Park in the early 1890s when it was developed as home grounds for the Schenectady entry in the State League. William Hathaway, a livery owner, and Fred D. Cherry, a cigar-smoking newsroom proprietor, were partners in the enterprise.

The crowds which crossed the pontoon bridge spanning the Binnekill at the south end of the island often numbered more than 3,000 persons, and after the grandstands were packed they spilled over into the fringe of the outfield grass. Baseball was then a new and exciting game that produced local athletes capable of giving the fans their money's worth—which usually consisted of whatever amount of change they wished to put in a cigar box that was passed around by a park attendant about midway through the game.

The State League games continued at the island park diamond until the Schenectady franchise shifted to Scranton in 1903. It was not used for regular play until the original Mohawk Giants took it over for weekly games with any and all competitors. The team was a strong one, featuring catcher Chappie Johnson and his fire-balling pitcher, John Wickware. Had it not been for the color line in major league baseball in those days, both Johnson and Wickware—and no doubt several other Mohawk Giants who came along later, such as Buck Ewing and Harold Perry—would have been big league material.

There was the afternoon in the fall of 1913 when the famed Walter Johnson and his all stars stopped by to take on the Giants during a barn-storming tour. They had been bowling over all local competition up to now, mainly behind the strong arm of Johnson. But Wickware was not impressed. He derailed the "Big Train" by a score of 1-0 and it was said the major leaguers were chagrined at the loss.

Incidentally, the local team staged what was probably the first sit-down strike in area sports. When an overflow crowd of an estimated 6,000 showed up for a close look at the great Washington Senators' pitcher in action, the Mohawk Giants decided it was time to ask for a bonus and refused to play until they got it. When the crowd began to get impatient after an hour's delay, Manager Bill Wernecke decided to give in "just this once."

Wickware sometimes antagonized his opponents while enjoying a comfortable lead. He belittled their efforts by calling in the outfielders, and there is no record that this bit of show-boating ever backfired. The Chappie Johnson crew deserted the island park after 1916 and played for a time on a ball diamond at the end of Broadway.

Then, shortly after World War I, the Mohawk island site was taken over by Knights of Columbus Athletic Association and from then on it was called Columbus Park. It ushered in an era of strong competition among several teams of the area—especially between the KC's and Scotia—but most of all, heralded the frequent appearances of major league squads both during schedule breaks in mid-season and in post season stints.

Henry Bozzi, who steered the fortunes Or the KC's, also was active in booking other sports attractions in Schenectady. In so doing, he arranged for many big league teams to stop by for an afternoon game in those days when a $1,000 guarantee was suf ficient.

One of the first was the Brooklyn Dodgers (or "Robins" as they were sometimes called) who beat the KC team on the island in the summer of 1921. Bozzi recalls that this was the day the old pontoon bridge was so weakened by the crowds crossing to the park that everyone had to be taken off by scows when the game had ended. But at least they had seen the fabulous Zack Wheat. The bridge, by the way, was at the end of what was then Water Street and is now near the end of Washington Avenue towards the boulevard.

The Cincinnati Reds, who finished fifth in the National League race in 1927, came here in late J uly of that year before moving on for a series with the Boston Braves. They were pitted against what was known as the Police team, but actually most of them were members of the original KC's. The game had been slated for the island park, but at the last minute was changed to the GEAA field (which later became the site of the GLAA club-house.)

Although the locals lost, 9-6, they gave the major leaguers a battle and pleased the throng of some 4,000 fans. Horace Smith pitched for the police squad and was opposed by the Reds' Ray Kolp. Others in the police lineup were: Lobby O'Brien, catcher; Hal McConvery, first base; Andy Marone, second base; Joe "Apple" Jablonski, third base; Ed Matthews, shortstop; Red Schilling, right field; Ted Karis, center, and Joe Petcrs Sr., left field.

Bozzi booked the Philadelphia Phillies at Scotia's Collins park in the mid-1920s against the GE Refrigerators and the St. Louis Browns soon after took on the police team. A game between the Boston Braves and the local cops actually had to be called at the top of the seventh inning during an exhibition tilt on Union College's Alexander Field on June 28, 1928—because they ran out of baseballs. So many fans refused to throw back foul balls that the three dozen baseballs on hand were used up. Most of the balls were used by the fans to obtain autographs of the major leaguers.

The Dodgers came back in September that same year to play a stubborn Scotia team at the village park and barely eked out a victory. On the Scotia team were such local standouts Bill and as Sig Makofski, Stan Cole and Al Harris.   The KCAA continued to use the island park, however, until the mid-1920s. After that, the site was used sparingly for exhibitions and gradually was replaced by other ball yards, principally Central Park. One last word about the old Island Park. There was a persistent story that one or two balls had been hit to the outfield and into the river beyond. Bozzi claimed this couldn't be true. .."unless the batter was a superman."

"It would have been a drive about 650 feet because the diamond was laid out so that the outfield faced the longest portion of the island," he said. "The longest ball I ever saw hit in that park was by Hal McConvery. lt went past the scoreboard to right center field, probably about 450 feet."

Bozzi, long-time barber in downtown Schenectady, organized the second edition of the Mohawk Gianls in 1924 and, after a few games on the island, played mostly at Central Park. This was another era in Schenectady baseball history and throughout the 1930s, the Schenectady Twilight League offered nightly entertainment and relaxation for depression-weary residents—still for the price of a nickel or a dime in the collection box.

Such local stars of the past decade as McConvery, Harris, Bill Makofski, Karis and Cole for a time kept pace with the newcomers and fans covered the hills of the "A" diamond in Central Park to watch them. But always in the midst of stiffest competitions was Bozzi's team of young stars—the Mohawk (Giants. There was Buck Ewing, Eagle Durant, "Duck Soup" Milton, Rags Roberts and Scrappy Brown, among others. to delight the crowds with superb play that often was spiced with good-natured clowning. Memorable are the hotly-contested series between the Giants and such as the Edisons, Jerseys or GE Refrigerators. Then there were the special exhibitions with the Detroit Clowns, Cuban All Stars and House of David.

This particular era in Schenectady baseball was brought to a close in the days preceding World War II. A little more than a decade of professional ball followed with the Blue Jay era, but since its demise after the 1956 season, nothing has approached the enthusiasm which local sports fans once showed for the game that Abner Doubleday devised on a Cooperstown pasture.

Entrance gate to the old Brandywine Park shortly after the Schenectady Railway Co. purchased and redeveloped that "uptown" facility in 1896..

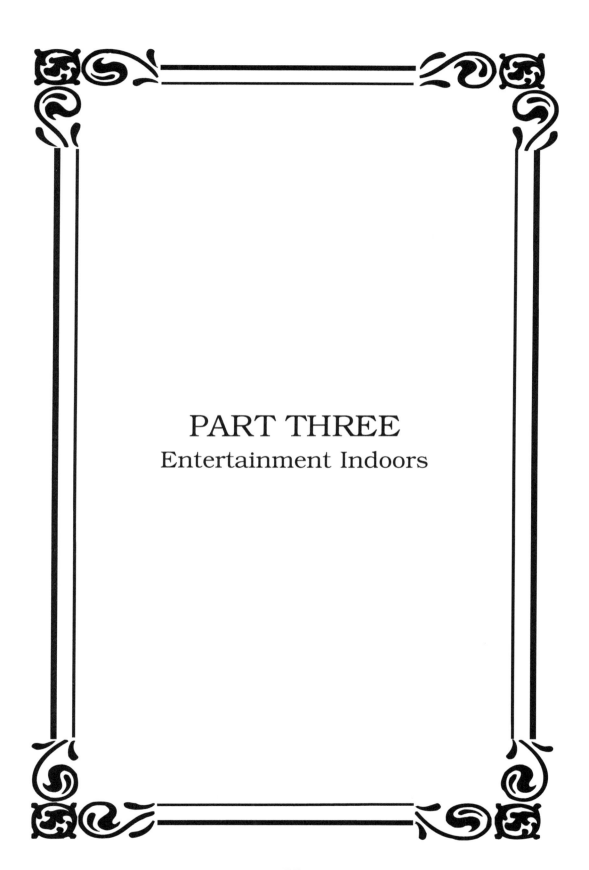

PART THREE
Entertainment Indoors

The Van Curler Opera House turned to burlesque during the 1920's alternating it with dramatic and comedy productions. In its later years, the theater showed motion pictures almost exclusively.

12—Van Curler Opera House

$\mathcal{C}$harles H. Benedict the young manager of the newly built Van Curler Opera House in Schenectady, had such a case of jitters on its opening night, March 1, 1893, that he could not go on stage before the opening performance as planned. Instead, he asked the leading man of "Friend Fritz" to do the honors.

So John Mason obligingly went before the footlights and told the huge first night audience how proud they should be of their new showplace the "best and biggest this side of New York City" – and that the management thanked them profusely for making it such a grand occasion.

Everyone was in a festive mood and it certainly was one of the biggest events to happen in Schenectady within anyone's memory. The "carriage trade" began arriving well before curtain time, and people lined both sides of Jay Street from State to Franklin to get a glimpse of the well-dressed people alighting from the fancy cabs and livery "hacks" to enter the arched foyer of the new theater. The carriages were lined up Jay Street for nearly a solid hour, business was that good.

Plans for the Van Curler were brought to fruition in late 1890 by a group of associates comprising Henry S. DeForest, George W. Van Vranken, Jacob W. Clute, John McDermott, Albert Shear, Charles E. Palmer and John W. White.

Ground was broken for the structure Sept. 5, 1892, after the lot had been cleared of the small frame buildings on the one-time mill lane of old Jan Baptiste Van Eps. The citizenry took great interest in the work of construction from the start. particularly the excavation. It was before the day of the steam shovel, and winding lines of laborers pushed wheelbarrows up steep inclines from the bottom of the "big hole."

Then came the foundations and gradually the big structure began to take shape. At last it was ready for the tinsmiths, roofers and interior decorators, and then came the furnishings. Before long, the time had rolled around for the long-awaited grand opening.

Down at the newly built Edison Hotel, a week or so before the opening, a local character by the name of Ford one evening began auctioning off the boxes, then the loges, then the seats in the orchestra, and so on as Schenectady's beloved musician, George Rivette and his Van Curler Opera House orchestra played popular tunes of the day. Interest in the opening was at high pitch. It was the gala event of all time here in the field of legitimate entertainment.

Edward Ellis, president of the Schenectady Locomotive Co., bought the first box, putting up $50 for the right to view Manola Mason from it on opening night. Richard Fuller grabbed the box nearest it, and it cost him two dollars more. John W. Smitley, the financier, and J.G.L. Ackerman, a banker, out bid all others for the next two boxes across from Ellis and Fuller, paying $29 and $31 respectively. Then followed the loges, and these were taken by E. T. Van Vranken, Charles Brown of the Edison Hotel, J. W Clute and the Delta Phi fraternity. These were bought from $16 to $20 each. Other loges went to L. B. Close, Edward Church, J. W. Clute and Charles E. Palmer, bringing from $12 to $15. Seats in the orchestra brought $3 and those in the first row balcony from $1.50 to $2.75.

What was this new theater like, inside and out, which so thrilled the citizens of this area?

In an illustrated edition of the Daily Gazette in 1898, there was this complete and rather glowing account of Schenectady's newest theatrical center:

"The location of the Van Curler, at the southeast corner of Jay and Franklin Streets, is central. It is only one short block from State Street and the electric cars and, while close to the principal hotels and the railway station, is far enough removed from the latter to be beyond the disturbing sound of the steam cars.

"The opera house building is an imposing and substantial structure of brick and stone. The front is of Philadelphia pressed brick and cut brown stone; it is in the Mooorish style of architecture, and is elegant and attractive in appearance. The building has a frontage of 98.5 feet on Jay Street and extends back on Franklin Street 144 feet. The main entrance to the theatre is 20 feet in width and equal to two stories in height. The front of the building above the entrance is four stories high. There are three stories south of the entrance on Jay Street and one to the north, at the corner. The entrance, or lobby, is 40 feet in depth.

"To the right, as you enter the lobby, is the box office, about half way down to the doors opening into the foyer. The box office is connected with the manager's office on the east. To the left of the lobby is a cloak room. The gents' retiring room is at the left of the foyer, the ladies' at right. Three sets of folding doors of polished cherry open into the foyer, which is about 40 feet by 12, extending across the rear end of the auditorium from which it is shut off by heavy silk draperies which are substituted for doors. The floor of the foyer is of mosaic stone. At either side, or end, of the foyer are broad stair cases leading up to the balcony.

"Separating the silken draperies, you pass from the foyer into the orchestra circle occupying the ground floor of the auditorium which is about 63 by 63 feet. This floor is saucer shaped and the seats are so arranged on an incline that a clear and uninterrupted view of the stage is obtainable from any and every seat. The orchestra seats are separated from the orchestra circle by a very ornamental partition. Directly in front of the orchestra circle are four loges, partitioned off by polished brass rods. The loges in the central portion of the floor contain five chairs, while the two at either side hold only three. The chairs on the entire ground floor and in the balcony are of the latest improved pattern with the best wire-spring cushions, upholstered in coral crushed plush.

"The cap of the rail dividing the circle and orchestra is upholstered with plush of the same color and surmounted by a brass rail. There are eight boxes, two on each side of the orchestra and two more above on a line with the balcony. The height from the floor to the dome is nearly 68 feet. Gracefully circling above the orchestra circle is the balcony, and towering above this, away up toward the top of the theatre, is the gallery or 'heaven.' The balcony contains 350 chairs, precisely the same as those on the ground floor, while the gallery has 450 folding seats. The line of sight is perfect from every seat in the balcony or gallery or on the first floor.

"The ornamentation of the interior of the opera house is magnificent. The general color on the sidewall is terra cotta. The ornamentation on the proscenium arch, the private boxes and on the fronts of the balcony and gallery is sterro-relief and finished in old ivory, light pink and gold. The center of the ceiling forms an immense dome and around this are four figures representing those four of the muses who are supposed to exert an especial influence over a Temple of Thespis, Viz.: Euterpe, goddess of music; Melpomene, goddess of tragedy; Terpsichore, goddess of dancing, and Thalia, goddess of comedy. Each of these figures is a real work of art. The figures are eight feet in height.

"The entrance to the gallery is on Franklin Street. The gallery ticket office is up stairs. There are five exits from the first floor, six from the balcony, six from the gallery and three from the stage. Fire escapes lead from the gallery to the ground, meeting plat form exits from the balcony.

"The stage of the Van Curler is one of the largest and best appointed theatre stages in the country. The stage is 72 feet wide and 40 feet deep from curtain line. The height of the stage from the floor to rigging loft is 60 feet; to roof, 80 feet; to fly gallery, 30 feet. The proscenium arch is 36 feet wide and 30 feet high. There are five sets of telescoped grooves, adjustable to scenery from 16 to 28 feet high. There are two lines of workbridges . . . and 350 lights on stage with 99 foot lights (electric) with red, white and blue globes, to use instead of calcium effects.

"There are two curtains, one fireproof asbestos, and one scene curtain representing the Towers of the Alhambra after a Moorish sketch by Sir David Roberts. There are 63 separate scenes in all, including mountain, garden, horizon, wooded landscape old street and new street scenes, palace, light and sides rocks, vases, statuary, prison and kitchen scenes, dark chamber scenes, gothic, bridges, set houses, set cottages and in fact everything necessary for a well regulated stage.

"There are 17 dressing rooms, about 9 by 12 feet. They are in an annex on the south of the stage, which is cut off by fire proof doors. In the cellar beneath the annex is the heating plant, the steam for the stage and theatre being furnished by a 40 horsepower boiler. There are six fire plugs on the stage and each furnished with 100 feet of hose. The stage is entirely shut off from the auditorium by a fire wall, added to the original plans at an extra cost of $1,480, and the fire proof asbestos curtains. All the wiring in the theatre is covered by fire proof pipe, and in fact every possible precaution has been adopted to render the theatre as near fire proof as stone, brick and mortar can be made.

"The plans for the Van Curler Opera House were furnished by Leon H . Lempert & Son, architects, of Rochester. The following are the contractors who built it: John McDermott, mason work; William G. Caw, carpenter work, John Allen, steam fitting; Stevenson Bros., plumbing."

So, on that March evening of 1893, the stage of the Van Curler was set for its premiere performance. The dressing rooms were alive with last minute attentions and stage hands scurried about checking their assignments. In front of the drop some 1,600 ardent theater-goers waited in almost breathless expectancy. The moment was at hand, when the new $100,000 playhouse was to be christened.

Rivette started the opening air. The big asbestos curtain slowly ascended, exposing to view a gorgeous set of hangings on which was a magnificent painting. Applause broke forth and the curtains parted. The great Manola Mason and her male supporting star, John Mason, were about to transpose their audience from expectancy to intense rapture, to leave memories that were to live for many years after. "Friend Fritz" was the play, and it met with wave upon wave of applause.

Everything seemed in step. The charm of the play, the closeness of the leading actors to their audience, the music and the grandeur of that auditorium combined to make an unforgettable evening.

Two days later, Lew Dockstader and his new minstrels were at the Van Curler Opera House and the place was sold out early. All available standing room was sold.

The story was much the same in the next two decades as leading players and top flight plays were brought to the Van Curler. Among the performers were such names as Eddie Foy, Chauncey Olcott, Lillian Russell, Joseph Jefferson, Otis Skinner and Robert Mansfield. Mae Desmond was a particular favorite and a delight to Van Curler audiences.

Olcott was one of the last actors to grace the Van Curler stage while it was still called the "opera house." He appeared on Thursday night, March 20, 1924, in a play called "The Heart of Paddy Whack," a tale of Ireland in the 1830s.

Of course, the opera house management did not ignore the growing popularity of motion pictures in the days before World War I. A huge projection screen was installed, which could easily be lowered to stage level, on which was shown many of the early movie classics. "Ben Hur," which starred Ramon Navarro and Francis X. Bushman, ran for a week because of its drawing power. Movies, especially Saturday matinees, were regularly shown throughout the 1920s.

Beginning about 1910, the Van Curler promoted the movie travelogues produced and presented by Lyman K. Howe. It was a new field for motion pictures and the photography for the times was excellent. Howe came in for three days of showing, matinee and evening performances, and played to capacity houses. The afternoon programs were attended mostly by school children and their mothers or aunts, but though it was predominantly a juvenile audience, there was nothing of the "kids'" matinees" in days to come. Everyone was well behaved, Howe saw to that not only by giving a good program but by instructing them to pay attention when it began. There was always a piano player who played the appropriate mood music. He also played during a brief intermission. In later years, Howe managed to insert a short comedy movie.

After the first year, Lyman Howe's pictures were something to look forward to They became topics of conversation in many Schenectady households for weeks afterward. Eventually, the movie industry got the idea that there was money to be made in travelogues, which it began to produce with increasing frequency. Thus, shortly before World War I, Howe's audiences began to dwindle and he ceased his annual presentation at the Van Curler Opera House. He did continue to put out short travel features which were distributed to the smaller movie houses, but they never had the same impact as when shown at the elegant Van Curler.

In 1925, the big entertainment center was sold to the Farash Corporation and its name was changed to Van Curler Theater. Burlesque was introduced. On March 5-8 that year, "The Girls from the Follies" played there, followed by Betty Palmer and her "French Follies" show. Amateur nights and auctions were held from the stage as the manager, Adelbert J. Rochelle, did his best to try to offer varied entertainment to keep the theater in the black.

But it was a losing battle. By 1930, the doom of the legitimate stage in any place but metropolitan areas sent the old Van Curler and its sister playhouses into the discard.

The front portion, which once housed the foyer and lobby, was rented out as store space while the theater section was closed for good. It remained that way until August, 1943, when wreckers moved in and took down the big hall east of the front offices and converted it into a parking lot. The front part finally was demolished in 1953 and on that corner site was built a modern two-story commercial building.

A view of the Van Curler Opera House on July 20, 1943, shortly before the large stage loft and auditorium were demolished. This is on Franklin Street looking toward Jay Street.

13—The Hudson Theater

*F*or the short time they were destined to provide live theater entertainment in Schenectady only a half century ago, the Harry Bond Players managed a rather astounding impact on the social life of much of its citizenry. But it all ended on a tragic note, the accidental deaths of Harry Austin Bond and Edward "Tedd" Brackett on the Schenectady-Albany Road, culminating in a real life melodrama which had local theater — goers in shock or tears.

The Roaring Twenties had hardly begun to warm up to the zany tempo of the jazz age when the affable Bond brought his stock company to Schenectady in the fall of 1924 to open a season of "decent family entertainment" at the Hudson Theater, 10-14 South College St. It was a switch from the baudy vaudeville and burlesque that had performed there as recent as the year previous.

They were brought here from a successful run in Pittsfield by A. Vedder Magee, who had bought the theater property at a foreclosure sale. He and his backers knew they were taking a chance on the venture, as vaudeville acts and "girlie" shows were rated the top money-makers in the entertainment field.

The Bond Players reopened the Hudson Theater beginning Monday night, Nov. 17,1924, with the week's run of John Golden's New York City success, "Thank-U." The entire proceeds of the first two performances were given over to the Crippled Children's Fund in Schenectady.

Soon after the first show opened, the box office at the Hudson began to show a profit. The Bond Players drew more and more regular patrons as they were treated to a variety of plays ranging from comedy to romance to murder.

Whenever "The Night of January 16th" was performed, a new jury was selected from the audience to sit in the jury box on stage and render a verdict. The cast was prepared to act out the scene no matter which way the jury found, conviction or acquittal. Probably the best thriller was "The Cat and the Canary."

Spicy incense permeated the old Hudson during performances of "Ming Toy" when Bond starred as an oriental merchant, and the pretty usherettes were dressed as Chinese girls.

It was not necessarily only the well-dressed, well-heeled and cultured element of this area which frequented the Hudson once the Bond Players caught on. These people may have purchased season tickets for box seats or reserved most of the orchestra seats for the Friday or Saturday night performances, but the "plain and ordinary" folk also were faithful patrons – and many of these would wait along the stage door alley left of the front entrance to get autographs or congratulate their favorite actors.

The Hudson's interior was typical of the Gay-Nineties theater houses — with the decorated ceilings, rococo moldings, gold leaf, crystal chandeliers and rich, textured drapes. There were two boxes on either side of the big stage, an orchestra pit, balcony and a wide center aisle with narrow side aisles on the main floor. The theater was constructed in 1904 and opened as the Mohawk Theater for vaudeville productions.

Harry Bond shared the spotlight with his character actress, Richie Clark Russell. She acted as convincingly in the role of a feeble gray-haired lady as she did a cleaning woman or a haughty socialite. Miss Russell came to Schenectady from Pittsfield with misgivings. She told Bond that although she had never seen the place, there was much doubt that she would stay more than one season. "I just know I won't like it there," she had decided.

As it turned out, she stayed in this area until her death June 21, 1971. She was the well-respected widow of her former boss, A. Vedder Magee.

The others in Bond's company, too, were popular with Hudson audiences. There were Victor Sutherland and Mark Haight, both of whom handled the handsome he man roles; Tedd Brackett, a lean and thin-faced character actor who was perhaps Bond's closest friend; Rankin Mansfield, straight man; Harry Fisher, comedian; Lois Landon, a pert brunette who could sing "A Cottage Small by a Waterfall" or cry real tears in "Seventh Heaven"; Doris King, who in real life was Mrs. Bond, and Helen Spring, Clayton Flagg and Edmund Soraghan.

Bond's good-naturedness was infectious to the rest of the cast. "There was a kindness in his manner," Richie Russell often told associates, "that made a nice feeling even when a play wasn't going right."

Hudson theater — goers felt the rapport which Bond and his players established soon after their arrival here. They roundly applauded each performer on initial stage entrances and rarely did the evening end without multiple curtain calls. On occasion, Harry Bond would step from beyond the curtain and, customarily twirling a black onyx ring on a finger of his right hand, thank the audience for their support - and invite them to return for next week's play.

Sometimes the "flappers" could hardly restrain themselves when their idols appeared on stage. Such was one occasion in 1925, when dark-haired Mark Haight made his entrance early in the production of "Slippy McGee" and a young lady called out"Ain't he the cats!"

Stock company productions in those days were hard work, rewarded mostly by the applause and support of the growing audiences. The season was nine months long and new performances were given each week with a matinee on Saturdays and a day off on Sunday.

The actors memorized lines of a new play and rehearsed it daily from 10 a.m. until noon, always a week ahead of the current attraction. One morning, early in 1926, the police were notified that a young man was leaning over the railing of the new Western Gateway Bridge, staring into the water below and looking suspiciously like a potential suicide. Upon investigation however, it turned out to be Victor Sutherland – rehearsing lines for his next role.

The pit orchestra, usually about eight men, rehearsed any special cue-ins with the cast at the end of the week sometimes after the matinee. Some of the pit men preferred the dramas so they could play poker in the downstairs dressing rooms between acts.

On Saturday night, May 22, 1926, the Bond Players completed the performance of a play called, "In Love with Love." It was advertised, and many advance sales were made, that the show which was to play the following week would close the company's second season in Schenectady. It was to be Owen Davis' Pulitzer Prize-winning drama of 1923, "Ice Bound," a tale of modern day New England.

Harry Bond was particularly delighted with the audience response to this next-to last play for the season and he came out before the footlights to tell them so . . . and that the players were looking forward to opening the third season in September.

Then — seemingly at the height of their popularity in Schenectady — tragedy struck the stock company.

It was about 1:30 p.m. on Sunday, May 23, 1926 when an onrushing interurban limited of the Schenectady Railway Co. demolished the auto in which Bond, 41, and Brackett, 45, were stalled on the Schenectady-Albany Road crossing of Stop 15½. Both were killed instantaneously and thrown from the wrecked auto, parts of which were strewn some 500 feet along the tracks (although two persons thought they detected a pulse in Brackett and rushed him by private car to Ellis Hospital where he was declared dead on arrival). Schenectady Coroner William C. Treder assisted the Albany coroner at the scene.

Bond was driving Brackett's new Buick Brougham and apparently was confused by the new gear shift as he was backing the auto off the tracks, stalling it in the path of the trolley. The crash took place directly in front of the home of Mr. and Mrs. Charles Aussicker. In fact, it was established that Bond was attempting to turn around by driving into the Aussicker's driveway and backing out over the tracks.

Mrs. Aussicker later said she was working in her kitchen and observed the Schenectady-bound trolley from a side window "traveling at a great rate of speed" and, seconds after, heard the crash in front of the house. George Robillard, motorman of the non-stop interurban, estimated he was traveling about 50 m.p.h. and sounded the whistle when he saw the auto across the tracks but was unable to stop in time.

Arthur Aussicker, son of the Aussickers (since deceased) today lives in the house which figured in the accident. It is now listed as 1900 Central Ave., Colonie, directly across from the Tick Tock Tavern.

Mrs. Bond and Mrs. Brackett later told authorities that when the accident occurred, they were at the Maywood Hotel (about a half mile west of Stop 15 ½) where the men had dropped them off before dinner to "try out Tedd's new car."

A crowd of more than 10,000 persons swarmed about the accident site before the day was out. And all during the following day, the Bond-Brackett demise was the prime topic of conversation in Schenectady. Tributes poured from public and civic spokesmen, regretting the loss of the two actors who had become friends to many in the city and also of the probable end of the Hudson shows.

Schenectady Kiwanis, at its meeting the following Wednesday, recalled that Bond had spoken at its club exactly a year before and, as a Kiwanian, had been classified as "builder." The club tribute to the actor ended, "What a wonderful afterglow Harry Bond is leaving behind."

Hundreds gathered along the street in front of Timeson & Fronk's funeral chapel at 15 South Church St. (which building was later torn down for the Liberty Street extension) two days after the mishap as simple services were conducted within for Bond and Brackett in a double funeral. Later, Brackett's body was taken to his hometown of Cortland for a burial while Bond was cremated.

Although their death broke up the Bond Players, it was not the end of theatrical stock at the Hudson. Magee immediately notified Richie Russell, in St. Louis at the time, that he wanted her to organize a company to open the 1926-27 season. In her contract Miss Russell was to have sole charge of production and was to appear in at least three plays a month.

The theater was filled when the new company opened Labor Day weekend, orchestra and box seats having been purchased when it was first advertised "the show must go on." There were accommodations for 900 patrons at the Hudson, which included the circle, loges and balcony. The upper gallery, which was rarely opened, would have made it 1,350.

The public soon discovered Miss Russell believed in realism. There are no doubt many in Schenectady today who can recall the week one thriller, "The Gorilla," was presented and an actor costumed as the hairy monster ran up and down the aisles and scared all the ladies.

And, by her own admission, she was a "crank" on scenic production. Her all-time favorite was "Smiling Through," a sad but heart-warming story of a Civil War veteran. A new lighting technique was used for the dual set to denote the passage of time by fadeouts — it was called X-ray border lighting. Frank Finch, later electrician at the State Theater, operated the spots and cross lights for these scenes.

Mark Kent, who opened the first scene downstage as an old man playing checkers only to reappear as a young man a few minutes later, played the lead with Helen Murdock.

Other actors with Miss Russell's troupe were Victor Sutherland, and later Butler Hixon as leading man; Arthur Cartwright, character parts, and Grant Irwin, comedy. Stagehands were "Shorty" Tulloch, Joe Mack, Ed Fitzgerald and Finch.

The box office had to take in almost $4,000 for the theater to show a profit each week. Rent was $300, script rental about $300 and the leading man alone made $175. The whole company, including orchestra, stage crew and ushers, totaled 43 persons — and they all received a weekly pay check.

Nevertheless, one play called "Charlie's Aunt" netted a profit of $1,200. Another, "Seventh Heaven" played to a packed house (including the gallery) every night, and still lost money because of a high costume bill and the hiring of extra players.

It was not lack of public support which resulted in the demise of theatrical stock in those days just before the crash of 1929. When the Russell Players concluded their second season in May, 1928, and it was announced it would be the last, theater-goers found it hard to believe.

What they didn't know was that, though times were still as good as the country had ever known, the steadily rising cost of operating live theater was too much for a small stock company.

Still, there were two last gasps at theater production at the Hudson before 1930. First the Wilcox Players played part of a season there, transferring its performances to the Erie (old Wedgeway) Theater for the remaining months. Then the Abbey Theatre Irish Players came in for a brief acting stint before the Hudson closed its doors forever to stage shows.

It lay idle for a few years until it was leased late in 1934 to the Farash Theater Corp. owned by William Shirley, William T. Farley and Guy A. Graves (father of Justice Guy A. Graves). The interior was remodeled into a night club decor with the stage as a dance floor.

This new departure in public entertainment at the Hudson was to be short-lived, however. A fire of undetermined origin swept through the old structure the cold night of Dec. 18, 1934 and its charred walls were torn down as soon as the debris had cooled.

The site was leveled and blacktopped, as it exists today next to the northern extremity of the Burger King parking lot.

An in-house party was in full swing on the Hudson Theater stage in this photo of Feb. 18, 1934.

14—The Movie Houses

$\mathscr{B}$ingo, raffles, free dishes, amateur nights...they were all part of the extra offerings of the neighborhood movie theater, once a prime source of family entertainment but which has now virtually left the Schenectady scene as in many other localities across the land.

Once "The Great Train Robbery" was projected on the six-by-eight foot screen of the Crescent Theater in 1905, the motion picture business soon became a serious threat to the vaudeville and play houses. The "nickelodeons," as they were first called because of the standard five-cent admission fee, were centered at first in the downtown area — almost anyplace an interprising promoter might wish to rent a hall with folding chairs in the hopes that some one or two reelers would come his way. But as the suburbs grew, so did the neighborhood movie houses.

The first Schenectady downtown theaters recognized as legitimate movie houses were the Crescent, located on the second floor of a former high-stooped resident at 440 State St. a few doors from the new Parker Building; the Art Theater, which was jammed between the Parker Building and Taberski's first pool hall opposite Jay Street; the Dorp Theater on South Center (now the site of Skype's Gallery) which became the Happy Hour Theater after 1912; the Orpheum at 409-11 State St.; the Auditorium located next to the Orpheum in the Vendome Hotel building, later to become known as the Penny Arcade, and the Star Theater on Jay Street near State.

These were all small movie houses and for a time were able to accommodate the crowds which came to watch the short-feature "flickers," interspaced with such anouncements as "Ladies Please Remove Hats" and "No Smoking While Pictures Are Being Shown." It was about this time, shortly after 1905, that saloons vied for customers by augmenting singing waiters with the projection of prize-fight films. Just as "The Great Train Robbery" was the first film to tell a story on the screen, so D.W. Grifhth's "Birth of a Nation" in 1915 set high standards in the movie industry for many years. And as the film fare improved, so did the box office returns.

The Orpheum became the Palace Theater in 1918 under the management of Bill Shirley but in 1924 it was again changed to the New Strand Theater. The Barcli Theater was built on Barrett Street extending to Clinton Street (its name a combination of Barrett and Clinton) and opened in 1921. In 1930, the Strand on State Street was closed and the Barcli was renamed the Strand Theater.

The era of the large downtown theater was ushered in with the 1920s. With the construction of these plush houses, complete with loges, boxes, and sloping seating arrangement, the public was introduced to high class entertainment at reasonable prices (35 cents for matinee and 50 cents for evening for adults, 25 cents for children at all times.)

The first Proctor's Theater was built in 1912 next to the old canal bed, but the construction of the State Theater by 1922 — complete with an arcade from State Street with entrance to both theaters — was the talk of the town. The Albany Street Theater at the foot of Germania Avenue was converted from the old Empire burlesque theater.

The opening of the new Proctor's Theater on Monday noon, Dec. 27, 1926, was a big event in Dorp City. The 2,700-seat showplace, built by F. F. Proctor at a cost of $ 1.5 million, attracted a total of more than 7,100 paid admissions on that first day. It began with the purchase of the first ticket by 12-year-old Michael Riccio. The"old" Proctor's adjacent to the State Theater was renamed the Wedgeway and, still later, the Erie.

The new Proctor's, which also provided an arcade in from State Street next between the Parker Building and the Carl Co. store, was equipped for state shows with 18 dressing rooms and a mechanically-operated scenery loft. The premiere movie offering was Paramount's vivacious Bebe Daniels in "stranded in Paris." But first there were speeches by Mayor Alexander T. Blessing, Public Service Commissioner George R. Lunn and theater manager Ackerman J.Gill. The crowds which waited to get in for the first show began to gather in the arcade and along State Street long before the noon opening.

Theater patrons were thrilled with the plush carpeting. the cream and gold walls, marble staircases and the cerise velvet drapes and wall hangings. The arcade, which was advertised as "finally extending Jay Street to connect State Street with Smith Street," also was admired by those who came by for the big inaugural.

There was one note of disappointment connected with that opening day at Proctor's. The $50,000 three-manual Wurlitzer organ, with Stephen Boisclair at the console, was not heard at any performance on that auspicious occasion. At the last minute, it was discovered that a mechanical difficulty caused by heat expansion would prevent its being used until the next day.

The last big theater to be built in downtown Schenectady was the Plaza which on Aug. 26, 1931 opened with "The Smiling Lieutenant" starring Maurie Chevalier. By now, people were becoming accustomed to the grandeur of the picture houses so the Plaza's opening opposite Crescent Park where Christ Episcopal Church once stood did not evoke the same enthusiastic response as did the others of the previous decade. Still, there was much favorable comment about the decor, the air conditioning system and the interior, with its "moving clouds and twinkling stars" overhead and the Grecian garden sidewalls. complete with backlit statuary and floral urns.

But as the downtown theaters furnished top entertainment at prices the average family could afford only once a week, the small neighborhood movie houses blossom ed all over town for nightly shows at moderate admission fees.

Up in Bellevue, residents there flocked to the Broadway Theater at the top of Broadway hill near Fire Station 8. the Cozy Theater in Odd Fellows Hall at Thompson Street and the Cameo Theater just a few doors farther up Broadway.

Mont Pleasant families had several theaters through the years, beginning with the Crystal Theater on Crane Street between Francis and Fourth Avenues - the premises later to be taken over by a variety department store. C.J. Frame was owner-manager of both the Crystal and Park Theaters. Shortly after, about 1911, came the Pearl Theater, built at the top of Crane Street hill the adjacent to what became the PNA Hall site. Both buildings were demolished recently to make room for the new Rite Aid Pharmacy and Marcella's appliances. The Sylvan was built by 1913 on Crane Street opposite Second Avenue but did not last long.

The Bijou held forth at the Odd Fellows Hall at Sixth Avenue and Crane Street in which there were movable folding chairs, four seats to a section. The Capitol Theater, located halfway between Fourth and Main at 934 Crane St., later became the Mont Pleasant Theater — the last to survive the closings of neighborhood theaters after World War II. The Pearl Theater, incidentally, stayed in business until the early 1930s.

Over on Congress Street, between Fifth and Sixth Avenues, the Congress Theater was in business in the early days of motion pictures up through 1923.

George Fuller of Rotterdam told of the early movie houses when he was a young projectionist in some of them, including Bill Shirley's Palace. He recalled the strenuous hand-cranked projection machines before the electrically-driven ones came in. He started early in the "move business." When a boy, he was hired by the owner of the Cozy and Congress Theaters to transfer reels of film from one theater to the other — a method employed by some theater owners and managers of that day for cutting back the expense of renting film for the weekday or weekend. Young Fuller transferred the film, one or two reels at a time, between the theater on Congress Street and the one on Broadway by pedaling his bicycle as fast as he could. Two round trips assured day's showing of the same films at both houses.

A walk-up neighborhood movie house was located on Edison Avenue just west of the Crane-Veeder coal and feed yards. It was called, naturally, the Edison Theater. Another early movie house, lasting for a short time, was located at Nott Street and Park Place.

Scotians had some early motion picture shows in the Odd Fellow's Hall on Mohawk Avenue. It was called the Grand Theater. However, in 1928 the villagers got a bona fide movie theater when the Ritz opened on Mohawk Avenue later to be renamed the Scotia Theater.

The Rivoli was on upper Union Street, the Rialto on Van Vranken Avenue, the American on Albany Street near Hulett, the Lincoln on South Brandywine Avenue just in from Albany Street, the Brandywine at Albany and Elm Streets, the Colony on State Street near Robinson, the Star Theater on State Street near Willow Avenue, the Woodlawn still farther out State Street and the Central Park Theater on McClellan Street opposite the car barns, operated from 1915 to 1924 by Samuel Freed.

Movie entertainment matured with theater equipment and improved techniques in cinematography. There was a time, early in the days of the "flicks", when ushers strolled down aisles with disinfectant spray guns to fumigate the stuffy interior during intermission. And early customers were reminded of the shortage of seating space by this spot announcement: "You have paid to see one performance. . . kindly pass out before the next show."

At first, live entertainment supplemented the meagre film fare which before 1916 consisted mostly of scenic shots or travelogues anything simply for the sake of motion. There were illustrated songs in which the customers could join, perhaps some ancient vaudeville acts or a solo by the theater manager's son.

The showing of movies on Sundays was banned by state law until 1918 when, under pressure of a public which worked long hours for the war effort on the homefront and clamored for some Sunday entertainment for relaxation, the legislature decided to rescind the ban and leave it up to local governments to decide the issue. Newspapers carried stories and advertisements by the factions which were split on the Sunday showings. In the end, and before the World War I armistice, the Sunday movies were allowed in Schenectady.

The silent movies were accompanied by a pianist hired by each theater. The musician usually sat in front to one side of the screen so that he or she could portray the action of the picture by the tempo of a frangi-pangi piano. There were occasions when the pianist was far from accomplished and might have known how to play only "Nola" or "Glow Worm" without music; but that hardly mattered - just as long as the bass keys were thumped mightily when the Indian raid started or the cavalry came charging over the hill.

When the larger houses were built, huge concert organs were installed in stage pits . . . and to hear those magnificent swells, during the movie and especially intermission, was the height of enjoyment.

The musical accompaniment went out soon after 1927. That was the big year in the movie industry, the year Al Jolson's "Jazz Singer" was shown across the country to amaze theater-goers with the use of synchronized sound for at least part of the picture. Organs remained in the large theaters for a few years after that to be used for intermission music or during still projections of local advertising.

The depression years of the 1930s saw the introduction of "gimmicks" to entice the regular patrons to come to the neighborhood theaters. Double features came into full sway (and remained ever since) and such giveaways as dishes, candy or clay figurines were to be expected.

The bingo games and raffles were held on a certain night of the week and with each Saturday came the inevitable amateur night in which the customers hooted or cheered for contestants who vied for a $5 top prize. Saturday afternoon was a special showing for the younger set. The matinee. which for many years cost only a thin dime for each admission, featured the western idols — starting with William S. Hart down through Ken Maynard, Tom Mix, Buck Jones. Hoot Gibson, Gene Autry and Roy Rogers.

Foot-stomping and high-pitched shrieks greeted the "coming attractions" an anouncements at each matinee and the pandemonium reached higher levels once the main feature began. And the serials. . .they were a part of the early days of movie theaters, beginning perhaps with the thrilling rescues of a helpless heroine such as Pearl White in "The Perils of Pauline." Other death-defying. week-to-week serials were filmed in adventurous sequences especially for the Saturday matinees, with titles such as ' The Green Archer" and "King of the Jungle." However, the serials died out with the introduction of double feature programs.

The advent of the television age and the growing popularity of drive-in theaters after World War II thinned the ranks of neighborhood theater goers. The small movie house owners found it increasingly difficult to maintain a daily film schedule as box office receipts failed to cover the overhead. They turned to weekend shows, closed during summer months. . . but even that didn't help.

One by one the small uptown theaters succumbed to the changing times and "For Sale" signs were hung over the marquees. The new owners converted them into commercial establishments such as drug stores, auto parts supply houses, welding shops, restaurants and auto body work. Three small theaters began featuring foreign films as "art theaters." The Cameo closed in 1958 and soon was demolished. The Colony shut its doors in the early 1970s and later was leveled by fire. The Scotia Cinema once called the Ritz, is still in business.

Remnants of the real old timers still exist, such as the body shop at Albany and Elm Streets which once was the Brandywine Theater, the welding school and shop on the top of Broadway hill once called the Broadway Theater, the peaked building on McClellan Street and Eastern Avenue that was the Central Park Theater, the business block at 1615 Union St. that was once the Rivoli Theater, the American Electric Supply Co. at 778 Albany St, once the American Theater, an oriental restaurant at 14181 State St. once the Star Theater, etc.

In downtown Schenectady, the Erie Theater was razed in 1963 and is now a parking lot at the corner of Erie Boulevard and Liberty Street; the beautiful Plaza Theater was torn down in the fall 1964 which site is part of the an empty lot across from Veterans' Park; the Strand "old Barcli" had been long vacant when it was finally demolished in 1972 to make way for the Albany Savings Bank building in that block; and the State Theater was demolished in May, 1985 after standing idle for several years with a roof that was threatening collapse.

Thus Proctor's Theater, one of the brighter spots in downtown, remains the holdout in the city's business district of the era of in-town, movie houses.

(1) Old postcard view of Van Curler Opera House, pictured shortly after it was opened in 1893. (2) Matinee theatergoers on Jay Street the afternoon of Aug. 10, 1908, after watching a Burgess Stock Co. show at Van Curler, in center background. In far left backgound can be seen the spire of old Second Reformed Church, now site of Postoffice.

(1) The final curtain was ringing down for the opera house when this photo was made in early August, 1943. A week later, the wrecking crew moved in to demolish the cavernous stage auditorium, leaving the front portion until 1953. (2) A glass photo of an old Schenectady pool hall, supposed to be Kadel's on the north side of State Street near Jay.

*(1) This was 1934 and the Hudson Theater had just been closed to live theater —
for the last time. Later that year the 30-year-old building was gutted by fire and its
ruins leveled for a parking lot on South College Street. It was built in 1904 as the
Mohawk Theater and soon became a burlesque palace.*

Scenes at Albany Road Accident and Two Men Killed

Edward Brackett

Harry A Bond

(1) This was the Schenectady Gazette's front page pictorial spread on May 24, 1926, of the tragic accident which took the lives of Hudson Theater actors Tedd Brackett, left, and Harry Bond, right, the day before when their car was struck by a trolley at Stop 15½ Albany - Schenectady Road. (2) This was the Empire Theater on Albany Street at Germania Avenue after it was constructed in 1907 as a burlesque and vaudeville house. In 1911 it became the Majestic movie theater and from 1918 to 1935 was known as the Albany Street Theater.

*(1) The Parker Building, built in 1906 and still the city's tallest downtown struc-
ture, is shown in this 1910 photo. The Art Theatre is at right with the entrance to
Taberski's first pool hall in between, while the Crescent Theater was located in
building at left, now the site of Key Bank.*

Downtown Schenectady scene about 1912 as two long-skirted ladies cross the north side of State Street in the direction of the Vendome Hotel. The Orpheum Theater (later the site of the Lerner shop) is in right background. It became the Palace Theater in 1918 and the New Strand Theater in 1924.

15—The Pool Halls

Such old-time world champions as Frank Taberski, Ralph Greenleaf and Alfredo DeOro would shudder today at such recent innovations in the game of pocket billiards as beige or tangerine cushion cloths on tables set up in elegant surroundings of a "billiard recreational academy."

Pocket billiards — more commonly known as pool — is making a comeback on the American scene through the efforts of billiards equipment manufacturers. But the "new look" is nothing like the old days.

The pool craze has invaded family recreation rooms, college dormitories and public play centers often connected with bowling establishments. Even the ladies are taking the cue and, possibly through their influence or as a means of enticement, the manufacturers are "dolling up" the surroundings.

The traditional green baize has now been joined by such gaudy cushion cloths as tangerine, beige, blue, gray and gold. Vari-colored wood trims are in competition with the beloved mahogany. Tables once were a standard 10 by 5 feet, but they are now 9 by 4 1/2 reet for convenience of patrons. The old "string" leather pockets have long since given way to cone pockets with ball returns.

Possibly the only similarity to yesteryear is that there are still 15 balls plus the cue ball.

Back in the days of the spitoon-dotted pool halls, it was common knowledge—at least in the minds of strait-laced citizens — "to play the game of billiards well was the mark of a misspent youth."

There certainly was the opportunity. Every small town had its bowling alley and pool hall and every good saloon had a pool table...so did the recreation rooms of the fire and police departments. Cities proportionately had a larger share of cue clubs which likewise thrived through the 19th century and up until the depression era of the 1930s.

There also was an unwritten rule: No ladies allowed.

It may be mere nostalgia that lends enchantment to the smoke-filled pool halls of bygone days. They were at once a retreat, a hang-out, a social center — and a means of hustling a few bucks if you were deft with the cue stick.

Schenectady had its share of billiard rooms. Among those in more recent years (after the turn of the century) were Morris' bowling alleys and pool hall at 211 Clinton Street, once the site of the Union-Star plant, and Nick Murphy's cue club at 148 Clinton Street where Ter Bush & Powell is now located.

Murphy's originally was at Albany Street, near Schenectady Street, but Nick moved down to the Clinton Street spot where his pool hall became a popular meeting place for high school and college students. One of Nick's sons, Sennett Murphy, was a slick player and often cleaned up when he hustled in out-of-town halls.

Leagues sometimes were formed, such as the GE drafting association's pool league, and gave prizes for high total ball, high percentage and high average for the year. Most of the halls had membership cards available for a nominal fee.

There was a pool hall known as Kadel's in the vicinity of Wallace's store. Another was connected with the Star Bowling Center just below the old trolley waiting room. On the south side of State Street, four doors below Clinton, was once located a howling alley on the third floor and a pool hall on the second.

Private clubs usually had a pool room. The Elks Club, the Mohawk Club and the YMCA, then located at State and Ferry Streets, had their club champs. The lower club often invited well-known cue artists to give exhibitions in pocket billiards and three cushion billiards — as it still does on occasion.

Unquestionably the best known of Schenectady's billiard shots was Frank Taberski, originally from Amsterdam, who became world champion of pocket billiards in 1916 and alternated with other top-notch shots of the day until he became ill in the early 1930s and had to retire. He died in 1941 at the age of 51.

About the time Taberski began to astound area pool sharks with his cue wizardry, he opened a pool parlor back of the old Art Theatre, near the present site of Proctor's. While still a world's champion in 1928, he built a new place—Taberski's bowling and billiard center — at 138 Broadway.

This new billiard hall soon became a popular center and often was the scene of astounding matches between Taberski and other pool greats.

Some today can still recall how Taberski "tortured" his adversaries with his deliberate, often painfully slow, manner of shooting while he made fantastic runs of 130 or more. He especially agitated the great Ralph Greenleaf, who captured the championship several times during Taberski's best years and last won it in 1937.

While Greenleaf fussed and fumed, Taberski would walk slowly around the table pondering his next shot. The gallery was tense, quiet. Taberski chalked up, for the fifth time since he made his last shot. Then he finally crouched over the table, deftly sliding the cue stick below a crooked finger and moving it back and forth for an interminable minute. Suddenly, he stood upright, chalked up again — only to start another slow walk around the table as though to determine whether he might have a better shot.

It was partly because of Taberski's "calculated" method of shooting that the Billiard Congress of America later placed a three-minute time limit between shots on official matches.

But nothing could be taken away from Taberski's skill. For years his records stood, and he was champion during the years 1916-18, 1925, 1927, 1928 and 1929. Besides Greenleaf, he beat the best of the day — Erwin Rudolph, Thomas Hueston and John Layton.

Probably the greatest champion of them all, in terms of longevity, was Alfredo DeOro. He won his first world's pocket billiards crown in 1887 and held it alternately on other years up until 1913.

Of course Willie Mosconi has to be rated the best in recent years. The great Willie took his first world's championship in 1941 and held it consistently until he retired, undefeated, in 1955.

The old Taberski pool hall and bowling alleys continued operations right up until a winter's nite in 1964 when it burned to the ground.

PART FOUR
Sic Semper Transit

Taking a short break at Rosendale Road opposite St. David's Lane, the crew of this open bench car get ready to head back to the city in 1905. Ward Burns is the motorman and Charles L. Pierson the conductor at right. Man at left is unidentified.

16—What Was a Trolley Car?

The story of the streetcars in Schenectady is a fascinating one, especially because it is a part of Americana that has vanished but not so long ago that many folks around today can't tell what it was like to have worked on the "electrics" and to have been among the faithful who supported them. It was a time before the nation became infatuated with automobiles and when the American people had another love — the trolley car.

In these succeeding segments on the history of the Schenectady Railway Company and the impact of the electric transit system on the social, industrial and economic life of the community, we will endeavor to give an inside look at people and events involved in its fantastic period of development. But a nostalgic synopsis of that golden era of transportation might be a fitting prelude to the full story. Countless interviews with people who worked on the urban and interurban lines and those who rode the cars have exacted a picture which enjoys a special niche in early 20th century American history.

By the turn of this century, people in Schenectady and in about every other enterprising city of the nation took the trolleys to their hearts and rode on them into a marvelous golden age that lasted until well after World War I. And why not? They offered a freedom from lolling on the front porch after working hours, an opportunity for the whole family to enjoy a ride into the country on those wonderful "breezers" or open bench cars on a warm summer evening, maybe even a ride to one of the recreation parks where admission was five cents a head for trolley riders and free fireworks and dances on the premises could round out the evening.

Only a few cities in the U.S. today offer the thrill of riding a trolley (St. Louis and New Orleans are among them, and San Francisco still has its cable cars) but there are numerous trolley museums which have purchased some of the old cars of nearly every type and offer the chance to ride down memory lane. In the northeast, there are the Branford Museum at New Haven, Conn., the Kennebunk Museum at Kennebunk, Maine, and the Trolley Museum at Warehouse Point, Conn.

For the over-forty crowd there remains an overwhelming desire to recapture the thrill of riding a trolley, which is probably why these museums are doing well during their summer seasons with volunteer help by men and women who are dedicated to keeping it alive. There is also an urge to have the small fry climb aboard an "electric" and share the exhilaration of feeling the ponderous lurch as the old car rattles down the rails. Two generations have not known the once-popular, non-polluting servant of mass transit, so there is little wonder that older folks are mindful of Robert S. Wilson's wincing lines:

"But oh! may there never come the day,
When a child shall go to his dad and say,
'What was a trolley car?'"

Let's take those wonderful days when the SRC regularly ran its "twilight specials" on summer evenings, bound for Rexford Park across the river from Craig or on up to the east end of Ballston Lake to Forest Park. Usually there were four or five such cars, the open breezers, and with colored lights aglow they picked up crowds in the area of McClellan Street, then at State and Lafayette and started out along Van Vranken Avenue. The night air blew against your face with a blessed coolness. Up front the motorman pulled down the green curtain that shielded his face from reflections. Meanwhile, the conductor swung along the running board collecting fares, sometimes not ending his chore until the car reached its destination.

From the moment you stepped off the trolley at Rexford's park shed, there were the delightful sounds of the merry-go-round, the click and roar of the roller coaster and the shrieks of terrified riders. Action, life and enjoyment were everywhere and it did not cost much to partake of every bit of it.

The ride home, across the long Mohawk bridge and back to Schenectady, was just as deliciously satisfying. You were hot and tired but in a comfortable sort of way. Maybe there'd be harmonizing along the way on "Let Me Call You Sweetheart" or "By the Light of the Silvery Moon" and "The End of a Perfect Day." Usually, "In the Good Old Summertime" was somehow fitted in before the car reached downtown and the load of riders had thinned out by several key stops.

If there came up a sudden thunderstorm, the conductor loosened the side curtains on the open car and the black and yellow striped canvas flapped merrily in the breeze while the patrons crowded closer together to avoid getting wet. It was all part of the fun.

Funny thing about those open cars. They were instantly popular with the riding public when they came out in the mid-1890s, and when they were put on the lines along about Decoration Day the motormen and conductors knew better than anyone else that the people were overjoyed at the coming out. But towards the World War I period, trolley companies across America began replacing them with closed models with center aisles. Probably there were two main reasons. One was the higher accident rate on the bench cars as passengers tended to board or leave them in motion. Another was the suspicion among company officials that many of the nickel fares were never collected, as people jumped on and off before the conductor got around to them. The big 15 bench open cars, for example, seated as many as 75 passengers but a lot more swarmed aboard all along the sides — making it extremely difficult for the conductor to collect fares.

The author is old enough to well remember the orange cars with cream trim that plied the streets of Schenectady, particularly the No. 4 to Woodlawn and the No. 6 "A" and "B" belt lines. But he had never been fortunate enough to have had a ride in the open car. That is why it was especially enjoyable to finally board a breezer on a hot summer afternoon at the Kennebunk Museum a few years ago and ride the two-mile length of track, reversing the seats at the end of the line for the return trip. It was all there — the sounds of the noisy air brake, the clanging trolley bell, the busy nok-nok-nok of the compressor and the clicking of the "coffee grinder" in the steady hand of the motorman. There was also that unforgettable odor compounded of fresh paint, hot motors and track sand.

A good friend of ours and of many in Schenectady, Albert P. Bantham, once told us that, as a child, he could tell the type of car without seeing it—just by the sound of the motor. The introduction of the 600 series, he recalls, was a memorable event in the lives of the young, awe-stricken riders. "We had never before seen anything so big and beautiful, and they rode like the wind," he said.

Mr. Bantham also shared a recollection of the Saratoga run:

"I recall my father taking me to Saratoga one August day to see the races. The through cars from Albany were supplemented by others, including some of the 700 series, and they departed only minutes apart. Passengers were jammed so tightly that the cars were nearly to Ballston Spa before the conductor was able to worm his way through to collect the fares. About that time the voltage would drop and the cars would crawl slowly until suddenly they stopped altogether. The line simply did not have sufficient power to handle so many cars at one time. There was a great deal of grumbling, which became louder as the minutes ticked away and large cheers when motion was resumed. After spending all that money (I think it was 35 cents) each way, they wanted to be sure they got there for the first race."

Art Sylvester, who joined the Schenectady trolley firm in November, 1923, had a few memories of the trolley days from a motorman's point of view. He came on just after the big strike and was assigned to some of the big interurbans. A conductor on the Albany interurbans in the early 1920's would close the door of the Limited after the stop at the city line near the Stanford estate (now the Ingersoll Memorial Home) and give the motorman the go-ahead signal. There were no stops from there to the Albany city line near the railroad underpass. The best time Mr. Sylvester recollected was seven minutes from city line to city line.

The conductors wore black cap badges with white even numerals, while the motormen had white cap badges with black odd numerals. The company published a rule book which was given to each new employee to study, remember and abide by. A watch inspection card was issued to each streetcar operator and conductor after the monthly timepiece inspection as both motormen and conductors had to carry open faced pocket watches which kept perfect time.

The fares managed to stay at a nickel until just after World War I. The trolley companies in New York State had been clamoring for state per-mission to go to a six-cent fare because, as they explained, operating costs were rising rapidly. There were many public hearings in localities to be affected by the price rise and the hike was forestalled by reason of the war effort. But no sooner had the one-cent raise in fares been effected after 1918 than another request by SRC was forthcoming for a seven-cent city fare with graduating increases for the interurban routes. This was granted by the Public Service Commission with a warning, however, that the new rates must remain in effect for an appreciable period in the future.

No doubt many today will recall the times when smaller members of the family, perhaps a year or two beyond the five-year age limit when trolleys and movie theaters permitted free admission, were persuaded to "scrooch down a bit" to economize the family budget — until they were challenged by the conductor or the box of office agent on too frequent occasions.

The glory days of the trolley probably covered about the first quarter of the 20th century. Even though it was still well patronized in 1925, there was growing evidence that the gasoline era had overtaken it and each year that followed saw the streetcar's fortunes dwindling in diminishing passenger fares and increased costs for maintenance. The buses by then were coming into prominence, but it was probably the family car — with all the freedom and independence it offered — which by 1930 made riding the trolley seem utilitarian. A verse which appeared in the Sante Fe Railroad magazine summed it up:

"Any girl can be gay in a classy coupe;
In a taxicab all can be jolly.
But the girl worth the while is the one who can smile
When you're taking her home on the trolley!"

A young lady gingerly hops on a streetcar in Schenectady in the late 1890s as the motorman upper left affixes the trolley above.

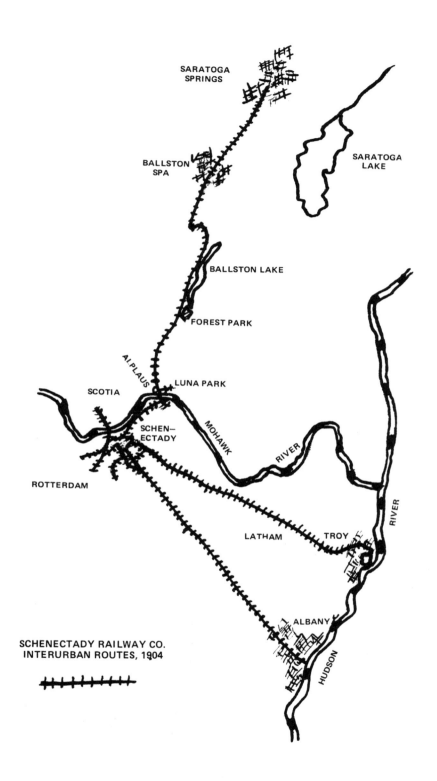

SARATOGA
SPRINGS

SARATOGA
LAKE

BALLSTON
SPA

BALLSTON LAKE

FOREST PARK

ALPLAUS

SCOTIA   LUNA PARK

SCHEN—
ECTADY

MOHAWK

RIVER

ROTTERDAM

RIVER

LATHAM   TROY

ALBANY

HUDSON

SCHENECTADY RAILWAY CO.
INTERURBAN ROUTES, 1904

108

17—The Rise and Fall of the SRC

THE BEGINNING

It has been over a century since J. Ezra McCue, 4th Ward alderman, reputedly paid the first five-cents fare on the first horsecar to run on the streets of Schenectady. That was in 1887 the year after Thomas A. Edison and his associates set up shop in 1886 along the Rotterdam flats—a move that was destined to have a profound effect on the future of the trolley car and, indeed, the city of Schenectady.

The history of the street railway in Schenectady formally began with dedication speeches at the foot of Crescent Park on the hot, muggy afternoon of July 16, 1887. That was the day McCue and other officials took the first ride in a Toonerville-type trolley, painted a gaudy red and yellow, that was pulled along trolley tracks by a team of white horses.

The Schenectady Street Railway Company had been organized Feb. 25, 1886, but it took time to lay the single track horsecar line from the Mohawk Bridge on Washington Ave. and up State Street to the Brandywine carbarn, a distance of about two miles. The equipment of the new company consisted of 30 horses, five cars and four sleighs.

The horsecars, open-sided in summer and closed the rest of the time, became a popular conveyance almost as soon as the dedication speeches had been made.

Of course, as with everything new, there were a few problems to be ironed out before the venture went smoothly. First, the teams of horses were new to the business. They tried to run away but could not, the weight was too great. The drivers could not hold them and the cars more than once were dragged from the tracks and bounded over the cobbles. Unused to the sight, runaways of other horsedrawn rigs were frequent and their drivers cursed the "dang-nab" new contraptions and threatened legal reprisals. However, inside of a month, this problem resolved itself as the horsecar teams became accustomed to hauling the rumbling vehicle.

Another problem was that of crossing the State Street railroad tracks, then at grade level. The city fathers, worried over possible fatalities, first decreed that passengers must leave the car and cross the tracks on foot before reentering the car on the other side.

Soon after a rash of protests over the order, however, the city officials recanted and the horsecars crossed the tracks under the watchful eyes of the crossing flagman.

The difficulty of halting so heavy a vehicle once it got rolling became a perplexing problem—especially when it went far past a prospective passenger before screeching to a full stop.

A foot pedal was used at first, but it was not effective. Finally, the situation was saved by the introduction of the "stemwinder," a large upright crank at the driver's right hand. The crank operated the brakes by winding a chain and holding it with a ratchet. The brake retained the right hand location throughout streetcar history.

Their main advantage over stagecoaches was that a horse could haul much more on smooth rails than over rutted roads or cobblestones. The horsecars had a door in the middle of the back, and seats facing inward on both sides. The driver stood on a plat form in front and received fares through a small door. No smoking was allowed inside the cars.

Although the simple-trucked horsecars had no wheel clearance problems, they retained the narrow bottom and curved sides of the stage-coach. These curved sides were divided into two lengthwise panels, with the lower one nearly always painted a light yellow or cream color—which led to the nickname of "yellow-belly."

Actually, Schenectady had been slow in getting a public trans-portation system. Horsecars had been in use, and proven successful, in a large number of U.S. cities since about 1850. When they finally did come to Schenectady, the stage already was set for mechanical cars. As important as it was to the early history of the street railway, the horsecar was doomed to early replacement here by an offspring of the wonder of the age — electricity.

The road continued to be operated by horsepower until July 3, 1891, when the motive power was changed to electricity. The first car in Schenectady was run at 9:45 that evening and not a few people were out along lower State Street to watch the marvelous spectacle of a car run-ning on its own power. Two Edison men were involved in a friendly wager on the occasion. William B. "Pop" Turner, who directed the changeover to an electrified line, won a $100 bet from Samuel B. Insull that he would have the cars running before midnight that date. There had been very lit-tle movement in the direction of extending the line that had existed with the horsecars. That would come, however, and at an almost incredible rate shortly after 1900. Schenectady was only seven years behind the start of the first successful street railway in the United States, which began operation in Cleveland in 1884.

The property and the franchise of the original company were sold on foreclosure Jan. 31. 1895 (much to the relief of local citizens who already had begun to complain about poor service) and the Schenectady Railway Co. was organized the following month. It was to serve the city and its surrounding area for the next half century.

The electric cars were very much like the horsecars, but were larg-er and heavier. They had monitor roofs, yellowbelly sides and open plat-forms. An electric controller was added at the motorman's left hand and a trolley pole sprouted from the roof. More elaborate trucks were intro-duced, with a place for the motors and an additional set of springs between the truck frame and the body.

In 1892, the Sprague and Thomson-Houston Co.s were merged with the Edison General Electric Co. to form the General Electric Co., which in that year introduced the first fully-enclosed cast-steel frame rail-way motor. There was little wonder that Schenectady got in on the ground floor of the rapid progress of the trolley car industry.

General Electric, owners of the Schenectady Railway Co., lost no time in converting the old State Street trolley route to electricity. The city's main thoroughfare was strung with overhead strands of copper wire to transmit power to the new trolley system and there were plans afoot to expand the network within the next few years.

Before the coming of the electric railway, the city extended only a little more than a mile from its center. Horse-drawn transportation was too slow to encourage living further out than that. But the electric trolley was at least twice as fast as the horsecar, and new suburban areas quickly developed. Uptown Schenectady can trace its growth directly to the electrification of the horsecar lines in the 1890's, just as many other cities across the nation must attribute their "uptown districts" to the coming of age of the electric trolley.

Since World War II, the trolley car has vanished so rapidly from the American scene that few members of the younger generation have ever climbed aboard a clanging streetcar.

In all the annals of human endeavor, never has so large an enterprise grown and disappeared so swiftly as the traction industry. In 1921, the electric railway business was America's fifth largest industry, accommodating 12 times the number of passengers carried by the steam railroads the same year. Yet today, only a handful of cities in the United States and Canada are still served by streetcars.

EXPANDING THE LINES

"The business revival in Schenectady is shown by the greatly increasing business done by the electric railway" stated an editorial in the Evening Star of July 23,1894. And yet, this was only the beginning of the part to be played in the city's expansion by the young Schenectady Railway Co., already rolling up its sleeves for the job ahead.

There were only a few single track routes in 1894, for the most part a retread of the original trackage laid down for the horsecars eight years before. Cars left Brandywine Avenue on the even quarter hour, reached the Edison Hotel (railroad depot) 15 minutes later; General Electric works, 22 minutes later, and the "white house" at the top of Broadway hill, 30 minutes later.

Citizens committees were being organized in many sections of the city and suburbs, holding public meetings and consultations with officials of the railway for the purpose of getting extension of the streetcar routes into their territory.

J. P. Ord, vice president of GE and president of the railway company, became the "champion of the people" along with his superintendent, R. H. Fraser, when he attended many of the meetings and promised the "acme of perfection in street railways and street lighting in Schenectady within the next few years." He was not making any rash promises. In August, 1898, General Electric purchased the interests and properties of Schenectady Railway, Schenectady Illuminating Co. and Mohawk Gas Co.

Henry Springstead's grocery store on Broadway in Bellevue was a favorite meeting place for those who wanted the line extended along that avenue to South Schenectady. Residents of the "northward" were generating enthusiasm for extension of the trolley lines through Nott Terrace and across the college pasture to Van Vranken. Mont Pleasant, a fast-growing "suburb" pleaded for passenger service to the city.

Naturally there were some objections to the prospect of trolley inroads to the heart of staid residential areas, where up to now the quiet of treelined avenues was broker, only by the occasional clip-clop of horse hoofs.

J. W. Smitley, owner of the property at the corner of Nott Terrace and Union Street (now the rectory of St. John the Evangelist Church), at first vigorously opposed the line that would run from State Street along Nott Terrace and Union Avenue, across Wendell to Nott Street. But in the end, a smiling Mr. Smitley agreed that it was best for the city's progress and on Oct. 20,1899, the first cars made the Nott Street run.

Objections were made by other individuals that the streetcars would spoil the street for horsemen and that "pupils of the Nott Terrace School would be ground and mangled under the merciless wheels."

The case of trolley service to Scotia was delayed pending legal interpretation of right of way. Several homeowners along lower Washington Avenue claimed their property line extended to the middle of the street—and they wanted no part of the rumbling cars that had to pass their homes in order to cross the steel bridge to Scotia. Despite numerous injunctions served on the railway company, temporary tracks and turnouts were installed to hasten the service.

At 5:30 p.m. on April 15, 1902, trolley No. 29 crossed the reconstructed steel bridge from the end of Washington Avenue crowded with cheering GE workers making the inaugural trip home.

Within the short span of five years, from 1900 to 1905, the city was gridironed with a network of street railway tracks as new routes were developed to satisfy the demands of a public anxious for the convenience of streetcar service. In many sections double track was laid to permit later schedules. By 1905, Bellevue, Scotia, Mont Pleasant, upper Union and Albany Streets, McClellan Street, Van Vranken Avenue, and Aqueduct all were included in the service provided by the fast-growing Schenectady Railway Co.

In addition, the interurban car had entered upon the scene and the Schenectady company early recognized its boon to business. While the smaller green and cream city cars plied the local routes, the fast and shiny behemoths began breaking speed records on the new roads to neighboring communities.

The double track line to Albany was opened Sept. 9, 1901; the one to Troy on Mar. 2, 1903; to Amsterdam on June 30 that same year and to Ballston Spa on June 30 the following year.

Most people who still remember the trolleys in Schenectady think of the bright orange bodies with cream trim, a long-standing color combination in the electric cars' 55-year history here. But there were earlier colors. The red and yellow of the horsecars were changed to dark green with silver trim. After 1910, the company's standard color was maroon with black and nickel striping, the name of the company glowing in large gold letters. The orange and cream came in shortly after World War I. For a time, in the early 1920's, SRC experimented with the "sunburst" design on each end of the cars-as though the headlight was exploding in brilliant rays of color. It was supposedly a safety factor to give oncoming vehicles greater perception of the electric cars, whether by day or night. This idea was soon dropped, however, as people complained of the gaudiness.

This brings to mind the brief advertising gimmick entered into by

SRC when Tip Top bread first came out in the mid-Twenties. One of the smaller city cars was painted to resemble a loaf of that particular brand and it became somewhat of a novelty for the year it was on the road. It also brought in a fair amount of revenue from the baking company for the promotional stunt. Advertising on the cars, at first only on the interior on an ad rack running above the windows, brought in about $1,200 a month. In later years. some ads were placed outside the car but mostly for community events and drives.

It might be well to describe a few of the routes for those who do not remember the trolleys rumbling through the city.

There were the A-Belt and B-Belt cars traversing in opposite directions on State, McClellan, Eastern Avenue and Nott Terrace. Rugby Road cars used State, Nott Terrace, a short block of Union Street, Union Avenue, half a block of Wendell Avenue, then Rugby to McClellan. The Woodlawn cars (No. 4) went up State as far as Frank Street. The Scotia cars were marked "M" and "B". They entered Scotia via the old iron bridge and traveled along the dike or Schonowe Avenue. The "M" cars went up Mohawk Avenue as far as Toll Street. The "B" cars went up Ballston Avenue, over Wallace and Fifth Street, turning up Vley Road and stopping at Sixth Street. After the Scotia run, the motorman changed the route sign to Crane Street because the Crane Street-Scotia route was one. When the cars entered from Scotia, again over the bridge and up Washington Avenue to State, they traveled up State and on up Albany Street to Schenectady Street, over Strong Street to the viaduct over the hollow to Francis Avenue and up Crane Street. Returning, they came straight over Hulett to State, then down to Washington Avenue and so back to Scotia. And then there were the lines that served Broadway, Campbell Avenue, Grand Boulevard and the Rexford-Aqueduct loop.

The through Saratoga-Albany cars came into the city by Van Vranken Avenue, down Nott Street and over Park Place and on over Lafayette Street where they waited on a special track at the foot of Crescent Park. Then they went up Albany Street to Elm, over to State and on out towards Albany. The Troy line went up State, across McClellan and on out Union Street.

CHANGING SCHENECTADY'S IMAGE

Modern inventions do not change human nature, but they do change human affairs.

So it was when rapid transit was introduced to America a little more than a century ago. Cities were of such small area that people could walk to and from their daily work without much loss of time. Nobody seemed to be in a hurry in those days, and life went on very easily and smoothly.

Invention of the electric trolley system soon changed all that. It became one of the most powerful factors in the evolution of cities, affecting not only the health and comfort of citizens but the very existence and prosperity of cities themselves. As the service of street railways increased, the faster the city population and suburbs grew and became more dependent upon that service.

The history of the Schenectady Railway Co, was not unique as, according to statistics, it experienced the same phenomenal success with its street cars as the other hundreds of roads which crisscrossed the nation at the beginning of this century.

In 1894, the Schenectady system consisted of two miles of single track with four cars. Its report of August,1904, showed an operation of 124 miles of track and 160 cars handling 10 million passengers in one year!

The city, both downtown and in far-reaching sections of all suburbs, underwent startling physical changes in that same decade. The railway company was constructing its vast network of tracks, building new car barns at Fuller Street and McClellan Street, steel bridges to span Cotton Factory Hollow (Pleasant Valley), the Mohawk River near Aqueduct and the canal at Washington Avenue.

Downtown Schenectady, in particular, was fast becoming a maze of sidewalk poles and overhead wires. No underground conduits were employed in those early days of electricity. Separate poles were used for main electrical service, for the telephone and for the copper wiring which supported the "witches brooms" of the trolley power lines directly over the streets.

In the summer of 1904, steam pile drivers were shaking the ground in the 400 block of State Street as construction was under way for the new "skyscraper" being erected for the Hon. John N. Parker.

Officials of General Electric and the Schenectady Railway Co. that same year hailed the opening of the Dock Street substation which would furnish the power needed to operate the fast-growing streetcar service. (It was razed in 1962).

In the summer of 1904, a huge steel gas tank was constructed on Villa Road by the Mohawk Gas Co. to improve the gas supply for the city.

The railway company, directly responsible for management of the Schenectady Illuminating Co., was also engaged that year in erecting new electric arc lights, complete with "artistic ornamental standards," from Church Street to Crescent Park.

Elimination of the steam railroad grade crossings throughout the city, a project which would take four years, began in 1903.

This is not to say that the invention of the electric railway was directly responsible for the entire boom of developments and improvements within the city at the turn of the century; the General Electric and American Locomotive companies certainly get more than a fair share of credit for they were contributing to the economic stability of the whole area.

But there is this fact: the Schenectady Railway Co., which seemed to come suddenly upon the scene and do everything well, captured the enthusiasm and the confidence of the citizens here. Perhaps it was part of the times, the vogue of doing new things and having new conveniences. At any rate, the street railway and its progressive outlook was in step with a growing Schenectady.

THE STATE STREET SIT-IN

During its formative years of rapid growth at the outset of this century, the Schenectady Railway Co. fought and won countless battles for improvement of its ever-widening system. Having been successful in conquering problems of the elements, pressure groups, legal maneuvers and rival transit outfits, the company suffered an ignominious setback one summer day in 1904 at the hands of that unpredictable entity — a woman.

Her name was Miss Ruth Levi, daughter of a Schenectady merchant reputed to be worth close to a million dollars, and the story of her defiance of the trolley firm and the Common Council not only made news here but was reprinted in newspapers throughout the Northeast. One even described her as "another Susan B. Anthony, one who stands not only for the rights of the weaker sex but for the rights of the common citizen against the encroachment of public utilities."

It all started when the city decided to install new electric incandescent lights along State Street. At a meeting of the Common Council Apr. 12, 1904, Public Works Commissioner George Holtzmann was authorized to install the lights on State Street from Crescent Park to Washington Avenue.

The new lights were known as "Buffalo lamps," the main street of that city being lighted with them, and would be arranged two in a series on a tall ornamental steel pole. One light was to hang over the sidewalk, the other over the street, and the lamps were to be wired separately so that the sidewalk lights could be extinguished after midnight. The old arc lamps which were suspended over the street at lengthy intervals would be removed once the new lights were installed.

"This will give us as well lighted a street as there is in the whole United States," enthused Commissioner Holtzmann when he turned over the installation contract to the Schenectady Railway Co.

The gang of workmen went to work on the project at once, beginning at the lower end of State Street on the job of digging troughs on either side of the street for the underground wire conduits. Power for the lighting of the new lamps would be supplied by the company's new Dock Street power station.

All went well until progress of the work brought the construction gang to the front of the Jonathan Levi residence at 428 State Street (That building still stands, the ground floor being occupied by Time Center). It was Aug. 15, 1904, the day Miss Ruth Levi defied and defeated the city and one of its strongest corporations.

About 5 p.m. that hot, sultry afternoon, the workmen had removed the flagging from in front of Levi's stately residence and had dug a deep hole preparatory to installing a light stanchion there. They were interrupted when Miss Levi suddenly came upon the scene, her gown swishing ominously as she dashed down the stone porch steps of her father's home and seated herself at the edge of the hole near the curb. She ignored the remarks made by the workmen and absolutely refused to budge until they had replaced the dirt in the hole.

Commissioner Holtzmann was called to the rescue; he tried unsuccessfully to reason with her. The lines of battle were distinctly drawn when another urgent call went out, this time to General Manager E. F. Peck. Meanwhile, news of the incident spread throughout the district and soon hundreds of curious and amused spectators thronged the street opposite Jay. Most seemed to sympathize with Miss Levi's cause which, foolishly enough, they seemed to feel was that of the underdog.

Peck sought to point out the urgency of getting the job done, but the lady would have none of it. She told the harassed official it was unnecessary to place a street light directly in front of a private residence of that business portion of State Street. And furthermore, she said, they already had one of two large elms in front of their house killed by the electric wires passing through its boughs.

Jonathan Levi, calm and patient businessman that he was, had all this time offered only token resistance and left most of the arguing to his daughter. However, he was about to agree to a proposition by Holtzmann that they remove the original pole from in front of the house, provided Levi would let the other pole be erected, when an agitated Miss Levi intervened.

"Father, you don't understand," she exclaimed, "he means to take up the old one but to leave the new one where the hole is dug. I will take charge of this matter, and if they raise that pole it will be over my dead body!" Whereupon, Peck called off his gang of workmen and retreated to the cheers of onlookers

But the battle was not over. The electricians renewed their attack under the Levi shade tree at 2:15 the following morning and dug three holes, thinking this would be an act of strategy on their part. The Levis were soon notified. The whole family came out in the dead of night, picked out a hole and sat in it while the men dug more.

Soon there were more excavations than Levis, but friends were on hand to sit in a hole as one was dug. Finally the workmen gave up digging and rigged up a tackle across two big railway feed wires and proceeded to hoist the big pole bearing the double lamps into position. But where? All the holes were occupied and another crowd of spectators awakened by the renewed "sit-in strike" obstructed work.

Thoroughly confused, the gang foreman went to the Fuller Street car barn for further instructions. When he returned he simply said to his men, "Cut it out!" The holes were refilled and the Levi family returned to its slumber, resolved that they would have no Buffalo lamps to light their front bedrooms.

Officials of the railway company and the city met the next day, conceded defeat to the Levis and decided to place the new light standard near the driveway of Dr. Harmon D. Swits' residence at 430 State Street (now the site of the Carl Co.)

The whole project was completed two months later and on Saturday night, Oct. 17 that year, the street lights were first turned on with a brilliance that amazed even the skeptics of the potential of electrical power.

On Thursday, Apr. 6, the next year, Jonathan Levi died at his residence. He had been identified with the city's commercial life for more than a half century, conducting a drygoods, liquor and grocery store at

218 State Street (opposite Barney's). Nearly all places of business in Schenectady closed at 2 p.m. while services were conducted at the Levi home the following Monday by Rabbi E. M. Chapman of Congregation Shara Schomajim.

ON TO THE NINTH WARD!

When it was announced June 13, 1904, that a contract had been awarded the Pennsylvania Steel Co. of Steelton, Pa., for the erection of the new Schenectady Railway Co.'s steel viaduct to span Cotton Factory Hollow, resident of the fast growing Mont Pleasant district applauded the move. They had petitioned the railway for such service two years before, pointing out that it would be a lucrative move for the company as they were cut off from the main part of the city without public transportation.

An editorial in the Evening Star that day said: "The day the Schenectady Railway Co. runs the first car over this line will mark the dawn of a greater increase in Ninth Ward property values and the entering of this section of our city into a closer relationship with the city proper."

Specifications called for a double track steel-girdered deck, 625 feet long and supported by five sets of steel pedestals set on solid concrete. The new viaduct was to have a carrying capacity of a 25,000-pound load designed to carry the heaviest of cars. The recently-opened Hulett and Schenectady Street line would run over the viaduct on 15-minute service up Crane Street to 9th Avenue.

As soon as trees and brush were cleared from the bridge area, steam-driven pile drivers were brought in to lay the foundations for the concrete footings. About 30 men and six teams of horses were at work grading the hills on either side of the hollow, and tracks were being laid by railway company gangs in the Mont Pleasant district beyond the point where the bridge would enter the Ninth Ward.

Crowds of people gathered along the banks each day to watch the progress of the bridge workmen, especially in the fall of 1904 when steel girders began to be hoisted into position.

The construction went on throughout that winter, with the exception of a few days lost because of extreme cold or snow. As the bridge surface began to take shape just before Christmas, the steel firm brought in an apparatus which amazed onlookers. It was a huge steel derrick called the "traveler," so named because it moved along the structure towering high in the air as it put the steel girders in place.

Finally the big day for the bridge opening arrived March 31, 1905. It was formally dedicated when a special car left the company's waiting room at 420 State Street 2 p.m. with a party of railroad officials and prominent residents of the ward and city.

The car had banners on both sides bearing the words: "Greetings to the Ninth Ward." Once it had crossed the new bridge and the barrier lifted, the occupants got out of the trolley to have their picture taken. Among them were John E. Yorkston, school commissioner; E. F. Peck, general manager of the railway company; George Holtzmann, commissioner of public works, and Henry Quackenbush, for whom Quackenbush Park in Mont Pleasant was later named.

The new line afforded transportation to about 5,000 persons, who now could board a trolley in the Ninth Ward and ride to the end of lower State Street without changing cars. Heretofore, they had to walk at least 1½ miles through some unpaved streets to reach the nearest trolley service at the foot of Crane or Congress Street hills.

Still in excellent condition, the Pleasant Valley bridge became strictly a crossover for automobiles and buses in the late 1940s when the bed of the span was torn up, the double tracks removed and the flooring replaced with steel-ribbed surfacing. This was after the railway company made the switch-over to buses prior to World War II, and found it expedient to turn over ownership of the bridge to the City of Schenectady.

It was Aug. 21, 1981 when the old trolley fixture was replaced by a modern bridge over the fully completed I-890. Of course the whole area had changed drastically since the days of Craig's cotton factory with its mills ponds and thick growth of trees and underbrush in the hollow long before the turn of this century. But before its demise, the old bridge witnessed another transition in its lifetime with construction of the Interstate that passed beneath its towering pillars.

This was after the railway company made the switch-over to buses prior to World War II, and found it expedient to turn over ownership of the old bridge to the City of Schenectady.

Of course the whole area has changed drastically since the days of Craig's cotton factory with its mills ponds and thick growth of trees and underbrush in the hollow at the turn of this century.

THE RUNAWAY TROLLEY

Shortly before 3 a.m. on Monday, July 13, 1903, motorman William C. McGraw and conductor Charles Gill pulled away from the Fuller Street carbarn on the No. 51 express, bound for the 'nighthawk" run to Albany. Within a half hour they would find themselves eye-witnesses to the wildest flight probably ever taken by a streetcar.

At the company's waiting room at 420 State Street, two Albany women boarded the car. They were Miss Clara Hammond, a young lady who had been vising relatives here, and Miss Mamie Miller, a domestic servant. No other passengers were aboard the express that early morning as the big 52-seat car rumbled up Albany Street past Crescent Park.

All went well until motorman McGraw guided No. 51 around the sharp curve at the corner of Elm and Albany Streets, heading into State Street. There was a noise underneath the trolley which sounded like a gun shot, followed by a loud hissing. Discovering the air pipe had been severed from the storage cylinder, rendering the air brake useless, the two men decided to return to the carbarn for another car.

Miss Hammond seemed distressed at the delay as they headed down State Street. Miss Miller, already drowsing in her seat next to a window in the middle of the car, certainly didn't mind.

When Hulett Street was reached, McGraw stopped the trolley to check the hand brake. At Close Street, two blocks farther down State Street hill where all cars were compelled to stop according to orders, the motorman again applied the hand brake. This time there was a brittle snap as the brake chain broke... and the heavy car began its plunge down the hill, the wheels of its double trucks squealing and grinding at the sudden burst of speed.

As the streetcar originally had set out for Albany, the emergency brake was not available—it was on the other end of the car. McGraw then tried to use the reverse brake, the fourth and final brakeage system, but could not throw it over. He hollered to Gill to pull the trolley pole off the wire, so that now the car's weight would provide the only momentum.

"I pray to God we can ride it out," McGraw mumbled as he stood frozen at the useless controls in the front vestibule of the darkened streetcar, which now careened wildly past the crossover at Nott Terrace, His words were a prophetic beginning to a weird experience.

The men expected the car to leave the tracks at Nott Terrace, but when this was passed safely they breathed again for a brief instant as they swung around the sweeping curve down past Crescent Park. The switches at Lafayette Street at the foot of the park were crossed so quickly they could scarcely believe the car was over, and then the switch at the waiting room was struck and also passed.

"The end will come at the railroad crossing" was the grim thought which came to both McGraw and Gill as the 30-ton behemoth shot crazily through the early morning gloom, raising clouds of dust behind it.

Up until now, the two women passengers had not known that anything was wrong. They knew the car was traveling at high speed (later estimated at a mile a minute), but they believed it was under control of the crew and had rather enjoyed the sensation of "rapid transit." But now, both conductor and motorman had come into the middle of the swaying car, and the look of apprehension on their faces struck terror to the hearts of the passengers.

They became hysterical and made a rush to get out of the car. The men seized them and flung them to the floor, knowing it would be certain death to jump. The frantic screams of the fear-crazed women were almost drowned out by the grinding of the wheels beneath.

The runaway car went across the street level railroad crossing just minutes ahead of an express train that was behind schedule, and when it reached the gentle slope of the canal bridge it leaped in the air and landed again on the rails. A few persons who were on the street at this early hour heard the roar of the approaching car, but they hardly turned to look up the street before No. 51 passed them in a whirl of dust.

The end of the blood-curdling ride came at the junction of State Street and Washington Avenue. At the foot of State Street (now the approach to the Western Gateway Bridge) there was a single car track with a double switch, one going north on Washington Avenue to the Glenville bridge and the other to Fuller Street and the car barn. The latter switch was open and the runaway car entered it, but at such high speed that it left the tracks as it was rounding the curve.

The trolley shot across the street, narrowly missed a large elm tree to the left, snapped off a telegraph pole and crashed into the Levi A. Young residence at 72 Washington Avenue (the location approximately what is now the driveway between the bridge and the community college). It struck the house with such force that it crushed the front of the brick facade like an egg shell and carried with it the upper part of the telegraph pole into the parlor.

Luckily the bedrooms of the house were upstairs. Its occupants were Mr. and Mrs. Young and three boarders. It was 3:20 a.m. when the crash awakened Mrs. Young, who looked out of the upstairs window and then awakened her disbelieving husband with the announcement that she "guessed there was a trolley car in the parlor."

One end of the car, its vestibule smashed, was indeed in the parlor. Brick and mortar and wreckage were all over the room, and the air was suffocating with dust and escaping gas. Despite the early hour, the street outside soon became congested with people who gathered about the wreck. By 6 a.m., the railway company had pulled No. 51 from its unscheduled stop and put up a tarpaulin over the gaping hole in front of the dwelling. Broken gas and water lines were shut off.

The occupants of the runaway car? Miraculously, even though they had been thrown violently about, they suffered only minor scratches and bruises. The women were treated at the scene by a doctor and then put aboard the next car for Albany.

The company not only exonerated McGraw and Gill but highly commended them, through a public statement by General Manager Edward F. Peck, for their good judgment in handling the car and caring for the women passengers. Both were given several days vacation to rest up from the experience that actually had lasted about two minutes.

McGraw had on brief statement for the press after the incident: "I've been a railroad man for seven years, both steam and trolley, and I have had a good many exciting adventures in that time. But I never experienced such a thrilling one as that ride down State Street . . . and I never want to go through another."

LEGAL SNAGS ALONG THE WAY

Prolonged litigation dogged the Schenectady Railway Co. early in 1900 as franchise fights, court injunctions and civil action accompanied its efforts to extend lines to Albany, Troy, Scotia and Ballston Spa.

No doubt the biggest doses of legal headaches were provided by the United Traction Co., the rival streetcar firm in Albany which sought to block the Schenectady company from expanding to that city. It all started when the 20th century was only a month old. That was when J. P. Ord, president of Schenectady Railway, announced with a flourish that "SRC is ready to branch out to surrounding communities" and probably would have a route to Albany in operation within the year.

Naturally, the Albany firm objected and took its case to the capital city's common council. UTC, which operated its red trolley cars within that city, argued it had plans to develop its own road to Loudonville and later to Schenectady. The vision of Schenectady cars running within Albany city limits was pointed out as a blow to city economy.

The Albany council mulled over the question for several months, staging public hearings at which representatives of both companies were queried as to expansion plans. Finally it decided the Schenectady company had the most advanced plans and, since the public was in favor of such a road as soon as possible, awarded the franchise to SRC.

The Albany line was opened officially Sept. 9, 1901, and was hailed by officials of the Schenectady company as "only the beginning of our plans for progress in this area." All of which was true — the Scotia line was opened Apr. 15, 1902; the Troy line on Mar. 2, 1903, and the Ballston Spa route June 30, 1904. But it was also the beginning of law suits against the Schenectady firm in its early development.

Looking back at the official records of the Schenectady railway, it seems the Albany line was most troublesome where litigation was concerned.

Even while construction gangs were laying the double track route along the 12 miles of turnpike between here and Albany, the county road commissioner complained of damage to the sidepath used mostly by bicyclists. In placing the poles for the cable to carry the 10,000-volt current, railway workmen damaged the path for several miles between the sub-station at Vly and Wolf Roads. Schenectady railway settled damage claims amounting to $250 and repaired the ruts and trenches which made traveling hazardous for the two-wheeled riders.

A taxpayers' action was brought against the company in 1903 when several residents of the settlement of Verdoy (formerly known as Morrisville) in the Town of Colonie complained the SRC had taken more than its rightful share of the highway granted in the franchise. Aaron Pearse was chief complainant. They also argued that one track, and not two; should run through that community. The SRC finally won out after a year's court action.

The United Traction Co. brewed more trouble for its rival company shortly after the Schenectady firm blossomed forth with "newer, larger and more comfortable cars for the Albany line that is the ultimate in modern public conveyances." They were the big 600 series, fitted with four double trucks and suspension springs, a glistening all metal exterior and upholstered seats within.

It was just before 9 a.m. on May 16, 1904, when agents of the Albany company were at the City line to stop these new cars from entering Albany. Attorney James O. Carr, summoned by the Schenectady firm, managed within hours to get a temporary injunction from County Judge A. M. Vedder restraining the UTC from interfering with its competitor.

Meanwhile, the case of the big cars went into the docket of the Supreme Court to be argued later that month. One of the charges advanced by UTC, besides the fact that the new cars were considered too heavy for the Albany city tracks, was that Albany residents were suing them for damages resulting from "quaking homes whenever the cars passed by."

The impasse finally was resolved when the Schenectady railway was allowed to maintain the huge cars on its Albany spur, provided it would abide by an agreement to reduce speed considerably while within Albany city limits.

A short time later, United Traction raised a similar objection against heavy cars invading Albany territory when Fonda, Johnstown and Gloversville Railroad was refused permission to run its newly-purchased interurbans, the 101-107 series, on those tracks. Consequently, with the exception of a few special runs to Albany and Watervliet, FJ & G restricted its southeast territory to Schenectady.

Before Supreme Court Justice Edgar A. Spencer of Amsterdam was able to arrange an agreement between the competitive Albany and Schenectady trolley companies on the heavy car issue, another incident broke out.

Schenectady railway had ordered six large electric cars from the J. M. Jones shops in Watervliet to be used on the new Ballston line. They were to have been delivered to the Fuller Street carbarn by June 6, 1904, but UTC officials refused permission to run the new trolleys over its Watervliet tracks on the grounds they were too heavy. They also claimed "it would be inconsistent with the objections already made against the running of such large cars in Albany.

Determined to get one of the cars to test its nearly-completed Ballston spur, the Schenectady company resorted to trickery. Long before daylight on June 21, it sent a crew to the Jones works and brought car 608 to Schenectady. That same day, a group of SRC and city officials rode the car to Ballston Spa and back to test the ballast of the road. It averaged 60 miles an hour on the straight run beyond the Rexford flats.

This latest dispute with United Traction Co. was settled within a week when the Albany firm was allowed to contract with Jones car works to deliver the remaining five trolleys to Schenectady. The Ballston line officially opened a few days after delivery.

In the years that followed, the Albany route proved a lucrative run with its chair cars, limited and express cars doing a thriving business. The lawsuit jinx stayed with it, though, right up until the bus gradually replaced the trolleys and the electric service to Albany was discontinued in 1933.

There continued a sizeable quota of lawsuits each year involving accidents for which SRC was held accountable. Some were for fatalities, others for personal injuries and the aggrieved were not always passengers. In many instances the company was sued for the loss of a horse or wagon that was hit while crossing the tracks.

THE CAR BARNS

As the young Schenectady Railway Co. began to prosper soon after 1895, so the need became acute for larger quarters in which to house the increasing rolling stock. The wooden barn at Brandywine Avenue and State Street had been adequate for the small horsecars, but not for the electrified open and closed streetcars.

The first barn to be built was the huge brick-sided structure at Fuller and Church Streets. Bids for the $25,000 building were opened in September, 1899. Andrew Kinum of Schenectady was awarded the brick and mason work, while the contract for carpentry went to Dennis Madden of Amsterdam. It was completed by the end of that year and was put into immediate use.

A year later, SRC erected another story on the front portion of the new barn and was arranged into club rooms for its employees, who were now organized as the Schenectady Railway Benefit Association.

It was said at the time that the rooms "left nothing to be desired." There were two smoking rooms, a reading room, assembly hall, steel lockers for 52 employees, lavatory and showers, a billiard room and — the pride and joy of every trolley man — two bowling lanes "which have no superior in this part of the state." There would be many bowling matches throughout the ensuing years, both in league play and special competitive meets against representatives of rival railway companies, police, firemen and Schenectady YMCA.

The new rooms were formally opened at an open house Oct. 1, 1903, complete with palms, flowers, flags and paper bunting. There was some entertainment (a juggler, tenor soloist and pianist) and some speeches, notably that of Hinsdill Parsons, who took over the presidency of the company from J. P. Ord in 1901. There was a power failure during the program (as so often occurred in those early days of electricity) and the orchestra entertained in the darkness for several minutes until the lights came on again.

As the interurban and suburban network rapidly spread out from downtown Schenectady, it was early recognized that even the large Fuller Street carbarn would not be able to handle all the new streetcars which were getting longer and more spacious. In May, 1902, plans were drawn up for another carbarn, this time in the "uptown" section of the then unsettled McClellan Street and Eastern Parkway.

Throughout that summer, workmen were busy with the construction of the new barn. The most difficult task was the filling of the land in that area to bring it up to street level; temporary tracks were laid and dirt was brought in by work cars to be emptied in the gully.

The belt lines have been credited with being largely responsible for the settling of the McClellan Street area after 1900. When the spur was constructed from the boulevard section across to State Street, houses rapidly began to fill in the wide gaps along McClellan. With transportation to the central part of the city now so close at hand, it no longer seemed "out in the country."

The new barn was considerably bigger than the Fuller Street carbarn. It was 350 by 120 feet, also built of brick, and had a capacity for 70 cars. There were eight lines of track inside and 150 feet of pit for mechanical repairs. The front entrances were equipped with the latest roll-up doors.

The barns were used by the railway company for 50 years, during which time they witnessed vast changes in the stylings and volume of streetcars as that mode of transportation continued its popularity. There were sleek and fast interurbans for the Ballston and Albany lines, the open-sided bench cars for "moonlight" and "twilight" tours in the summer and the big PAYE (Pay-as-you-enter) city trolleys in later years.

The decline of the electrified streetcar in the 1930s saw both carbarns gradually being converted to the storage of buses, now replacing trolley routes as fast as permission could be granted by the Public Service Commission.

The Fuller Street structure was sold in 1952 to IUE Local 301, which moved its offices from Liberty Street and located in the rooms which once were the chambers for the Schenectady Railway Benefit Association. After erecting its IUE auditorium on Erie Boulevard, the union built new offices partially on the site of the old carbarn which was razed in January, 1960.

The McClellan Street carbarn was sold in October, 1952 to the Golub Corporation which in turn added to the back and remodeled the interior. It was leased to J.M. Fields which operated a business there until 1973 when the owner opened a Price Chopper store. Finally, the former carbarn was pulled down in 1994 as finishing work was done on the new Price Chopper supermarket off Eastern Parkway adjacent to the rear. A wall sketch of the carbarn and trolley days was later mounted inside the new store in recognition of a historical site.

THE EMERGENCY CREWS

The people of Schenectady had come to depend on the service provided by the Schenectady Railway Co. even before the dawn of this century. As the city grew outwards, and the trolley lines expanded with it, the need for reliable service in all kinds of weather was apparent if the transportation company was to survive.

The Schenectady company, and others like it in major cities of the United States, soon found it needed more than passenger cars and newly opened routes to satisfy the public. It had to be ready to cope with any emergency — accidents, power failure and inclement weather being the chief trouble-makers — to keep delayed schedules at a minimum.

One of the first pieces of special equipment employed by SRC was an odd-looking, horsedrawn apparatus known as the tower wagon. Its specific use was to restore power whenever a break occurred in the overhead trolley wires, which was frequent in those early years before improved wire-stringing was introduced.

Elmer Rivenburgh, who lived at 906 Stanley St., was foreman of the first tower wagon crew, organized in the fall of 1901 and he remained at that post for a number of years. His driver was George F. Faircloth, an ex-fireman from Quincy, Mass., who trained the first team of horses, used to pull the tower wagon, in the same way as fire horses — even to the drop harnesses for fast getaways. "Barney" and "Maggie," a pair of dappled grays, learned fast.

The railway company leased a barn across from Ellis Hospital on Jay Street (now the site of City Hall) and set it up as the emergency station for the tower wagon crew. The men were on call day and night (each having one day off a week) and they responded to all emergency calls on the average of three a day. They also answered all fire alarms which came from a box on or near a street where street cars ran because it was their job to see that the cars were not delayed by fire-fighting operations.

If firemen had to string hoses across trolley tracks, the emergency crew brought out portable hose jumpers which made a bridge for the car tracks over the hoses. A big fire sometimes meant the cutting down of sections of trolley wire (later to be repaired) so that firemen were not hampered.

On a hot Sunday afternoon on July 19, 1908, at 1:40 p.m. there was a bit of excitement on State Street beneath the new railroad overpass. A trolley had just passed by when there was a loud report and some pyrotechnics along the eastbound trolley wire. A blaze shot up from the circuit breaker box on a trolley pole opposite Jay Street over a block away. In the excitement, someone turned in an alarm from fire box 551 at State and Clinton which brought Central Fire Station's apparatus, followed a few minutes later by No. 3's truck.

As these were swinging into view down the State Street hill, SRC's emergency wagon dashed out from South Center Street and railway officials were also soon at hand. No one was hurt in the mishap. In falling, the trolley wire fell across the tracks causing a short circuit. The firemen returned to their stations while the emergency gang picked up the charged wire for repair.

Soon the large crowd dispersed and normal traffic was again resumed, the trolley cars "drifting" past the break and picking up power on the other side.

Schenectady Railway kept its horse-drawn tower wagon until about 1912 when it was replaced by motorized units which used the same collapsible tower apparatus that could be raised about 25 feet. The equipment, too, was the same — strands of copper transmission wire, oil lamps and long boxes containing pliers, scissors, hammers and many other tools used in emergency repairs.

Accidents along the trolley routes often involved collisions with wagons. The railway company, anxious to avoid long delays in clearing its tracks of debris — such as bales of hay, furniture, stove wood or coal — added several work cars to its rolling stock to handle such emergencies. These crews would clear the tracks and, if need be, tow the damaged street car back to the carbarn. A derrick, or crane, car also was purchased, mainly to right an overturned trolley or pull it back on the track.

Ballast cars, which looked much like a railroad coal hopper, were in constant use to keep the track beds firm, especially after heavy rains. A real bad spot was the area between the foot of Crane Street hill and Broadway hill known as Villa Road (now Broadway) where summer rains brought down tons of earth from the surrounding hillsides.

During June and July of 1904, for example, the tracks were covered at various times by about three feet of mud after cloudbursts. Crews of workmen shoveled the mud into flatcars while the ballast cars made hurried trips to the company's Aqueduct gravel yards to bring back loads of stone for the undermined tracks.

Icy weather conditions were the most dreaded by railway men. Not only did sleet change the trolley tracks into useless ribbons of steel; it also insulated the power of overhead wires. At the first hint of freezing rain, emergency crews rumbled out of the carbarns with tower wagons to shake the wires free of the ice coating.

Before the automotive era came into its own, railway companies usually combatted slippery tracks by the use of sand spreaders. Salt was tabooed by city officials because it ruined sledding in the winter months when the only other urban transportation was by horse and cutter. The few times the Schenectady Railway Co. attempted to spread salt along its tracks on Broadway hill in the early 1900s, there was such a general outcry against the practice that the company promised to discontinue it.

Later, trolley cars were fitted with sand boxes and blower pipes so that they could provide their own traction except in cases of extreme conditions. Most of the early sand spreader cars were manufactured by the Westinghouse Co. of Schenectady.

Among the special equipment housed earlier by the SRC in its Fuller Street barn was a sprinkler car, which was quite essential to keeping the lines in operation. There were two outlet pipes at either end, used according to the direction of the car, and the water which gushed through them from the huge tank in the center of the car cleared the city tracks of dirt and debris during the warm weather months. There was only one sprinkler, Number 30W, and it had a water capacity of 2,480 gallons. The company discontinued the use of this car in the early 1920's when the city's street department began using motorized street sprinklers and made the rounds more quickly than with the former horse and "wash tub" wagon formerly used to wet down the streets.

The interurban lines used baggage compartments on a few models for transporting parcels and other materials principally for local firms who wanted "on schedule" deliveries to nearby communities. SRC had five huge double-truck express cars, numbered 1 to 5 E, which it used for an extensive period throughout the first part of this century while it was in the express business as the Electric Express Company. Through its inter-rurban lines, the express cars carried packages, crates, produce and dairy products to and from such points as Saratoga Springs, Ballston Spa, Troy and Albany.

For a time, just before and after World War I, Schenectady Railway also had a plush funeral car which was numbered 505. It was part of the vogue in electric car service such as was offered in larger cities (Baltimore, Washington, Philadelphia and Chicago, for example) in which a whole funeral party might be accommodated even in rides to out-of-town burials if connections could be made.

There was not enough demand for the car in this area, however, and by 1920 SRC's funeral car was converted into a regular passenger car for interurban runs. The car was so specially built, and decorated for funeral purposes, that it could not be used for other occasions; thus because it was idle much of the time it became it a liability among SRC's rolling stock. The carrying capacity was 32 persons. The front section was known as the "casket compartment," into which the casket was placed from the outside through a large glass door. A nickel-plated rail extending around the casket compartment held the floral displays, so that the coffin and flowers were visible from the street as the car rolled along to the cemetery. Individual over-stuffed chairs were used in the funeral car.

One Schenectadian recalls a rather unusual instance in which the SRC used a regular city car for a funeral before it got the funeral car. Mrs. Earl W. Henion said it was during the big snowstorm of St. Valentine's Day in 1914 when her uncle was to be buried from her mother's home on Crane Street. The hearse could not be used because of the storm, so arrangements were made with SRC to transport the deceased and the mourners on that day. The casket was put in the car through the front window and placed on the backs of seats. Then the car and its funeral party rolled solemnly to the Vale Cemetery gate on Nott Terrace, where the casket was carried to the vault to await spring interment.

Then there were the fabulous "chair cars," which were used mainly by executives of area industries for in-conference transportation to meetings or special events, say in Albany, Troy or Saratoga. They were as plush as the best lounge or smoker cars on the railroad, complete with upholstered furniture. This, too, was a luxury which, like the funeral car, was a passing fancy because there was not the demand for such specialties to warrant maintenance by the SRC.

It was a good piece of timing for SRC when the company decided, in the fall of 1903, to construct plow blades for four work cars. This was in addition to other snow removal equipment of one sweeper and three rotary plows. The new plows no sooner were completed and fitted at either end of the work cars when heavy snow began falling this area. Ten inches began piling up soon after noon on Dec. 10, the storm lasting well into the night.

The sweeper at first tackled the light, dry flakes, its huge rattan broom whisking the snow from the rails in quick runs over all the city routes. Later, however, the falling snow became damp and heavy and was coming down in greater quantity.

After 7 p.m. the four new plow cars were sent out of the Fuller Street carbarn to clear the city routes and those of Aqueduct and Scotia. By midnight, the two rotary plows were put into action, one on the Albany line, the other on the newly opened Troy line.

Crews of laborers were kept busy all night removing snow from the State Street crossing and in keeping switches clear in other parts of the city. A "B" belt car, derailed at Union Avenue at 9 p.m., was pulled back into place 20 minutes later by an emergency car. Railway officials were up all night, directing operations from the waiting room and Fuller Street offices. By morning, when the storm had subsided, the trolleys were still running.

This was by no means the worst snow storm faced by the Schenectady company, but it is an example of how the local company and others like it were determined to keep the public service in operation.

The falling of snow was like the sounding of a battlecry where emergency crews were concerned.

THE SARATOGA LINE

The peaceful repose of the village of Ballston Spa was abruptly interrupted one spring morning at the turn of this century. It came with such a suddenness that at first no one, not even the village officials, knew what was happening or what to do about it.

That day was Apr. 18, 1902. The Schenectady Railway Co. which had announced earlier it would begin laying track within the village limits "within a short time" to link it with the spur already begun from, the Rexford flats of the Mohawk, chose this day to send its equipment and working crews to Ballston. But they were in for a surprise.

A crew of about 100 Italian laborers had already entered the village from the other end earlier that morning and was ripping up a portion of Bath Street to lay trolley tracks — but for a different company. The Hudson Valley Trolley Co. of Saratoga, which had petitioned for the Ballston franchise a year ago only to have it annulled by the village in favor of the Schenectady company, had decided to take matters in its own hands.

It was later revealed the Hudson Valley group learned of the SRC's plans to begin work in the village and moved to take the initiative by disproving the Ballston officials' view that it never intended to carry out its petition.

Villagers, ogling the frantic race by the two rival working crews to tear up the streets within shouting distance of each other, lined the sidewalks fully expecting a brawl to develop. Meanwhile, Police Chief James J. O'Brien hurriedly conferred with village board members and foremen of the working crews.

By nightful there still had been no outbreak of violence. The workmen had been ordered to "keep digging, and never mind those other jackanapes!" The Hudson Valley crew had torn up the street and partly laid tracks from the corner of Bath Street to the railroad bridge. The SRC, which was to enter the village through Front Street, built a track from the bridge back through Charlton Street.

There had been sullen murmuring among the rival crews when they quit work late that afternoon, leaving the streets torn up and the peaceful citizens of Ballston Spa wondering what would happen when the lines met. To guard against any outbreak, the village authorities placed Chief O'Brien in charge and provided him with seven deputies — Terrence Bruckley, William Jones, Thomas McGuire, James O'Connor, Michael Fitzpatrick, George Steenburgh and William Morrissey. They were stationed all that night along the line of work.

The Schenectady workmen took up their pickaxes and sledges the next day, a Sunday, but hardly warmed to the task when they were ordered to stop work. The village officials had invoked the Sunday Law.

The trolley war came to a standstill for one year after that brief bloodless skirmish. It was a period of involved litigation: Hudson Valley swearing out a court injunction against SRC; the Village of Ballston Spa against Hudson Valley; the Schenectady Railway against Hudson Valley. The cases were argued before Supreme Court Justice Russell in Canton. All work in Ballston Spa had been ordered stopped, and the streets remained torn up.

Finally, on Apr. 21, 1903, the Ballston franchise was awarded SRC after court judgment, and once again the Schenectady work crews began laying the tracks through the village, across Front Street and down Milton Avenue.

In tracking out the route for the Ballston spur, engineers could not avoid areas where rock ledges had to be cut or blasted and where low-lying areas required heavy rock ballast before the track beds were level.

The cars assigned to the new line were the latest in trolley design. They were 51 feet long with a smoker compartment at one end. The interior finish was a solid mahogany, with ceilings painted a light green. The passenger seats were covered with imported English "Epingle" used on the British railway systems, and there were continuous shining bronze parcel racks and coat hangers. There was green opalescent glass over the side windows.

Once billed as the "longest trolley bridge in the world," the Schenectady Railway Co. steel bridge which crossed the Mohawk River to carry the interurban cars northward to Ballston Spa and Saratoga Springs was in service from the time the Saratoga line opened in 1904 until it closed in 1941.

The only evidence of the span today are the few stone piers left standing on either side of the river where the bridge once crossed from the community then known as Craig to Alplaus. The piers in the river channel were removed some years ago. The bridge itself was razed during World War II when, as the company officials announced at the time, the "steel went to war."

When it was determined that SRC would build a line to Ballston and Saratoga, there was much speculation about what route it would take. For some time, plans leaned heavily in favor of sending the cars across the steel bridge at Washington Avenue to Scotia, then out to East Glenville past Alplaus and cut northward from the area of Hetcheltown Road. But then, suddenly, plans were changed and announcement was made of the decision to build a new bridge across the canal and the river just west of the Aqueduct.

American Bridge Co. was awarded the contract in May 1903 and work was started the next month. It took a year to build.

When completed, the bridge was 1,800 feet long, set on 10 block piers which were 154 feet apart except those which spanned the Erie Canal at 175 feet. The steel girders were set into place by a unique mechanism known as "the traveler." A novelty of the bridge construction was that it was created in separate sections so that in case a river flood or ice jam carried away a portion of the bridge, it would give way where the sections were joined and could be easily replaced. However, in its nearly 40 years of existence, this feature was never put to the test.

While the bridge was being erected, other things were taking place which were pertinent to the Saratoga line. SRC decided to sell its recreation facility on upper Albany Street at Elm Street known as Brandywine Park because it was "no longer outside the city" and therefore was made attractive to developers for building lots. But the street car firm also decided to develop a new park, this to be located at Ballston Lake and to be called Forest Park. Plans for the new resort were announced early in 1903 when the company said it would spend $100,000 in improvements.

At the same time, work was going on for development of a park at Rexford to be known as River View Park (later to be called Luna Park, Dolle's Park and Rexford Park). A summer pavilion was being rushed to completion in 1904 under the direction of Charles Miller, the park proprietor. A trolley passenger shed also was being readied for the spur which SRC would build to the park from the Saratoga line.

People were anxious for the opening of the Saratoga line (although when it first opened it went only to Ballston for nearly a year before the rest of the route was completed) not only because of the scenic trip and convenience of hopping on a trolley car, but also because it would be cheaper than going by railroad. The Delaware & Hudson at that time was charging 45 cents for one-way and 85 cents roundtrip to Ballston Spa. The trolley company advertised its rates as 25 cents one-way and 40 cents roundtrip to Ballston Spa. For a trip to the park site at Ballston Lake, it was 15 cents one-way and 25 cents round trip.

A test run of the new route was made by company officers June 1, 1904, in a single truck city line car. They wanted not only to feel for themselves the sturdiness of the new bridge but also to check the road bed and tie rails along the way to Ballston Lake, which was as far as they went that day. In the party were Edward F. Peck, general manager; Frederick Smith, superintendent; J. F. Hamilton, assistant chief engineer; and J. N. Shannahan, general superintendent of the Fonda, Johnstown & Gloversville Railway.

The big day came the next day, when regular passenger service to Ballston Spa was started as Car 608 left the Schenectady waiting room at 420 State St. at 5:30 p.m. with a load of excited riders, anxious to be among those who afterward could say they were the first to cross over the new trolley bridge, "the longest trolley bridge in the world."

THE PARKS. . .'TRAFFIC GENERATORS'

Before the automobile appeared on the American scene to whisk families on their separate ways to places hundreds of miles from home the public looked to local facilities for weekend entertainment. In most localities the railway system and the amusement park usually combined to provide just such recreation for many years before and after the turn of this century.

Many people today can recall the "moonlight trolley tours" inaugurated by Schenectady Railway Co. about 1900 and continued for many years after. Hundreds of people would throng the downtown waiting room to get seats on the open cars which left after 7:30 p.m. for a ride out in the suburban country on the Troy line. The tour, which cost 25 cents, took about 1½ hours for a leisurely trip to Latham and back through the boulevard section of Schenectady.

However, the amusement park was by far the most popular summer playground. Whole families and organizations took the trolleys to the park on any afternoon and evening. There was usually a band concert, sometimes a fireworks display and always a dance and entertainment in the casino.

The SRC operated two parks, Brandywine Park at the "end of Albany Street," and Forest Park, on the east end of Ballston Lake. Forest was the bigger establishment and yet Brandywine never lacked patronage.

When SRC announced on April 1, 1896, it was taking over management of Brandywine Park, the company made clear it intended to erase the bad name the park had earned over previous years. "The park will be maintained as a family pleasure resort and picnic ground without fear of offense or molestation," the directive said. "Furthermore no intoxicating drink will be permitted or sold on the grounds, and anyone under its influence will be ejected."

The company renewed existing buildings and erected new ones, including a large dance pavilion. It laid out croquet lawns and a picnic grove. Finally all was ready for grand opening on Saturday, May 30, 1896—more than 6,000 nickel fares were taken that day as the SRC street cars shuttled holiday crowds to the renovated park grounds. It opened with a concert by the Citizens Corps Band and there was dancing until almost midnight.

The park soon became a popular place for group outings. In years to come reservations were booked solid for July and August for such organizations as the Meat Cutters Union, Polish National Alliance, First Reformed Church, Italian Benefit Society, Horsfall Post 14, Grand Army of the Republic, and Boilermakers Union.

The Schenectady Railway Company branched out in the amusement park operation when it opened Forest Park on Ballston Lake in 1904 to coincide with the opening of its Ballston line. The 50-acre site was leased from Everett Smith, who was president of Schenectady Savings Bank and who publicly acknowledged he purchased the old Baker "Castle" estate so that it could be developed as a public park.

SRC spent nearly $75,000 in making over the lake resort to an amusement center. Workmen were on the job almost a year building a casino, dance pavilion, waiting room, a 100-foot dock, boathouse, bathhouses and rustic theater, laying out promenades and groves, a baseball diamond and tracks for bicycle and foot races. The amusement concessions came later.

The lakefront facilities became a favorite with the crowds who paid a quarter for the round trip and admission to the park. There were 18 steel rowboats available for fishing and romancing, and a 31-foot motor launch regularly carried 25 passengers for trips around the scenic lake.

Gartland's Military Band for years gave the Forest Park midsummer concerts on Saturday afternoon and evening. The Saturday night dances at the pavilion also brought in a bumper crop of summer trolley fares. Sherman Brownell, Schenectady Railway treasurer, was the park cashier and usually sold the dance tickets at the pavilion.

Patrons of Forest Park were fond of the "twilight specials" which usually left the State Street waiting room about 8 p.m. on summer weekends. Identified as a park special by colored lights on the front dash in the form of a crescent, they carried about 80 passengers on the round trip (still 25 cents). The trolley crews enjoyed being assigned to this particular run because they could spend the evening at the park, making the return trip to Schenectady about 10:30.

As early as 1903, when SRC first leased the Ballston Lake site, the company directors intended to sell the Brandywine Park grounds because "it is no longer located in the suburb of the city." The early plans called for it to be cut up into building lots and sold. However, even though almost half the original site was sold to house developers, Brandywine Park continued to operate as an amusement and picnic resort almost as long as Forest Park.

Increased popularity of the automobile in the early 1920's spelled the doom of the amusement parks and the weekend rides to those resorts. Before long, it became a liability to the company to operate the park runs with half-filled trolleys; the park concessions began to close, too, because of a lack of business.

Brandywine Park was first to go. It was sold in the mid-20's to the congregation of St. Luke's Church. The original dance pavilion, the only remaining building from the old park, was enclosed with shingling and heated in 1933 and a kitchen was added at the rear. It was torn down and the former park site was replaced by St. Luke's School which was dedicated in September, 1955.

The Forest Park site was parceled into lots and sold to individuals who later built summer camps along the lakefront.

THE ELECTRICS COME TO SCOTIA

"The people of Scotia are tired of floundering around in the darkness. . .so let us do something about it!" Walter Price told his committee and a group of interested citizens which met the night of Mar. 22, 1903, in Good Templar's Hall on Mohawk Avenue to discuss the possibility of illuminating the village streets with electricity.

Price was chairman of the Citizens Association of Scotia, organized for the express purpose of improving the street lighting when it was learned an electric power line was to be strung to Scotia by the Schenectady Illuminating Co. Now it had been almost a year since Schenectady Railway Co. had run its first trolley across the steel bridge spanning the Mohawk, but still the streets of Scotia were dismally lighted by oil lamps spaced far apart.

Those same oil lamps were purchased for $100, a gift from the Edison Machine Works (which became General Electric Co. in 1892) to the village for its assistance in putting out a fire in the Edison tube building in 1891. But now, as it was pointed out by those attending the meeting in the lodge hall, the outmoded lamps had outlived their sentimental value these 10 years. . .and it was time for modern lighting.

A petition was drawn up and signed first by the committee, other members of which included Charles Snyder Jr., J.C.F. DeGraff, Edwin Egner and Peter Brogan. Later it was presented to Glenville Supervisor J. B. Houck, who also was interested in the project and promised to work with the committee in getting the new lights for Scotia.

Houck and the committee started at the top. They went to GE officials, who referred them to C. F. Peck, general manager of Schenectady Railway Co. (In those early years, GE owned the railway company, which in turn regulated the business affairs of Schenectady Illuminating and Mohawk Gas Companies). And action came fast.

The railway company, Peck told the Scotia group, was very anxious to cooperate with its new patrons across the river and also preferred to have its Mohawk Avenue line better lighted at night for safety and convenience. Not only would the company install the lights, but it would have it done within a month without charge to the town!

Seven arc lights were hung before that summer of 1903 so that Scotia's main street seemed to glow with the wonders of a new age—as did this report on the accomplishment in the Evening Star: "We are realizing that Scotia is fast becoming a village of importance in Schenectady County, and that its prospects for the future are bright."

These were the new 2,000 candlepower outdoor electric lamps developed by GE. They already were being installed over many streets in Schenectady to replace the earlier, less efficient type that had been hung about 10 years previous by Thomas Edison's new branch company.

The old type carbon arc lamp, which burned and sputtered in open air, required almost daily trimming and dusting. But now, as with the lamps installed in Scotia, the longer-burning carbons were enclosed within a glass globe and needed trimming only two or three times a month. They were provided with tightly-fitting waterproof castings to keep out the rain.

GE had also perfected this lamp to run on alternating current instead of the earlier direct current so that they could be operated with the same power source which ran the electric streetcars.

The Schenectady trolley firm early recognized Scotia's potential in terms of car fares. It had fought hard in the courts to get access for its tracks through Washington Avenue in order to cross the Mohawk bridge to Scotia. Once trolley No. 29 made the initial crossing at 5:30 on the afternoon of Apr. 15, 1902, the village across the river became more closely linked to Schenectady than it ever had been.

SRC inaugurated "pleasure trips" to Scotia on warm summer nights, using its open bench cars which would be filled with people anxious to cool off during the river crossing.

The first Scotia trolley line did not extend up Mohawk Avenue many blocks beyond the Dyke (now Schonowe Avenue) but in a few years, SRC had constructed separate routes to Reeseville (Sacandaga Road) and up Ballston Avenue. By 1915, the cars went as far as Toll Street on Mohawk Avenue while on the other route, the cars veered into Wallace Street, over Fifth Street and up Vley Road to Sixth Street.

THE FJ&G IN SCHENECTADY

On the afternoon of Nov. 29, 1870, a train hauled by a sleek and brassy engine called the "Pioneer" chugged its way along a new road laid from Fonda to Gloversville.

This was the first train to make the run and signaled the beginning of operations for the Fonda, Johnstown & Gloversville Railroad during the boom days of the post-Civil War period.

The Gloversville company's close association with Schenectady trade began with the purchase of the "Pioneer," a funnelstacked McQueen-American type locomotive, from the American Locomotive Works here. In later years, as it combined steam and electric roads to form a massive short-line operation, the FJ&G played a significant role in public transportation from Schenectady to points north.

One of its biggest contributions to the immediate area was the building of the Amsterdam-Schenectady trolley line, which was formally opened June 30, 1903. It was heralded in the press as "the consummation of long cherished hopes of speedy interurban connection between the cities of Schenectady and Amsterdam, and Fulton County." No one could quarrel with the fact that the opening of the new line was a boost to convenience and prosperity.

On opening day, a group of about 30 FJ&G officials and guests met at 9 a.m. in the Gloversville yards and boarded a yellow trolley, the sides of which bore streamers reading: "FJ&G RR—Connecting Schenectady, Amsterdam, Johnstown, Gloversville and Sacandaga Park." (It was one of several cars recently purchased from Lehigh Valley Transit Co. so the signs conveniently covered the name of the former owner.)

Brief ceremonies were held in Amsterdam before the car started the maiden trip over the new interurban route at 10, piloted by motorman Abram Nellis, with conductor Robert Stewart, two of the oldest and most trusted of the company's employees. During the 17-mile trip, the trolley was greeted at numerous places by cheering, flag-waving crowds.

This is how a reporter of the Amsterdam Evening Recorder was impressed by the new line: "The route is decidedly picturesque, as the view of the Mohawk Valley to be obtained from the cars as they spin along the hilltops from Cranesville eastward is most delightful to the eye. The Mohawk River, through which the aborigines were wont to ply the canoe, the old Albany turnpike, the Erie Canal, through which the packet boats were operated in the early days of the past century, the New York Central with its great steam railway of four tracks, and the double-tracked electric line, all parallel, give striking evidence of the remarkable advances in the way of transportation facilities in the valley of the Mohawk during the past hundred years."

When the FJ&G car reached the Boston & Maine Railroad bridge (end of N. Ballston Avenue) in Glenville, it was met by a group of Schenectady officials in a Schenectady Railway Co. trolley. They included SRC Superintendent Frederick Smith, Mayor Horace S. Van Voast and Fire Chief Henry Yates. At this point, the road connected to the SRC's Scotia line which crossed over the steel Mohawk bridge and entered Schenectady through Washington Avenue.

The Gloversville car was in Schenectady about 40 minutes. It left the SRC waiting room at 420 State St. and returned to Gloversville with additional guests for a luncheon held at the Kingsborough Hotel to celebrate the day's event.

Regular service on the new route started the next day, July 1, leaving both cities on the hour beginning at 6 a.m. from Amsterdam and 7 from Schenectady. J. L. Hees, president and general manager of FJ&G, announced that all cars from Schenectady would be run directly into the station of the steam railroad at Gloversville where quick connections could be made with the steam cars for Sacandaga Park. The Gloversville rail company operated the 750-acre recreation and amusement center just above Cranberry Creek for many years until the flooding of most of that area in 1930 for the Sacandaga Reservoir.

A big feature of the FJ&G's new expansion was the construction of a huge $600,000 power plant at Tribes Hill, capable of generating a maximum load of 6,750-horsepower. The road also had transformer stations, at Johnstown, Amsterdam and Glenville.

Within a few months, seven new cars of the 101-107 series arrived on order from the St. Louis Car Co. and immediately were put into service on the Schenectady run. Costing $14,000 each, they were at the time considered the most luxurious ever constructed for trolley service.

They were big cars—55 feet long—built of wood, finished with mahogany on the inside and painted dark green with gold trim on the outside. Fifty-six passengers could be accommodated in two compartments, one for normal use and the other for the men who liked to smoke. Other features: Hot water heating system, red plushcovered seats, head and foot rests, washrooms and individual seat lights. These cars were so popular that four more were purchased in 1904, and some of them still were in operation 35 years later when the electric road was totally abandoned.

It was at first planned for the new FJ&G trolleys to provide service to Albany and Troy, via the Schenectady Railway Company's trackage and that of the United Traction Co. of Albany. However, the idea was abandoned when the UTC refused to permit the big cars to run on its tracks, as it did those of SRC, on the basis that the interurbans were too heavy.

The FJ&G trolleys continued to be part of the Schenectady scene through later years when steel and aluminum cars replaced the slickly varnished wooden models of earlier days. However, the Gloversville company decided to abandon its electric lines in 1938, replacing the service with buses. On the night of June 28 that year, trolley No. 176 made the last run over the route from Gloversville to Schenectady, returning to the car barn about 2 a.m. At 4:50 that same morning, the first FJ&G motor bus started out for the Amsterdam run to Schenectady.

The company operated its buses over nearly the same routes as the trolleys until the bus business was sold in 1956 to the Mohawk Valley Transit Co.

TROLLEY STORIES TOLD AND RETOLD

There were many humorous incidents and stories that came out of the halcyon days of the trolley car, up through the first two decades of this century. They are told and retold even today whenever railway men get together.

Many remember that groups of boys used to get the one-man "Toonervilles" bouncing like a baby carriage by jumping up and down on the rear platform.

Everett T. Grout, who later was to become an influential figure in the Schenectady school system as director of its physical education program, worked for the Schenectady Railway Co. as a young man. He was known then as the "railway sprinter." He earned that title on early evening, June 2, 1904,when he bet a conductor $10 he could cover the distance from the McClellan Street carbarn down to the waiting room at 420 State St. in 10 minutes.

With trousers rolled up, cap in hand, the long-legged paymaster ran down Union Street to Nott Terrace, down Liberty Street and across Jay until he reached the company's waiting room nine minutes later, panting, but a 10-spot richer.

That same year, 1904, the SRC was presented with a problem at the Mohawk Golf Club, where members frequently complained they were often late in returning home after golf matches because they had missed a trolley. The Troy Road cars never stopped at the club entrance unless someone was standing there.

A company electrician came up with what was then thought an ingenious plan. A buzzer system was installed so that when the wheels of a westbound trolley passed over a certain spot a half mile from the club house, golfers were warned that they had 1 1/2 minutes to get out front and catch the car for home. That year the company also in stalled a huge bell at the grade level railroad crossing on State Street, as there had been numerous incidents where streetcars passing over the tracks were narrowly missed being struck by trains.

Trolley conductors and motormen on both urban and interurban lines maintained strict decorum in their cars. Moreover a rule of the company required that all employees wear their coats and ties and caps even in the warmest weather—and woe unto the motorman who took off his coat and was reported by a company "spy." These so-called spies, or spotters, were hired by the railway company to ride the cars at random and check on the conduct of the streetcar crews and the taking of fares. If a soft-hearted conductor let too many over-age children ride free, he would in due time be called on the carpet of the company offices.

Many peculiar incidents happened aboard the trolleys, and it was usually up to the motorman or conductor to set things straight.

A man got on a Rexford car one fall evening of 1903, returning from a hunting expedition. As the car neared Schenectady, a sudden jolt discharged the shotgun the hunter had between his knees. Fortunately, the charge passed through the roof of the car, barely missing the face of Motorman J. P. Waldron.

A streetcar conductor once found himself the "middle man" in a family squabble that began at the new waiting room built at State and Lafayette Streets after 1913. An irate wife had stormed onto the trolley, found her husband sitting with another woman and then began to pull him out of the car by the hair of his head while screaming accusations at the startled woman passenger. When the conductor interceded, the battling spouse doubled up her fist and hit him in the eye. "That'll teach you to mind your own damn business!" she cried, still holding her cringing mate by the hair.

The story is told about the passenger who boarded a Troy-bound trolley in Schenectady. Being very sleepy, he asked the conductor to tell him when the car arrived in Troy and then settled back to sleep. The car arrived in Troy, started on its return and was well on its way to Schenectady when the conductor noticed the huddled passenger sound asleep in the car: He puzzled over what to do.

When the trolley pulled down State Street and made the turn into Broadway, stopping in front of the Hotel Mohawk, the conductor shouted at the top of his voice, "Troy depot!" The drowsy passenger jumped to his feet and dashed out of the car and into the Mohawk where, it is said, he sleepily asked for a trolley ticket to Albany.

It was a thrill in the early days of the system to board the electric car for a ride, particularly the express trolleys on the interurban runs where they sometimes attained speeds of 60 and 65 miles an hour on the straight routes without making a stop between cities. The Albany cars were considered fast but the big Saratogas were notably the speediest once they passed the east curve out of Ballston Spa.

Racing with other vehicles was of course against company rules, but many a time the motorman with sporting blood "just happened" to be alongside a speeding railroad train, such as on the Saratoga Springs or Amsterdam run. The trolley passengers invariably crowded to the side next to the train, excitedly urging their motorman to outdistance the puffing engine.

Later on, when automobiles came into their own, the Albany Road became a favorite "drag strip" for interurbans and high-powered autos.

On Sunday afternoon July 19, 1908, two men stood outside SRC's waiting room, then at 420 State St. just above Broadway, discussing the current spell of hot weather. They were company agents, one Passenger Agent Weatherwax and the other Inspector Teagle. When they saw the Twilight Special lumbering down State Street, they decided to board it for a cooling ride out to Forest Park.

When the specials were placed in service that year, an order had gone out from the office of the passenger agent restricting the use of the car to paid fare, barring all passes. As the two men got on the car, the conductor approached them to collect the fares but they each took a pass from his pocket and showed the conductor that they were, indeed, company officials.

"Sorry, gentlemen, my orders are to accept no passes," the conductor told them. There were some protests on the part of the agents but the conductor insisted he was boss of the car, officials or no officials.

Agent Weatherwax finally paid his fare but Inspector Teagle prolonged the argument. He informed the conductor he would be replaced as soon as the barn was reached. "All right," said the conductor, "replace me but you will pay your fare or get off."

A rule permitted the inspector to ride with the motorman so Teagle immediately stepped forward and rode at the front of the car. When the trolley reached the Fuller Street carbarn, where it would soon begin the return trip to Ballston Lake, the conductor walked up to the inspector and asked for his relief.

"Never mind your relief, get back where you belong," barked the inspector.

The conductor did so, but the next day he refused to take out the special until the matter was cleared up. As it turned out, Inspector Teagle lost. He had to pay his fare and was reprimanded for his actions.

THE WAITING ROOM

The opening of the Schenectady Railway Co. passenger terminal at the foot of Crescent Park in October, 1913, coincided with that company's peak business year. It was the heyday of intercity trolley systems. No one could foresee then that the huge pile of brick and stone, described as "one of the finest interurban trolley stations in the country," would in three short decades stand only as a monument to a passing era.

The need for a large terminal in Schenectady became apparent soon after 1904, when interurban lines connected this city with Albany, Troy, Ballston Spa, Saratoga Springs, Scotia, Amsterdam and Gloversville. State Street had become a focal point for daily commuters and the small waiting room on the ground floor of the SRC building at 420 State St. usually was overflowing with customers.

The Schenectady company moved into the latter building (next to the towering Clark Whitbeck building) on Oct. 1, 1902, setting up its business offices on the two other floors. Before that, trolley passengers used Cherry's Newsroom — but that was before the days of interurban travel.

Schenectady Railway spent almost 10 discouraging years on prop-

137

erty negotiations before coming to terms on the 512 State Street address, where the terminal finally was erected. First choice was the property at 440 State St., for which St. Paul's Lodge 17, IOOF, turned down an offer of $62,000. Neither would attorney William W. Wemple sell the premises at 514 State St., corner of State and Lafayette, which he bought from the Chauncey O. Yates family in 1906. (That building still stands, although the third floor was removed and the entire structure remodeled in 1938).

When it finally did locate at 512 State St., SRC also purchased property around the corner on Lafayette Street so that it could erect an office building to adjoin the waiting room.

Although its official name was the Schenectady Railway Co. Terminal, the new trolley station was always referred to as the "waiting room." No matter what, for a few years the $500,000 building was a source of pride to both the railway firm and the city.

Its exterior was a gray block stone, with a two-story high archway that had a large circular clock on either side of its plate glass frames. There were five separate doors to the entrance.

The cavernous interior of the waiting room, typical of a railroad station, was lighted by electric globe lamps on the sides of the stone walls. . .and from any daylight which filtered through dusty skylights high above the three-story building. Sounds echoed sharply through the place, punctuated by the station master's regular announcements about arriving cars.

A dozen rows of varnished wood benches were at the left of the front section, the cashiers' windows on the right. In the back were vendors' booths, a shoeshine parlor, telephone booths and lavatories. The building was heated by steam boilers.

The waiting room, which at the outset was hailed as one of the finest in the country, became a liability when the railway company began to turn to motorized service in the early 1930s and when passenger service had declined. The terminal fell into disuse, becoming a grimy and empty shell of its former splendor.

It ceased to be used for trolley connections after the Saratoga Springs line changed over to buses on Dec. 7, 1941, and was used as a bus terminal for the interurbans.

The property was purchased in February, 1948 by Samuel Scheinzeit, Schenectady businessman. After being leased to private interests for exhibitions and meetings for a few years, the building was closed in 1950 to undergo a complete facelifting.

The stone facade was ripped from the old waiting room, and a modern brick exterior was built over that space and the adjoining property to the west. Two extra floors were constructed within the terminal building and now are commerical offices.

THE 1923 STREETCAR STRIKE

The year 1923 was bad for the Schenectady Railway Co. That was the year its employes' union had grown strong enough to dictate terms for higher wages, the result of which was a costly strike and rioting in the streets.

The union, formed in 1912, was known as the Amalgamated

Association of Street and Electric Railway Employees of America, Division 576. Almost at once it comprised about three quarters of the 400 SRC employees, and yet was not taken seriously by the company.

While it had not recognized the union, the SRC did listen to its suggestions for improved working conditions. This, it contended, was exactly what it had done in previous years with the Railway Workers Benevolent Association that was now replaced by the union.

A strike was called in May, 1916, the new association demanding the company raise its weekly payroll of about $13,000, but it proved ineffective. Too many private citizens depended upon the trolley for transportation and the union found itself unable to cope with strikebreakers hired by the company. The strike served notice, however, that there would be a day of reckoning in the near future.

That day came on May 16, 1923, when the union met in Trades Assembly Hall and again called a strike. Only four of 248 members opposed the action, and the results of the vote were cheered that night with the threat that "this time it will be different."

General Manager Harry B. Weatherwax already had informed association officials "the company will not do business with a union that is not incorporated or bonded." The union men sought to point out that the wage scale was unfair—that after 1912 the men were paid 60 cents an hour as long as the trolley fare remained seven cents, but later (1921) the company reduced the wages to 45 cents an hour. Now the union was asking not only reinstatement of the original wage scale but even higher rates for veteran railwaymen. But Weatherwax would not listen, and the strike was on.

The streets of Schenectady were unusually quiet that first night. No streetcars left the McClellan Street or Fuller Street barns after 10, and cars on night runs returned as soon as word reached the crews. The company might well have hoisted storm warnings atop its carbarns because this strike cast an ominous shadow over its fortunes.

It was apparent at the outset that this time the public was in sympathy with the strikers. Schenectady Railway continued to send out its cars on all routes, importing strikebreakers from out of town who were broken in on the Albany and Troy lines by older employees who returned to their jobs when the company threatened all on strike would lose their jobs. But the cars rumbled with an emptiness, save for the few "decoy" passengers hired by the company to encourage the public to patronize the lines.

Physical opposition to the running of the cars by strike breakers began in about a week, with isolated incidents such as cutting the overhead wires and placing obstacles on the tracks. More violent reaction set in about the first of June, however, and once it had erupted, the company knew it was in for a fight.

Boys joined adults in stoning episodes, and many were arrested by police. The company countered by fitting heavy wire mesh to the windows of all its trolleys.

On June 6 a streetcar was stoned heavily at the end of the Crane Street line and the motorman escaped from several men who were chasing him by jumping aboard a freight train on the New York Central road nearby. The conductor ran into the J. C. Dearstine lumber yards on Catalyn Street and later was taken away in an auto manned by SRC men.

It was not uncommon, during the worst of the rioting in June and July, for street cars to be halted by cars blocking the tracks and then stoned by shouting mobs. Sometimes the trolley crews would stay inside their cars until rescued by police; other times, depending on the mood of the crowd, they would be dragged outside and beaten.

Weatherwax denounced the attacks on the railwaymen and street-cars as "barbarism" and added that it might be well for rioters to keep in mind that the cost of repairing damage done "is very likely to appear on the tax bills of Schenectady citizens since the city is held responsible for this loss to the company."

The railway hired "guards" to protect the trolley crews. They rode in cars and brandished revolvers; some used their guns (although no one was reported killed or wounded by gunfire) and were hauled off to the city jail. The company called off their guards as soon as it appeared the violence was subsiding.

Mayor Clarence A. Whitmyre pleaded with the citizens to aid the police during outbreaks by not taking part in the fight between striker and strikebreaker. His words fell on deaf ears. When they were finally heard, the strike had run its course.

The worst period of widespread violence probably was June 6, between 6 p.m. until midnight. About a ton of glass was broken in eight cars. "B Belt" Car 805, badly battered and burned, pulled into the Fuller Street carbarn after its crew had spent a harrowing one-hour siege by strikers on upper State Street.

Riots broke out that night on Crane Street, Armory Place and downtown in front of the Wallace Co. An attempt was made to burn the trolley trestle at Kellum's Crossing, on which the SRC tracks of the Saratoga line crossed the Troy division of the New York Central Railroad. Gasoline was poured over the ties and ignited, but the fire was put out by nearby residents before it did much damage.

Tag days were held for the benefit of the strikers and their families after the strike reached its second month. Married men received $12 a week, single men were given $8.

City officials, the Chamber of Commerce and citizens' committees sought to end the crippling strike by mediation conferences between the two factions. Even A. H. Smith, president of New York Central (half owner of the railway company with Delaware & Hudson) came here from New York City to make a personal investigation. But he left in two days without finding a solution.

Licenses for 900 jitneys were taken out during the strike—and it has since been said this got the public in a more general habit of not depending on the trolley for a ride downtown. The railway company unsuccessfully sought an injunction against them.

Meanwhile, Weatherwax, aptly characterized as a man of indomitable will, stuck to his statement made the first day of the strike: "We cannot recognize unionism among our employees." William Walker, union president, and Mike Ward, business agent, finally urged the mayor to use his influence with the company for a resumption of streetcar service under "peaceful conditions conducive to the workers."

As the men were returning to their jobs at SRC, the story came out that Walker and Ward were the real reasons in back of the strike. They had become so "bossy" the company said it would not recognize the union but would be willing to talk settlement if they were replaced. The men, however, voted to stick with their leaders although once the strike was over, many of them said they were "damn fools" not to have elected new union leaders at the outset. This hindsight was like bitter almond to those who lost their seniority and, in some cases. their jobs.

By the end of August, many of the strikers were returning to work under the company's promise to give special compensation to those who went back to their old jobs within the month. More than 60 per cent of the company's 128 cars were in operation, although the public still was not patronizing them in large numbers.

The strike resolved itself before the summer's end with no clear-cut victory for either side. The union had failed to force the company to accept its demands, but all the men were given a pay raise soon after and—what was more important to union membership—it had waged a good enough battle to establish itself as a power to be reckoned with.

As for the company, it would claim the lion's share of perseverance throughout the strike for it had not backed down from its original stand. However, what it had lost in widespread public patronage could not be retrieved. The strike in reality was a harbinger of darker days ahead for the electric streetcar.

THE END OF THE TROLLEYS

The trolley era in its day attracted as much attention in the press as the steam railroad had a generation earlier, but in the late 1920s newspapers and magazines were filled with glowing accounts of the new marvel of the modern age—the automobile. This was a tipoff on the trend toward a new mode of transportation, and it was reflected in dwindling fares aboard the streetcars.

The Schenectady Railway Co. had enjoyed more than three decades of phenomenal growth and prosperity in the Schenectady area before the internal combustion engine proved its worth. Now, by 1930, the golden age of the clattering, swaying trolley was nearing its end for paved highways and mass-produced autos brought even more convenience to the public.

As automotive traffic increased, and Schenectady's downtown streets became more congested, the streetcar became cumbersome in its straight-line travel. In bygone days, horsedrawn wagons lumbered along the sides of the tracks. . .but now, no matter how hard the motorman stepped on the foot gong, double-parked trucks and cars could not be budged from the rails until they were ready to be moved.

The street railway firm made its first concession to the inevitable on June 16, 1930, when it inaugurated motor service on the Rosa Road and Crane Street lines. Of course it first obtained permission from the Public Service Commission to make the switch, something which was being done all over the state at that time. It was found that additional transportation service could be given, too, once the buses were put on the road. The Carman-Curry Road district was the first to benefit by a new bus route.

In a way, it was ironic that one of the first lines to be converted to bus service was the Crane Street-Scotia run because that particular route had always been the most consistently lucrative one in the trolley firm's history. It was not unusual in the early 1920s for the Crane Street-Scotia route to clear in excess of $1,000 in one day—which was not at all bad for a city route. The Broadway-Albany Street run was another profitable city route during that period, netting about $900 per day.

Of course, the interurbans brought in huge amounts, particularly on weekends. David Washburn, who retired in 1974 from 57 years of service in the area transportation field, well recalls his earlier days with the Schenectady streetcar firm after he began his transit career in October, 1917 as a register boy at the McClellan Street carbarn. As night cashier a few years later, he saw many a Saturday or Sunday night's receipts from the Albany line total more than $2,500. A conductor on the Saratoga line or the Forest Park run to Ballston Lake often came back from a round trip run with more than $250 in receipts.

One by one, the old trolley routes which had been opened 30 years before with ceremonies and dedication were being substituted by buses. The Scotia trolley line was abandoned in 1932, the motorized service taking over via the Western Gateway Bridge. On Aug. 1, 1935, the SRC's orange and cream diesel buses began running on the Grand Boulevard, Wendell Avenue, Union Avenue, Rugby Road and Union Street routes for the first time.

Now the only trolley routes left in the city were those State Street lines leading to Elbert Street and over McClellan. The interurban routes remaining were Aqueduct and Saratoga.

Schenectady had 140 miles of track up to 1930, but in 1938 there were 71 buses crowding the trolleys out of the picture, covering about 62 miles of routes. Of the more than 100 streetcars once used by SRC, now only 30 remained to service the sparse routes.

It had originally been planned that the closing of the Saratoga line in favor of buses would officially close the trolley era here. Elaborate preparations were made for what was to be the last streetcar ride for those in the Schenectady area and car 650 was selected to make the run with Earl Wheeler at the controls. It returned to Schenectady about 2 a.m. and pulled into the McClellan Street carbarn battered and stripped by souvenir collectors. The day? It happened to be Sunday, Dec. 7, 1941—the day of the Japanese attack on Pearl Harbor.

The advent of World War 11 gave the trolley a reprieve several more years because it helped the war economy to save gasoline and tires. The only routes in which the electric cars could be used, however, were the State Street and McClellan Street runs—all of the other lines were torn up or covered over with asphalt.

Thousands of tons of rail were ripped up to meet wartime demands for steel and old copper trolley wire was melted down for use in electrical equipment.

The streetcar's demise in Schenectady came not long after the war's end. The Public Service Commission held a hearing March, 1946, on the final abandonment of trolley lines here and granted the SRC's request to operate solely by motorized service. Most of the streetcars already had been sold before the war, and now the last of them were bought by a traction firm in Santiago, Chile.

One summer morning in 1946, a C. M. Gridley flatbed trailer pulled away from the McClellan Street carbarn (later J. M. Fields department store) with a low-bed trailer. Its cargo was the last trolley to leave Schenectady a J. G. Brill city car, No. 114, that now had the "Schenectady Railway Company" lettering on its sides painted out in favor of a crude sign: "Santiago Chile, via Valparaiso." It was on its way to the freight yards.

The fortunes of the electric streetcar in Schenectady coincided with the industry across the nation. Never had so large an enterprise grown and disappeared so swiftly as the traction industry. It had flourished amid the surroundings of the era during giant and world power that it is today. Of the hundreds of interurban railways that once criss-crossed the nation, less than half a dozen still remain.

The trolley era officially ended in New York State in July, 1960, when the PSC wiped out all the rules and regulations that applied solely to the streetcar industry. Actually, the PSC said, trolley operations ceased in the state on April 7, 1957, when the Queensburg Bridge Railway Co. in New York City substituted buses in place of trolley cars.

(1) This was the SRC interurban car that was involved in the wild ride down State Street in 1903 after its brakes failed. It is shown here in front of the Fuller Street carbarn (with canal lift bridge in left background) after its number had been changed from "51" to "551" for the "500" series. (2) This is a funeral car, "Elmlawn," once used by International Railway Co. of Buffalo. Built by Brill in 1895 for $5,798, it had four GE motors. It was typical of the funeral cars that were in general use in the early 1900's.

(1) The horsecar barn on Brandywine Avenue, near State Street, in 1888. (2) The tower wagon at Fuller Street carbarn in1900. "Barney" and "Maggie" are dappled grays. The driver is George Faircloth. Others, front to back, are foreman Elmer Rivenburgh, Michael Duggan and Charles Myers.

(1) Laying Nott Terrace tracks from State Street, Sept. 9, 1906. (2) New crossover being constructed on east side of State Street at Broadway, Sept. 26, 1906.

(1) Schenectady Railway Co. plow working in front of interurban car at Ballston Spa. (2) Saratoga interrurban, Car 609.

(1) The "traveler" in action during 1904 construction of Pleasant Valley trolley bridge. (2) Dignitaries pose for picture as first car crossed the trolley bridge to the Ninth Ward on Mar. 31, 1905.

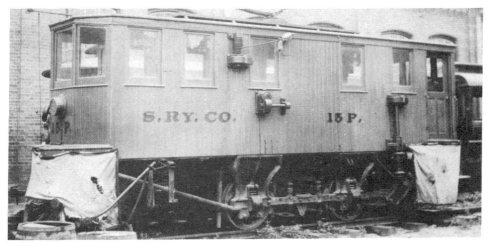

(1) Car 400, an open bench trolley used on the Albany Street-Scotia run shortly after Scotia line was opened in1902. (2) Sweeper Car 15, one of four operated by SRC. The heavy rattan rotary brooms were at either end. (3) The sprinkle car at the Fuller Street barn, No. 30W was the only sprinkler owned by SRC and it was discontinued in the early 1920s.

(1) Old No. 10, later renumbered 108. The company had four of this single-trucked type, the others being Nos. 103, 106, 107. (2) The big and beautiful 651 on South Church Street, assigned as a limited on the Albany interurban run.

*(1) SRC managed to keep the trolleys running, here at State Street and canal cross-
ing, when the big snow came on Feb. 14, 1914. (2) Traffic "tieup" on lower
Broadway in early 1920s as quitting time at factories drew near.*

151

(1) Trolley car interior, wooden seats, in the early 1920s. When the motorman changed platform controls at the end of the line, the passenger seat backrests were reversed. Heaters were beneath the seats. (2) An early bus on the Ravena to Albany run, 1913. Gus Snyder, driver, owned the line and often carried the mail between Coeyman's Hollow and Albany.

(1) Crowds waiting to board SRC trolleys at State Street and boulevard in 1924. (2) Fleet of Schenectady Auto Co. buses in 1914 in front of Parker Building. Art Theatre, now entrance to Proctor's Arcade, is in center.

(1) SRC waiting room at right, about 1915. Crescent Park is in left background.
(2) Scene on State Street, Broadway in right background, about 8 p.m. on June 6, 1923, as mob surrounded and stoned two stalled SRC trolleys during height of bitter strike.

(1) Westerly view of Albany line, looking toward Schenectady, at Stop 4¾– between Chiswell and Van Zandt Streets, Highway is at right. View made Oct. 8, 1926. (2) Construction of Eastern Avenue extension in 1906. Brandywine Avenue is in foreground.

(1) Bench car crossing "longest trolley bridge in the world" across the Mohawk River between Alplaus and Craig, about 1910. (2) Aqueduct Car 200, a convertible type, on Van Vranken Avenue extension. (3) Unidentified man on the trolley river bridge.

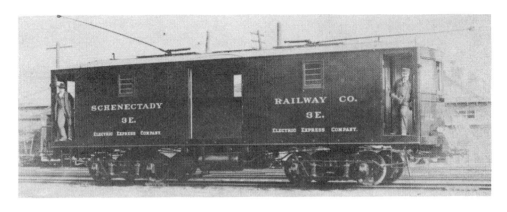

(1) SRC's Electric Express Co. Car 3E in Fuller Street yards. (2) SRC's sleek chair-car, Car 505, at Eastern and McClellan. (3) SRC experimented briefly with this huge double-truck, No. 856, arranged for one-man operation. Entrance was through turnstile in center, exit from front. Photo made Sept. 27, 1922, from front of McClellan Street barn.

Three views of SRC's trolley "graveyard" in late 1930s as the electrics were fast being replaced by diesel buses on most routes. Some cars were sold, but most were left to deteriorate in the company's gravel pit at the end of Van Vranken Avenue and later were burned.

(1) Typical Schenectady downtown scene about 1940, showing the traffic congestion which made it increasingly difficult for electric trolleys to maintain their schedule. (2) Car 202, a No. 4 Woodlawn trolley which went up State as far as Frank Street, stalled by a car parked on track in 1942. Old state armory is in left background.

(1) This was a warm afternoon in August, 1946, as a flatbed Gridley truck was loading the last trolley car to leave Schenectady, bound for its new home in Santiago, Chile. It is rolling out of the McClellan Street carbarn. (2) On its way to the railroad yard and shipment to South America.

PART FIVE
In Public Service

18—County Courthouse

$\mathcal{S}$chenectady County celebrated its 100th anniversary on Jan. 5, 1909, by hiring an architect to design a new county courthouse near the summit of the State Street hill.

That the building has served the county well in these intervening years is quite evident, the recently renovated structure being made an important coordinate to the adjacent county office building. In connection with the construction of the courthouse 65 years ago are these interesting sidelights:

Instead of being built in an estimated 18 months, the courthouse was not completed until three and a half years later.

Cost of construction and furnishings came to about $400,000 — which was nearly $150,000 less than the cost of remodeling and equipment a half century later.

Agitation for a new courthouse began just after the turn of this century when it was decided the old quarters were antiquated and outgrown. County and Supreme Court sessions were held in the building at 108 Union St., ultimately purchased by the city and up through 1974 used for its public school administration offices. The county sheriff and the jail also had been located in this building.

Just down the block, at 11-13 Union St., was an old two-story brick building used by the supervisors, surrogate and county clerk. That structure, known afterwards as the county annex, was purchased by the Mohawk Club and torn down in 1966 to accommodate a club parking lot. The contract with W. L. Stoddart, New York City architect, was negotiated with the county board in the supervisors' chambers in the latter building. Stoddart drew up the elaborate plans for the new courthouse; the supervisors were pleased with the results and bids were advertised for construction. The contract for general construction was awarded to John McDermott on May 25, 1909, calling for completion ready for occupancy by the county within 18 months from that date at a cost, including furnishings, not to exceed $400,000.

In October, 1910, McDermott asked for an extension of one year which was granted by the Board of Supervisors without penalty. Additional extensions without penalty were also given the contractor on Nov. 26, 1911, and Aug. 1, 1912. The building finally was completed Jan. 1, 1913 — 29 months after the time of completion specified in the contract.

The county moved its departments uptown into the new courthouse on March 1, 1913, and formally accepted it one month later. The acceptance on the part of the supervisors was unanimous and the general opinion was expressed that the building "is one of satisfaction and pride on the part of the citizens of Schenectady County."

The new county jail also was under construction on Veeder Avenue and was finished nearly a year after the courthouse.

Then the county board received a bill from architect Stoddart for an additional $5,908 incurred, he said, as a result of the extensions given the general contractor. In his threatening lawsuit, after the county balked at payment of the extra fee, Stoddart claimed his contract with the county stated specifically that no extension of time be granted without written consent of the architect and that he had had no notice of the extensions given McDermott. This necessitated Stoddart keeping George Talbot, supervising architect, on the job longer than had been agreed upon.

It appeared that William Dewey Loucks, county attorney from 1910 to 1911, had not required the consent of the architect to be given in writing for the extension in time. Stoddart told the board the building was to have been completed by Nov. 26, 1910. Finally, the county board agreed to give Stoddart the extra fee and in paying the bill expressed gratitude for the "outstanding job" he had done in designing the new courthouse.

When the $2 million county office building was finished in 1962, all county departments were moved into it from the courthouse. Under the renovation program, work then was started by Wade Lupe contractors under a $498,000 contract to transform the courthouse interior into a modern judicial building.

It was finished early in 1964 and the courts and affiliated departments moved back into it that summer. An open house was held in September, 1964, and formal dedication of the renovated courthouse took place on Jan. 16, 1966.

AT LAST - The new Schenectady County Courthouse at right as it looked when completed in March, 1913. The Central Fire Station is at left.

19—The Fire Dept.

$\mathcal{U}$ntil 1900, fire-fighting chores in Schenectady were left to the volunteer hose companies which had been around since the Revolutionary War. It was about time, both the officials of the city and its citizens figured, that an industrial center such as Schenectady had become should have an organized, paid fire department.

On Nov. 15, 1898, the Common Council appointed a special committee to devise a plan for reorganizing the city's fire protection system. Within a few months, the committee finished its work, adding the recommendation that a central fire station be erected in the vicinity of Crescent Park on the State Street hill.

There were six fire stations in downtown Schenectady at the time, all of which housed volunteer companies. Under the new system — a paid department to supplement the volunteers — the Schenectady Fire Department would utilize those old stations until new ones could be built. Most of the stations being used today were built by 1913, but the first to be inaugurated into the new department was the central fire station.

Work on the three-story brick structure was started in 1899 across from the park and just a few doors from Veeder Avenue. The first floor was designed to house the fire apparatus and horses. Firemen's quarters and administration offices were on the second floor, while the top floor had recreation rooms and volunteer company meeting rooms. The exterior was of red sandstone on the ground floor and light-colored brick on the upper stories.

Although the reorganization of the fire department officially began Jan. 1, 1900, the central fire station was not opened until July 1 of that year when open house ceremonies were held.

Schenectady's first fire chief under the paid department setup was Henry R. Yates. He was one of 18 candidates, most of whom had been volunteer firemen many years, who took a Civil Service examination for the position on Nov. 9, 1899. Yates, who had been a member of Van Vranken Hose Company No. 2, made his headquarters at the old South Church Street station until the central station was completed.

Yates started his term as chief with nine paid firemen — August Derra (who was to become the city's second chief in 1924 at Yates' death), John Bath, Maurice Baum, Jerome O'Leary, Edward Connery, Edward McGee, John Cregan, Edward McCormick and John Shaffer. The newly organized department consisted of only one wagon, a steam fire engine, five hand-drawn carts and a hook and ladder truck.

However, there were 18 paid firemen and several more pieces of equipment when the department held its first parade down State Street on Sept. 11, 1900. Yates loved parades. While he was chief, Schenectady residents were treated to frequent full dress reviews of the fire department's personnel and equipment. Invariably, the chief would be at the head of the procession, either riding in his horse-drawn red carriage or walking jauntily in dress uniform with a chief's silver megaphone tucked under one arm.

The department was almost fully mechanized when Yates died Aug. 31, 1924, and Derra took over. It was growing with the city and already plans were in the offing for a revamping of stations.

When the filling in of the Erie Canal was nearly completed in 1924, plans were readily approved for the construction of a new central station on what was to become Erie Boulevard. That building, the present central fire station, was officially opened May 1, 1929, and simultaneously marked the closing of the old central fire house opposite Crescent Park. Although it was to be used no longer as a fire station the building was soon taken over by the Schenectady Police Department as a headquarters for its traffic division. In time, American Legion Post 21 and the Jewish War Veterans took over the upper floors for clubrooms.

During the depression years of the Thirties, the traffic barn was used frequently as a bundle station for clothing and furniture to he distributed by the welfare department. When the building was earmarked for condemnation in 1950, the police moved out and relocated the traffic division in the Smith Street police station. Post 21 left the next year, dedicating its new post home at 740 Union St. in 1951.

Actually, the Schenectady County government was owner of the old fire station as early as 1935 when it gave the city $10,000 plus the old county almshouse at Duane and Steuben Streets in return for the station. The station was now located next to the county courthouse.

By the early 1950s, plans were made for the construction of a new county office building at the corner of Veeder Avenue and State Street — so now the fire station had to go.

It was in mid-October of 1956 that many local "old timers" gathered in Crescent Park (now renamed Veterans' Park) to watch with nostalgic twinges as across the street wrecking crews began tearing down the former central fire house. Some of them, in their mind's eye, could still see the spirited fire horses pulling the rigs out of the arched doorways, spurred on by the loud gonging of the tapper bell from inside the station.

And it was in mid-July of 1981 when crowds gathered at 360 Veeder Avenue, corner of Hamilton Street, to see the formal opening of Schenectady's new central fire station. The gleaming red trucks and other apparatus were lined up in front of the sprawling single-story headquarters. It was the beginning of another era. The former headquarters down on the boulevard was sold to private investors and turned into a handsome business center.

SCHENECTADY'S FIRE CHIEFS

Henry R.Yates	1900-1924
August G. Derra	1924-1937
James J. Higgins	1937-1951
Edward M. Moffett	1951-1960
Ernest H. Berger	1960-1962
Thomas L. Meaney	1962-1963
Milton C. Kling	1963-1977
Ralph Marshall	1977-1983
Ralph Ruggiero	1983-1987
Thomas Varno	1987-

20—The Police Dept.

*L*ikely there was not a Schenectady police officer around during the first week in May, 1973, who could shed a tear over the fact that the department was leaving its old headquarters at Clinton and Smith Streets in favor of the new $3 million station on Liberty Street. And yet, this much should be said about the former headquarters — it provided a home base for our city police for more than 40 years since it was remodeled from an old school building, which was a lot longer than had been anticipated.

In 1868, only three years after the end of the Civil War and the assassination of President Lincoln, a six-room brick schoolhouse was built on the Smith Street site at a cost of $5,000. It was a successor to the city's first free common schoolhouse which was constructed in 1848 near the corner of Liberty Street and what was then Willow Street, later White Street and, still later, Clinton Street (this two-story brick building stood until the late 1920s when that entire block was cleared for erection of the present City Hall).

About 1898, an eight-room addition was built towards the Smith Street side of the second school building at a cost of $30,000 to form the structure which exists today on that site.

It was declared "unfit for educational purposes" in the late 1920s and was last used as a school in June, 1929.

That same year, the Schenectady Police Department was about to lose its headquarters, then located in the old City Hall on the southern side of the present City Hall block. The suggestion that the police might take over the now vacant Clinton Street School building as its new headquarters was swiftly acted upon by the City Council. At that time, it was not necessary for the city school district to turn it over to the city — much less sell it to the city — as this was before the school system was fiscally independent.

The school building was renovated for police use by Works Progress Administration funds and by 1932 was ready for occupancy by the Schenectady Police Department, then under Chief William H. Funston, the fifth in the department's history.

From 1798 to 1832, Schenectady's ordinances were upheld by the mayor in his dual capacity as both administrator and protector. From 1832 to 1866, an appointed official known as a "high constable" kept the peace.

Probably Schenectady's first police headquarters might logically be said to have been a room rented by High Constable Roswell Perry after 1833 in a building which was the former rectory of St. George's Episcopal Church. The room was advertised by a "Mr. Cooke...who will rent a room in his building on Ferry Street for two dollars a month."

Besides the high constable, each ward of the city in those early days also boasted its ward constable — whose duty and privilege it was to serve legal papers, the fees derived from so doing being his only recompense. Lewis Vrooman was the last Schenectadian to hold the position of high constable.

The State Legislature created the Capitol Police Force in 1867 to uphold the law in the cities of Schenectady, Albany and Troy. The Capitol police commissioners, having jurisdiction over an appointed force, were appointed by the governor. Under the law establishing this commission, Schenectady was a precinct, the local members of the force being under the supervision of David J. Caw. This was the first uniformed police in the city. A police headquarters was located on Wall Street, near State.

For Schenectady, the brief period of the Capitol police was an unhappy one as the force had been established without the city's consent and much resentment followed. However, an act of the Legislature passed in 1870 gave Schenectady the right to govern its own police — and the present police department dates from this act.

The city's police force moved into the new City Hall, a three-story brick structure, when it was built in 1880 with funds largely donated by William K. Fuller, prominent Schenectadian. In addition, Schenectady's long arm of the law was strengthened by four district precincts scattered throughout the city.

In the rear of the City Hall, towards Clinton Street, were barns in which horses and equipment were kept. A horsedrawn patrol wagon was put into use in 1903 when William L. Campbell was still chief. Capt. James W. Rynex (who would become chief the following year upon Campbell's death) had earlier become the first Schenectady patrolman to ride a horse on his rounds. The first motorcycle patrolmen in Schenectady made their appearance about 1906.

Looking back into the early records of our police department — even before the horse patrols and the two horse hitch "Black Maria" — there is quite a contrast in police dress and equipment between today's force and that of a century ago.

In the early days, policemen were dressed in knee-length blue coats with high collar and two long rows of brass buttons. They wore Keystone Cop-like helmets and, for the most part, handlebar mustaches. Patrolmen carried lanterns and six-foot staffs while on night duty. Some were supplied with small lanterns that fastened to their belts.

Our police department has, indeed, come a long way in our city's history of law enforcement and peace-keeping.

SCHENECTADY'S POLICE CHIEFS

Isaac G. Lovett 1870-1872
Charles H. Willard 1872
William L. Campbell..1872-1904
James W. Rynex 1904-1925
William H. Funston 1925-1938
Joseph A. Peters, Sr. 1938-1951
Joseph Foley 1951-1952
Ambrose P. Mountain...1952-1955
William F. Brandt...1955-1958
Stanley A. DuCharme 1958-1966
John P. Murphy..1966-1977
Joseph A. Peters Jr. 1977-1981
Richard Nelson 1981-1991
Commissioner Charles Mills................................1991-1994
Michael G. Moffett 1994-

21—The Sheriff's Dept.

$\mathcal{W}$hen Schenectady County was established in 1809, the office of county sheriff was among the first to be organized within the new governmental structure. In so doing, the county added an extra dimension to the arm of the law within and outside the city since up until that time, private citizens were hired as a constabulary force in the wards and townships — mostly to check on such things as whether the street oil lamps were lighted or to give warning in cases of fire. They tried to keep order best they could, but usually it was a matter of persuading neighbors to behave themselves.

Along with the first county sheriff came the first lockup, located in the basement of the building on the northeast corner of Ferry and Union Streets, the same building in which Union College was founded in 1795.

The first sheriff was James (Jacobus) Van Slyck Ryley, who took office April 2, 1809. A more colorful personality than he could not have been selected to launch the county's law enforcement agency.

Ryley was born in Schenectady on Oct. 3, 1761, the son of Philip Ryley, a civic leader in the community that grew out of the ashes of the 1690 massacre. Young James enlisted in the Second Albany Militia in the last stages of the Revolutionary War and saw action at Stone Arabia, qualifying him for a federal pension. Then he became an Indian trader, traveling throughout the Great Lakes country and becoming well known among the Indians in that territory.

He soon joined the federal service as an interpreter and exerted great influence over the Chippewas in the government's Treaty of the Saginaw. Ryley married a Chippewa girl named Me-naw-cam-e-quoqua who bore him three sons, John, Peter and James. He later divorced her and returned to Schenectady (his sons all were given grants of land in the area of present day Detroit.)

He married Janetje Swits, daughter of Isaac Swits, in August, 1792, and bought land on Washington Street south of State Street. In the 1830s, he was part owner of the house at 31 Front St. and in the 1840s lived at 42 Union St.

Once in Schenectady, he took an interest in politics and public service. He was an active member of the Schenectady John Jay for Governor Committee in 1798 and became known in Albany circles as an energetic civic worker — which did not hurt him one iota whenever he applied for local government jobs. He was confirmed in 1805 in the First Reformed Church.

Ryley was a man of many talents and many jobs. He was a fire warden and a city constable in 1803, a "superintendent of the watch" in the First Ward and an inspector of chimneys the following year. When the new position of county sheriff became available, he applied for and was granted the post by action of the new Board of Supervisors. He served until 1813 and was replaced by John Brown, but again became sheriff in 1835 for a short while.

He was not inactive in between jobs. He was Schenectady's third postmaster for about 15 years after 1820, then after his second stint as sheriff, was named an associate judge of Common Law in Schenectady.

Ryley's wife Jane died in 1838. He died in 1848 at age 86. Both were buried in the Green Street Cemetery and their remains later were reinterred in Vale Cemetery.

After 1831, when the county built its new courthouse at 108 Union St., the sheriffs department was moved into it to preside over maintenance of the building and the jail cells that had been built into it. The sheriff made the courthouse building his residence.

Up until 1905, the county board paid its sheriff a daily rate, taking into account that he also had the benefit of lodging, heat and light in the courthouse. The sheriff was paid $3 a day, the undersheriff $2 a day and constables $2 a day at the turn of the century.

It was in 1905 that the county made the office of sheriff a salaried one. Instead of a daily fee, he was to be paid $3,500 annually — but included in said amount was the obligation of the sheriff to pay his undersheriff, jailer "and all other help required by him to run the jail, courthouse, courts etc." It was duly stipulated that he was to continue to receive fees from civil cases and would be allowed to live in the courthouse building. Merritt Hammond, county sheriff from 1905 until 1907, had the distinction of being the first salaried sheriff in Schenectady's history.

Likewise, another "first" was recorded by Sheriff Louis A. Welch Sr. who was in office when the sheriff's department moved uptown into its new jail and offices on Veeder Avenue in 1914, the rear courtyard abutting the back lot of the new county courthouse which had been opened the year before.

Following are the Schenectady County sheriffs since the turn of the century:

William G. Caw	1900-1905
Merritt Hammond	1905-1907
Thomas E. Leavitt	1907-1909
William Hathaway	1909-1911
Christian L. Staver	1911-1913
Louis A. Welch Sr.	1913-1917
William A. Cryne	1917-1920
Daniel Manning	1920-1923
John G. Myers	1923-1926
George E. Ramsey	1926-1929
Edward C. Klein	1929-1932
Carroll A. Gardner	1932-1935
Thomas W. Walsh	1935-1938
Ernest H. Blanchard	1938-1943
Harold Armstrong	1943-1946
William H. Dunn	1946-1952
Harold Calkins	1952-1971
Bernard T. Waldron	1971-1990
William Barnes	1990-

22—The Education Dept.

*P*ublic education is virtually taken for granted by today's society—but only a century ago in Schenectady as most everyplace else in America it had not even worn off the newness of a radical departure in our social order.

Under the direction of its first city school superintendent, Dr. Samuel Howe (for whom Howe School was named), Schenectady's school system made remarkable strides in reaching out to all families within the growing city — wealthy and poor, native-born and immigrant alike — to make at least an elementary education available to all children.

But, like so many other facets of endeavor in Old Dorp, public education here made its greatest progress after 1900. Most of the school buildings still being used today were constructed during the first quarter of this century and innovations now considered commonplace — such as free textbooks and school supplies, playgrounds, lunch programs and extra-curricular activities — were also initiated in that era.

Until a Board of Education was established in Schenectady in 1854, there was no such thing as a tuition-free school. There were small private schools — including the Lancaster School, Schenectady Female Academy and the Schenectady Lyceum — but until the new Board of Education purchased West College (at Union and North College Streets) from Union College for the sum of $6,000 and opened it as a public school for about 550 pupils, there was no such thing in Schenectady as a free school.

In 1872, the classical department was moved to a building on the corner of Church and Union Streets (designed by the famous colonial architect, Philip Hooker, as was West College) and became the city's first high school, known as the Union Classical Institute. The old U.C.I.,the building now occupied by the Mohawk Club, was the only high school here until the north building of Schenectady High School was built on Nott Terrace in 1903 and replaced U.C.I. The south building of Schenectady High School, which was adjoined to the north building with a second and third floor bridge, was constructed in 1911. Schenectady High School became Nott Terrace High School in 1931 when Mont Pleasant High was completed.

Incidentally, it was the newer portion of the old Nott Terrace High School—the south building—which was torn down in 1962 when Liberty Street was widened. The north building was used for a time as an elementary school but that since has been razed and the space occupied by a restaurant.

After 1913, when the county moved into its new courthouse building on State Street opposite the park, the city school system took over the old courthouse at 108 Union Street as an administration building. It is an old building, constructed 1830-33, but remains a sturdy and picturesque structure.

Listed at the end of this segment are the city school system's school buildings and the date of their construction, but first we would mention those schools which long filled their purpose but are now gone or no longer used for classroom instruction.

There was the old Mohawkville School, a wood frame building constructed in 1875 at the end of Crane Street almost at the city line. It operated much like a prototype of the little red schoolhouse—one schoolmaster and children of all grade levels. In 1922, it was equipped as an open air school for tubercular children but shortly after was torn down.

Nott School, also built in 1875 at Nott and Devine Streets, was a substantial brick structure which at first had four classrooms until a later addition doubled its size. It was phased out as a school in the mid-1930s, used for storage of welfare furniture for a time, then as the headquarters for the War Price Rationing Board during World War II and finally as the administration building for the Schenectady County Social Services Department. It is still serving in that capacity—a far cry from its original purpose a century ago but yet serviceable.

In another chapter on the police department's old Smith Street headquarters, we mentioned the early schoolhouse built on White Street (later Clinton Street) on the present City Hall block in 1848 and that the Clinton Street School was built in 1868 and later enlarged. The latter school is still around at this writing even though the police department deserted it in 1973 for their new station. The Clinton Street building is presently used by the Schenectady Off Track Betting Corp. From schoolhouse to police station to betting parlor—as curious a transition as one could ever imagine.

The first Euclid School up in Bellevue was a wooden schoolhouse built next to the Broadway plank road in 1888. A new brick school was being built when the old building burned to the ground on a cold winter's night in 1925. Euclid School was closed after the 1973-74 semester and is now occupied by the Spirit and Truth Christian Church.

The Third Avenue School at the corner of Orchard Street in Mont Pleasant was also a well-used school that had been built in the 1880s when the Ninth Ward began development. It was later used as a police precinct and razed in the late 1930s.

Park Place School, built in 1892, was torn down in the 1950s and is now a playground at the South Avenue corner.

Seward School was another Mont Pleasant elementary school which was torn down after being phased out of the school system. It had been built in 1908 at the corner of Congress and Fifth Streets.

Halsey School, which many referred to as the Albany Street School, was built in 1890 as an eight-room schoolhouse and later was given an extra floor with two more classrooms and an auditorium. Located at the corner of Albany and Steuben Streets, the brick structure was razed in 1970.

Nott Terrace Elementary School was a stylish brick building of eight classrooms when built in 1884 at the corner of Nott Terrace and Chapel Street. It, too, was enlarged a few years later and served the community well until it was vacated and torn down with the urban renewal clearance of that area in the mid-1950s.

Union School, sometimes called the Union Street School, replaced the old West College building at Union and College Streets in 1892. It was in use up until the time of World War II, after which it was remodeled into apartments for low income families. This latter project was short-lived, however, and the former school building was demolished in 1960 and has since been a parking lot on that corner.

In 1908, the Broadway School was built as a vocational high school and next to it, in the same year, was built the Edison School, both fronting on Broadway with Van Guysling Avenue in the rear. They have since been discontinued as educational centers but are still used by the city school system. The Broadway School is now a curriculum center while Edison School is a collection point for maintenance supplies. They have since been discontinued as educational centers.

Much has transpired in the 145 years that Schenectady has had a free public education system. Understandably, it was once a problem—not only of logistics but also of convenience to neighborhood families—to attempt to locate schools where they could be most easily accessible by pupils in that area. As time went on, this became less of a problem than simply finding the funds to build new schools. More and more pupils were going to school as the city's population increased but, beginning with the post-World War I era, they were also remaining in school after the elementary grades.

The introduction of the junior high school system in the early 1920s was intended to combat the early dropouts (many children before that time quit school after the sixth grade and went to work) and encourage a smooth transition into secondary school. Vocational or trade schools on the high school level were also an innovation.

It is difficult today, when a college education is within the grasp of any young person, to comprehend the days of over a half century ago—when graduation from high school was a rarity among the offspring of a working class family. It was a big event, to be sure, but many friends and relatives would be wondering why that young person "hadn't been to work by now."

Schenectady has a fine school system today, offering equal opportunities to all pupils with the best that modern educational technology offers. It still has problems, mainly budgetary, and is presently engaged in a consolidation program designed to be of greater service to the community as a whole while staying within its tax structure. The closing of Brandywine and Euclid Schools in June, 1974 was part of that program. Since that time, the school administration offices moved out from 108 Union St. and into the vacant Brandywine School. In 1994, since Mont Pleasant High School became a middle school, the administrative function followed suit and took up its duties there.

September, 1992 saw some drastic changes on the scholastic front. Extensive additions to Linton High School had been made and finished by then so when the student body filed into the classrooms there were many more pupils and the school had changed its name to Schenectady High School. Now it combined student bodies of both Linton and Mont Pleasant and its school colors were red, white and blue to please both sides. After 61 years, MPHS had become a middle school, as did Central Park Junior High after 69 years.

Schenectady School Superintendents

Samuel Howe 1868-1905
John T. Freeman 1905-1908
Abraham R. Brubacher 1908-1915
Herbert Blair 1915-1917
Oscar W. Kuolt...1917-1918
E. R. Whitney..1918-1925
Granville B. Jeffers 1925-1926
A. J. Stoddard 1926-1929
W. Howard Pillsbury 1929-1946
Harry J. Linton 1946-1954
Robert E. Murray 1955-1968
Bruce Brummit 1968-1970
Charles Abba 1970-1981
Frank Mayer 1981-1987
Richard Holzman 1987-1990
Frank Laplant (acting supervisor).......................1990-1991
Michael Coury 1991-1993
Raymond C. Colucciello 1993-

City School Buildings and Dates of Construction

Brandywine School 1904
Central Park Junior High School...............................1923
Clinton Street School 1868
Edison School...1909
Eliphalet Nott (Street) School 1875
Elmer Avenue School 1905
Euclid School 1925
Franklin School 1907
Fulton School 1908
Grout Park School 1953
Halsey School 1890
Hamilton School 1914
Horace Mann School 1908
Howe School 1910
Dr. Martin Luther King Jr. School 1966
Lincoln School 1908
Linton High School 1958
Mont Pleasant High School 1931
Nott Terrace Elementay School 1884
Oneida Junior High School 1923
Paige School 1953
Pleasant Valley School 1922
Riverside School 1923
Seward School 1908
Steinmetz School (former McKinley School).............1908
Union School 1890
Van Corlaer School 1914

Area preservationists became concerned over the uncertain fate of the old county courthouse at 108 Union St. after the city school system in 1975 moved its administration offices from there up to the former Brandywine School at 108 North Brandywine Ave. The Schenectady County Historical Society investigated the possibility of selling its headquarters on 32 Washington Ave. and purchasing the former courthouse as a replacement. However, after many months of careful consideration, weighing practicality and cost factors against the desire to save the old building, the society's trustees rejected the plan. The school board then put the Union Street property on the block, setting a date for a public auction.

In March, 1976, it was announced that the new owners would be a Schenectady couple, Mr. and Mrs. Albert W. Lawrence, who submitted a successful bid of $81,000. Lawrence, the owner of an insurance firm with eight offices in New York State, has since moved some of his operations into the former courthouse.

Old Nott Terrace High was not far from demolition in this 1956 aerial view of Nott Terrace in foreground and former South Seward place in background. It was replaced by Linton High School in January, 1958

23—The City Hall Block

The construction of the present City Hall building during 1929 and 1930 drastically changed the character of the block bounded by Jay, Franklin, Clinton and Liberty Streets.

In addition to the three-story brick building of the original Ellis Hospital facing Jay Street, other structures on that block which were demolished early in 1929 to make way for the new City Hall included several dilapidated frame houses, a small brick building once known as the White Street School and a building at the rear of the old City Hall used for street equipment, the water department and police vehicles.

Under perfect skies but before a crowd estimated at only 400 persons, the cornerstone of the new City Hall was laid Saturday afternoon, May 10, 1930, with Mayor Henry C. Fagal wielding the trowel.

The speakers, city officials and some members of the mayor's committee were seated on a small platform, about 12 feet square, erected in front of where the cornerstone was to be placed — at the northwest corner of the building's foundation at Jay and Liberty Streets. The platform was decorated with red, white and blue bunting and a public address system was rigged up — but failed to function.

Not many except those real close to the stand heard much that was said, but that did not seem to matter; they were there for an occasion and not necessarily to listen to speeches.

The ceremonies opened with the playing of "America" by the 105th Infantry Band. Mayor Fagal then made introductory remarks, followed by an invocation by the Rev. John C. Meengs, pastor of the Second Reformed Church. James Kellum Smith, of the New York City firm of McKim, Mead and White, architects for the new building, was called upon to say "a few words" but it turned out rather lengthy.

"Some time ago, when our firm was invited to enter a competition for the design of a new city hall for Schenectady, we accepted with enthusiasm in spite of our distaste for this method of selecting an architect," Smith said. "We were influenced by our admiration for the architectural beauty of many of the city's older buildings. In spite of its fair share of indifferent work, Schenectady is a city of distinct architectural flavor. There is much quality here, expressive of a fine building tradition. . .

"The situation here has been unusually gratifying. Those representing the city administration have realized the peculiar nature of a city hall — its relative permanence compared with other types of buildings, its intimate relation to those subtle but highly important elements of public spirit which, for lack of more precise terms, are called civic pride or general morale. They have recognized that they are now erecting a building which may still be the material and spiritual center of civic life in the Schenectady of 100 years from today. . ."

That was the tenor of the architect's speech, one that lasted nearly 10 minutes. It was followed up by a bit of nostalgia provided by the city's oldest living ex-mayor, T. Low Barhydt, who had served a two-year term in 1887-88.

He told of the small city of his boyhood days, giving the location of streets, buildings and other places by referring to the streets or buildings now occupying the same areas. The former mayor described the tremendous growth which followed the coming here of the General Electric Co. He compared living, working and governmental conditions of the mid-1800's to 1930, closing his speech by telling of the inaugura tion while he was city water commissioner of a water system which replaced the one by which Schenectadians drank Mohawk River water.

The band struck up a marching tune at that point, during which some frolicking youngsters followed the cue by stomping heavily in and around the mud near the speakers' platform—until some spattered bystanders prevailed upon them to go out to a clearing to pursue their close order drill. Hugh R. McPartlon, president of the Common Council, then described the contents of the copper box to be placed in the cornerstone. It had been sealed shortly after 10 a.m. the previous day in City Engineer Frank R. Lanagan's office. So well did Lanagan arrange the packing of the wealth of records, there was room enough left to include the printed minutes of the Council, the Board of Contract and Supply, and the Board of Estimate and Apportionment for 1928 and 1929. When these were packed into the box, not a hair's space remained.

Isaac Y. Burgess, who constructed the copper box and presented it to the city for the cornerstone, had placed the slide cover upon the box and soldered every edge. In the office at the time, in addition to Burgess and Lanagan, were City Clerk Douglas K. Miller, Deputy City Clerk William H. Fowler Jr., Frank D. King, secretary to the mayor, Public Works Commissioner Walter H. Mischler, Deputy Public Works Commissioner James W. Lewis, Deputy Comptroller C. H. Greene and a newspaper representative.

"This, in brief, Mr. Mayor," concluded McPartlon at the ceremonies," is a general description of the records contained in this sealed copper box which I now have the honor and pleasure of handing to you to be placed in the cornerstone of the city hall."

Mayor Fagal took the box and placed it inside a cavity hollowed out trom the bottom of the cornerstone. As the latter was at that time suspended in air, wedges were placed by workmen to keep the box in position.

The mayor was then handed a silver trowel on which was engraved, "Trowel used by Mayor Henry C. Fagal in laying the cornerstone of Schenectady's new city hall, May 10, 1930." (That still-gleaming tool today is among the archives of the City History Center in City Hall.) When the mayor scooped up the mortar to place under the stone, incidentally, he used one of the workmen's trowels rather than dirty up the ceremonial trowel.

There was some difficulty in getting the stone to settle into its proper position, much pounding by workmen being necessary before the heavy granite block finally reached the proper level.

"We must turn our eyes to the new Schenectady if we are going to keep pace with civilization," the mayor said during his speech. "This cornerstone laying should be an inspiration for the achievement of other big things." He expressed the hope that local merchants and businessmen "will see the light of day and make improvements which should have taken place in this city long ago."

Mayor Fagal advocated a long term improvement program. He praised the widening of State Street at Crescent Park, performed during his administration, and recommended the following improvements: A viaduct across Vale Cemetery which would provide a north-south connection between Union and State Streets between Nott Terrace and Brandywine Avenue; more and improved approaches to the city, including the extension of Albany Street to Albany; the widening of Weaver Street and the extension of it to Pleasant Valley Park; and the extension of Hamilton Street to Erie Boulevard on the west and Brandywine Avenue on the east. Forty years later, many of the same things were still being advocated.

The mayor closed by saying that he and the Common Council could not accomplish these things alone, but they must have the sentiment of the people behind them

The Right Rev. Msgr. John L. Reilly, pastor of St. John the Evangelist Church, pronounced benediction followed by the band's playing the national anthem.

The onlookers, which had been comparatively attentive during the festivities despite the fact that they had to stand in the hot sun during an hour and half of speechmaking which most of them couldn't hear—walked around the premises for awhile to inspect the footings and other construction work that had started in early spring. Many of them took a closer look at the cornerstone, upon the front of which was carved the Roman numerals MCMXXX. The stone was four feet, eight inches long, two feet high and two feet wide. The copper box now inside it measured 14 by 10 by 8 inches.

The city had rented offices in the downtown section, most of them on Clinton Street, for its departments as temporary quarters until the new City Hall was finished.

When the city decided to utilize the whole block for its new City Hall, it was necessary to acquire only a few parcels since the city already owned more than half the block. This cut the initial outlay considerably, but the cost of such a magnificent building soon prompted the inevitable cry of political critics to label it a "folly". . . in this case "Fagal's Folly." They also dubbed it the "Million Dollar Palace." It might be noted, however, that although Henry Fagal was defeated in 1931 after a four-year term he was returned to office two years later in the midst of the depression.

Until 1880, the only place the city administration could call home after the city's founding in 1798 was the old West College building at Union and College Streets. The city twice took possession of that building, as a city hall after 1813 and as a school in 1854. In the interim, between 1854 and 1880, the Common Council met in the county building at 108 Union St. with various city departments being housed in leased offices in the downtown area.

In 1878, Gen. William K. Fuller led the campaign to find a permanent City Hall for Schenectady. In that year, the Daily Union reported that General Fuller gave the sum of $10,000 to the city to enable it to erect a proper building on Jay Street "which for a generation has been an eyesore to the public." This was the impetus needed to construct a city building capable of accommodating the administration and its departments.

Construction began in 1880 and in less than a year a three-story brick building was sufficiently completed to allow the police department and assessment office to move into it. By 1881, it was entirely finished and was now Schenectady's City Hall.

Who was General Fuller? He was the son of Jeremiah Fuller and the grandson of the noted colonial architect, Samuel Fuller. He studied law with Henry and John B. Yates and as a young man was named adjutant general of New York State (and as such issued orders on the official reception of General Lafayette during the latter's visit to Albany in 1824.) General Fuller, a wealthy man by birth who became richer by virtue of his vocation, retired to his home at 2 Church St. (the old Fuller House, built about 1792 by his grandfather) about the time of the Civil War. It is said he never took much of an interest in local politics in his waning years to the extent that he did not even vote in local or national elections. And yet, apparently he was concerned enough about the city government to spark the move toward a new City Hall.

In those days, $10,000 was a sizeable start towards a building fund of the kind that the city needed, roughly one-third of the total cost. It was accepted from General Fuller with gratitude and plans went forward for the new building. The general died Nov. 30, 1883, so he saw its completion.

There was not much to be said about the Jay Street block from an aesthetic standpoint. Most of the buildings in the block fronted on either Clinton (then White) Street or Liberty Street. On the Franklin Street side were a few ramshackle wood-framed dwellings.

When "Fuller's" City Hall was erected, a vast improvement was at once noticeable. Its interior was much like a schoolhouse—wide, oil-soaked floors with offices on the sides and a central staircase in the middle. The police department, which shared the building on the right front side, had several jail cells in the basement. In later years, the cell block was called "a vile den" by tenants and officials alike.

When the city took over the former Ellis Hospital building and called it the annex, people referred to the City Hall as the "white building" and the annex as the "red building." In the rear of the old City Hall was a second county building fronting on Clinton Street which housed the department of public works and the water department.

In the early 1920s, when agitation began for a more spacious city headquarters, it was pointed out—and rightly so—that such a small building was not capable of holding so many departments in a growing city. It must be understood that when the first Jay Street hall was built in 1880, the city's population was only 13,655, whereas in 1920 it had risen to 88,723.

The building had roughly a half century of use before it was taken down and replaced by the picturesque structure that is today's City Hall. There are two reminders of that old building still around. One is the cornerstone, with its huge "1880" in full prominence, that was installed in the ground floor of the new City Hall near the stairway. The other is the keystone of the front entrance, kept on the premises of the Schenectady County Historical Society, bearing the name of William K. Fuller.

"Fuller's" City Hall, as afore-mentioned, was the last of the old buildings on the City Hall block to go. In fact, the new City Hall was well along in construction when the wreckers finally moved in on the doomed building. When it was taken down, work was started at once to widen that portion of Jay Street between Liberty and Franklin. Just to get an idea of how narrow that section once was, one could stand today halfway across the street at Jay and Franklin Streets and be in the approximate vicinity of what was the entrance to the former City Hall.

So, Jay Street—which had officially been opened as a public thoroughfare in August, 1831—really became Schenectady's City Hall block in 1880. But it was a century later, in 1931, when the present City Hall was opened, that the block came into its own.

The clock tower of Schenectady's City Hall is always a glow in the dark.

(1) Schenectady's paid firemen in 1901 in front of the new Central Fire Station opposite Crescent Park. (2) Firemen on parade Oct. 5, 1907, coming down State Street. Lorraine Block is at left and Wasson's Park House in center, corner of Barrett Street.

(1) Schenectady police force of 1887. Chief William L. Campbell is seated center. (2) The Clinton Street School about 1930, shortly before it became the city's police headquarters.

(1) Three-horse hitch pulls hook and ladder along lower Union Street during 1905 parade. (2) The Schenectady Police Department's "Black Maria" in back of old City Hall, about 1908.

(1) A 1910 view of Schenectady's City Hall which was built in 1880. The annex, formerly Ellis Hospital, is at left, and the water department building in right background. (2) Just before the razing of the Jay Street block in 1929 for the new City Hall. Looking northeast from old annex, with Liberty Street side of postoffice at extreme left.

(1) Cornerstone ceremonies for new City Hall, May 10, 1930. Clinton Street is in far background. (2) Progress by July 5, 1930. The front steps and first floor walls were being put into place.

(1) By Sept. 6, 1930, two stories of exterior walls were in place. (2) The clock tower of City Hall going up, Oct. 8, 1930 (Construction photos by Herman Zamjohn).

(1) Jay Street was twice as wide as before this 1931 view after completion of the new City Hall. Van Curler Opera House is in center background. (2) A formal photograph of the city's magnificent City Hall in 1934.

(1) Work had just started on the foundation of the federal building (postoffice) at Jay and Liberty Streets when this picture was made Nov. 1, 1911. (2) The finished building, Jay Street side, 1912.

(1) Laying the foundation for the postoffice addition, Aug. 1, 1934. City Hall tower is in right background. (2) Nearly completed, Jay Street side, Dec. 12, 1934.

(1) The old County Courthouse, built in 1831, to become the city school system's administration building after 1913 when the courts moved up on the hill. (2) This building at Church and Union Streets has been put to many uses over the years. It was the Mohawk Bank, a residence, the Union Classical Institute and, today, the Mohawk Club.

(1) An architect's drawing of Schenectady's new courthouse that was completed in 1913. (2) The south side of State Street opposite Crescent Park had just been repaved with cement-topped granite block when this shot was made in November, 1913. The new courthouse is at right, central fire station in center background and the park at left.

(1) The north building of old Schenectady High School as it neared completion in 1903. The south building was erected in 1911 and the two became Nott Terrace High School in 1931. Both are now gone. (2) Built in 1875 as the Eliphalet Nott School, this old structure today is headquarters for the county's Social Services Dept.

A family crossing the old iron bridge in a horsedrawn rig from Scotia in 1889. This was before the automobile and trolley car traffic made it such a busy bridge that by 1914 the public was clamoring for a new and larger bridge.

PART SIX
Whinnies, Wheels & Wings

24—Hathaway's Livery

"*A*h, those were the days," invariably is the comment of today's motorist, a victim of traffic jams and parking problems, when he is shown a picture typical of the freewheeling but relaxed atmosphere of the horse-and-buggy era.

Before the automobile came into its own about 60 years ago, even before the mocking cry of "Get a horse!" greeted each new owner of a Stanley steamer, the pace of daily living was not gaited by horsepower under the hood. However, one's social standing definitely hinged upon the quality of stable and trappings.

Happiest in these surroundings was the owner of a livery stable. The business was steady, non-ulcerous and certainly made the proprietor an important businessman of the day. And it was most prosperous if the stable included more than run-of-the-mill riding or carriage horses.

Liverymen who offered for lease a complete line of vehicles, from gaily-decorated sleighs to somber funeral coaches, were the ones who cashed in on the times. Only the wealthiest families kept their own stables, and certain types of horse-drawn conveyances were in demand by everyone at one time or another.

One of the most enterprising men in Schenectady during the heyday of the livery business was William Helmer Hathaway, owner of Hathaway's Livery Sales and Service. It was known as one of the finest liveries between New York and Buffalo.

The Hathaway livery, long since torn down, was located between what was Ryan's Garage and the State employment offices. In those days the address was 324-26 South Center Street (now changed to Broadway.) The building was almost adjacent to the old John Wiederhold mill on Broadway at Hamilton Street, later the Saveway Market.

No matter what the day or hour, it seemed that a rig of some sort was driving in or out of the arched entrance to the Hathaway livery. Sometmes a hearse and several black coaches would leave on their sorrowful appointment; or a tally-ho, pulled by two teams of high-spirited horses, would be bound for a gay outing. Closed coupes were popular on Sunday afternoons as young men took their best girls for a drive. And there always was a great demand for light delivery wagons and family carriages.

Bill Hathaway, known to one and all in this part of the state, was born in 1857 in the family home at 299 State Street, where the Plaza Theater building was located. He had hardly outgrown knee breeches when he and his father, Robine Hathaway, began hauling freight between Schenectady and Albany. Their rigs plied the stone wagon tracks of the old Albany Turnpike.

The elder Hathaway, once a canal boatman and later superintendent of the Erie canal section here, enjoyed a successful partnership for years with his son. Soon after his father's death, Bill Hathaway decided to convert the firm into a livery and by 1890 had made it one of the best in the state.

He and his wife, the former Jessie Smith, bought a three-story brick house at 304 Clinton Street, where their two children, Edward and

Mabel, were born. Their neighbors were among the city's most illustrious families—the Coffins, Hastings, Furmans, Mac Taggerts, Kuhns and Barhydts.

Hathaway's Livery business boomed after 1902, when he replaced the original wood building with an expansive pressed-brick structure on the Broadway site. While the work was in progress, Hathaway housed his horses and equipment under huge canvas tents in what now is the market square. All during that spring and summer, it looked as though the circus was in town.

The new building, spotless with varnished wood ceilings and concrete floors, was a model for up-to-date liveries. A sloping ramp led down to the basement where the horses were quartered in spacious stalls. The coach room, on the ground level, contained rolling stock most in demand—hearses, wagons and light carriages.

The "specials" were kept on the second floor and were lowered on call by a hydraulic elevator. These included the ultimate in refinement—phaetons, victorias and coupes.

Cowhorn Creek flowed beneath the foundation of the new building so that almost every spring the concrete flooring would be upheaved and flooded by surging water. The horses then took over the first floor until the flooding subsided.

Hathaway believed in keeping up with the times. When the hansom cab—a low, two-wheeled cab with the driver's seat on top—became the vogue in New York City about 1908, he purchased one and had it available to meet trains at the railroad depot, a silk-hatted driver perched on the rear top seat.

At the height of its prosperity, about 1905, Hathaway's livery stabled about 65 fine horses purchased in Buffalo or New York sales markets.

These included gaited horses for four-in-hand and team rigs. There were also five teams of pure whites, used mostly for funerals or parades. The whites were on call every summer to pull the floats in the annual floral fete at Saratoga Springs.

Funerals often meant the lease of a hearse and about 15 or 20 coaches. Ministers always preferred to ride in a two-wheeled coupe with a single white horse, whether for funerals or weddings. Hathaway had three black ornamental hearses and a smaller white one for children's funerals.

The hearses and coaches used on these occasions were made by Cunningham of Rochester, later the builder of one of the most expensive automobiles. A hearse cost $4,500 and coaches $1,500 each, because the interiors were lined and tufted.

The white horses which pulled the hearse were draped in heavy black nettings and sometimes wore black plumes on the crown pieces.

Hathaway's son, Edward Hathaway, had charge of the lucrative business of hauling scenery for the Van Curler Opera Co. Often, on one-night stands, the stage props would be loaded on a huge flat wagon pulled by four horses and taken to the opera house at Jay and Franklin Streets in the early afternoon.

When the performance was nearly over, usually near midnight,

Edward and his crew brought the stage equipment back to the yards to be loaded on freight cars.

Bill Hathaway was a stocky man with brown, wavy hair, which later turned snow white. He was fond of good clothes and had a penchant for red neckties. Although he had a fiery temper, it was quick to cool and he had many friends.

Probably it was this last quality which led him into politics and election as sheriff in 1909—the first Democrat to make the grade here in 40 years. He served several terms as a Fifth Ward alderman and also was police commissioner.

Mass production of the "horseless carriage" sounded the death knell for livery stables, especially the introduction of the Model T in 1908.

Still it was years before Bill Hathaway conceded the auto would replace horsedrawn transportation.

"Can you imagine one of those sputtering, back-firing machines leading a funeral cortege?" he would say.

Liveries in urban areas throughout the country soon went under when the sales markets for horses failed in the larger cities. Hathaway closed his business shortly before World War I, suffering an extreme loss on the sale of livestock and equipment. He died in 1922 at the age of 65.

The Hathaway home near Clinton and Smith Streets was purchased in 1914 by the Schenectady County Humane Society, which remained there until moving to its present headquarters at 210 Union Street in 1949.

The old brick building was razed in February, 1960, the first of the buildings between Clinton and Dakota Streets to be taken down.

More parking space was needed for automobiles.

25—The Horseless Carriage

LOOKING AHEAD IN 1900

$\mathcal{T}$he following is an excerpt from a letter written April 11, 1900, by Henry W. Darling concerning a lecture on the prospects of the automobile given the previous evening in the Van Curler Opera House:

"We went to Professor Elihu Thomson's lecture last night on the automobile. The curtain rose. Mr. Rice (E.W. Rice Jr.) and the professor rode on stage in Mr. Rice's electric vehicle, jumped off and then, on removing their overcoats, they were in full dress.

"Mr. Rice introduced the professor very nicely. A good audience. Mr. Ord, Mr. Coffin and Mr. Emmons were in a box with Mrs. Rice and the boys.

"He first traced the horseless carriage historically, then assumed that only a mechanical carriage was in existence and showed the objections to the use of horses in comparison—tearing up the roads with their shoes, eating the cribs (holding hay and oats), unsanitary, always running away, costly to feed and maintain, apt to die with limitations uncertain, requiring a servant to clean etc.

"Then he explained the various kinds of electric, steam, compressed air and other motive power for driven vehicles and was very frank in explaining all the advantages and defects of each, ending up with some poetry of his own composition about the defects of the horse, ending up with 'Ain't no sense nohow,' as David Harum says.

"It was interesting and instructive but created little enthusiasm until the close when he got a grand clap."

THE ALCO CAR

The chugging, backfiring "horseless carriage" still was considered an impractical nuisance in 1905 when the American Locomotive Co. of Schenectady highballed its way into the automotive picture by offering rugged but luxurious automobiles at fancy price tags.

Soon after its decision to invade the auto field in April 1905, Alco (the forerunner of ALCO Products) became the licensed U.S. manufacturer of the French Berliet auto, a gasoline-powered car of established prestige and quality. A branch company of the American Locomotive Co., was incorporated in Schenectady for $300,000 and plans were immediately drawn up for its first model.

The public got its first look at the "Locomotive Car" in 1906, with the Berliet name also used on the insignia. Presented with a 25 and 40 horsepower engine, the car was a brassy square-framed model that resembled a junior locomotive. Production was limited to 200, a practice that was to be continued throughout the company's brief history.

The hand crafted autos, a far cry from the assemblyline product which was to catapult the industry into public acceptance, were turned out at a plant built in Providence, R.I. The plant manager was Arthur Pitkin, son of Albert J. Pitkin, Alco's president from 1904-06.

Administration of the auto firm's policies, however, came from the directors in Schenectady.

In 1907, the Alco branch introduced a full-floating rear axle and shaft drive — steering away from the raspy, unsightly chain drive — and a combined radiator and water tank. Both were radical departures for the times. And new words — berline, limousine, vestibule sedan, landaulet — began to appear in the promotion language and were common listings in the Alco catalog.

Alco drew attention too, when it dropped the conventional make-and-break ignition system in favor of the new jump spark.

The company entered other fields in the automotive industry in 1909. It began to make taxi cabs with a light 16 horsepower entry, trucks, ambulances and fire engines. All were built strictly on order and therefore were not manufactured in any great quantity.

Meanwhile the passenger car line was upgraded with a 60 horsepower model.

Harry Grant, behind the wheel of a speedy Alco "six" stock touring car, brought considerable attention to the Alco products by winning the coveted Vanderbilt Cup Race for two successive years, 1909-10.

Alco's last big year was in 1912, when it offered its big berlines and limousines with prices in the $8,000 bracket — a price for luxury even in these days. The cars combined roof ventilators, 25½-inch-wide doors, 10-inch deep upholstery and lights that illuminated the running board when the doors opened.

A few Alcos were built in 1913 — but that year proved to be an unlucky 13 for the company as heavy losses were red-inked into the ledgers. The pinch of strong competition, particularly Henry Ford's cheaper models that were being turned out daily on the assembly line, was being felt by companies offering specialized high-priced cars on an ever-widening market.

Many of the stockholders in Schenectady firm fought the discontinuance of its automotive production after a glowing seven-year venture, but the Alco was put on the blocks for good in 1913.

The locomotive department, though, kept chugging along.

PIONEER MOTORING

Those among us today who can hark back to the early days of motoring at about the turn of this century are the best authorities on what has transpired in the automotive field since the time it took real courage and determination to venture forth in what many at first called the "devil's contraption."

There were no decent roads to speak of, at least the kind that might accommodate an automobile. Motor car drivers were frowned upon as reckless individuals, and a mite stupid to boot, who scared horses and disturbed the public peace. They customarily put their cars up for the long winter months before the 1920s, relying on the trolley cars or their own two feet for transportation. There were no driver's tests or licenses to worry about in those early years, but then it was a time when the motorist was self-reliant and ignored by the politicians and the general public.

Along about 1912, however, the love affair between the American citizen and the automobile came into full bloom. Henry Ford had a lot to do with it, making his Model T's available (in the standard color black) at a down-to-earth price and with few mechanical complications. Even the amateur mechanic could keep his car running by following the simple directions of the owner's manual. All he had to beware of was the "kick" of the starting crank. The Tin Lizzie actually made its debut in the fall of 1908, but the red hot romance with it and other cars of the day really began a few years later. The electric car had a moment in the sun in the late 1890s and early 1900s (Dr. Charles P. Steinmetz loved his Detroit electric) but it was later deemed impractical because of the short distances it was capable of traveling between charges. The internal combustion engine, once it got a foothold, took over the motoring field.

A lot of people in Schenectady, as almost everywhere else in America, bought Ford's flivvers in the pre-World War I era. Picnicking in the country, anywhere a dirt lane might lead, became a Sunday pastime. As a matter of fact, there are many fond memories yet today of the "refreshment stops" along the road (Mother simply spread out a blanket and brought out some sandwiches, pickles and a fruit drink whenever Dad had to make one of those frequent stops to fix a blown tire) even when the trip that day might have consisted of 30 or 40 miles to a distant relative or a lakeside resort.

Getting a Model T started required some strength, willpower and a fair amount of agility. You retarded the spark and advanced the throttle levers on the steering column, then stepped around to the front and pulled out the choke wire emerging from the radiator. Then, you spat on your hands and cranked. As soon as the engine started, you shoved in the choke and rushed back to the driver's seat to ease off on the gas and advance the spark. A really smart operator learned it was safer to lift the crank smartly from the 9 o'clock position to 12 o'clock. A backfire simply yanked the crank off the end of your fingertips. Spinning the crank all the way around was done at one's own risk, for a backfire when pressing down was the one that could break an arm.

When people began driving their cars in the winter, they emptied the radiator every night, filled it with a couple of kettles of hot water from the kitchen in the morning. Drivers carried a jug of denatured alcohol for anti-freeze when parking for any length of time in town.

In 1915, acetylene headlights on most cars were replaced with electric and by 1919 the self-starter was widely offered as an "extra." Another popular innovation about that time was the introduction of demountable rims which soon replaced the clincher tires. The latter was one of the curses that had to be endured by the early motorist. To fix a puncture, you had to somehow pry the tire from the wheel, remove the tube, patch the hole, return the tube to the tire and try to get the tire back in place. It often required an hour to do the job — then there was the added task of hand-pumping the tire, which was good for any number of punctures but lasted only 3,000 miles.

Along about 1915, local newspapers (including the Gazette and Union-Star) began recognizing the immense popularity of the automobile by publishing daily features of several pages covering mechanical hints, new legislation concerning automobiles and roads, the new cars on the market and suggestions of places to visit by auto. In a few years, the automotive page was joined by feature installments on another craze — radio.

Car owners in the 1920s, whether they knew it or not, were indebted to an organization known as the Society of Automotive Engineers (S.A.E.) which was founded in 1905 and took over the work of automobile standardization which had been inaugurated by the National Association of Automobile Manufacturers in 1900. The effects were evident in the manufacturing, servicing and use of cars and trucks, especially. For example, it was through the pressure of S.A.E. that spark plugs were standardized as to diameter and thread.

For many years, New York State drivers had black and white license plates on their vehicles (the very first, when there were few motorists on the road, were an expensive and ornate heavy enameled steel, cherry and white in color.) On Dec. 1, 1925, the New York State motor vehicle department inaugurated the once familiar orange and black (alternating between numerals and background each year) plates. John J. Merrill, an employe of the state tax commission who was the designer of the new plates, noted that outdoor tests showed the new colors could be read at a distance and in any time of day or night with 50 percent greater accuracy than the others.

"Next year there will be 1,500,000 pleasure cars in the state and we needed a license design easily read and remembered. We have succeeded," said Merrill in 1925. The orange-black combination lasted until 1965, when New York State went to royal blue and cornflower yellow.

Automobile clubs, both state and local, were organized in the early decades of this century not so much as social groups but to work towards better roads and direction signs. These clubs usually issued monthly bulletins for the membership and also lobbied for driving improvements. They petitioned the state legislature for improved state roads, requested city and village officials to erect more suitable signs giving speed limits and, above all, the names of towns so the motorist might find his way easier when passing through. It was in 1925, through the urging of auto clubs, that New York State abandoned its plan by which main routes were designated by colored bands, rather adopting the number system whereby state roads were numbered, north and south bound routes with even numbers, east and west routes with odd numbers.

Auto clubs also started a movement to encourage commercial firms to put their trucking on a 24-hour basis to avoid congestion in towns during daylight peak hours of traffic.

At the outset of World War I, the Ford Club of America, which counted thousands of Model T owners among its members, came forth with the idea that there would be many volunteers in its club who would work with the army to organize a "citizens' task force" should they ever be needed for defense on the home front. The plan was for a machine gun to be mounted on the Tin Lizzie of each volunteer minuteman, the forces to be organized locally and on call whenever emergency beckoned. It was a magnificent gesture — but the war department turned down the idea flatly.

Back in the 1920s, people began to be concerned with speeding autos. In the automotive section of the Gazette in November, 1925, was this caution against the urge to drive fast:

"In the first place, the motorist is usually not on the road to break any speed records or to get anywhere in the shortest possible time. His should be a trip of leisure. He should not be under the stress and strain of fast driving...Going a distance of 30 miles at the rate of 35 miles an hour, there is a saving of about 30 minutes over a rate of 25 miles an hour. That saving, anyone will admit, is insignificant, especially to the automobile tourist. Besides, the half hour saved by speeding may mean several hours lost telling the story to a justice of the peace. Or it may mean doctor or funeral bills. Lose a minute and save a life!"

Probably the biggest single factor to make the auto less a plaything and more a family affair was the building of roads conducive to motoring. Although nothing like the four-lane strips which today stretch across the nation in concrete ribbons, the roads that were constructed after World War I did add immeasurably to the joy of driving a motor car.

There was gradually less use for the dusters and driving caps, worn by both men drivers and women passengers in the earliest days of motoring, because the new roads were either oil-treated and rolled smooth (usually with the "humped" middle to avoid puddles) or made of concrete. However, it was still the custom throughout the 1920s for the cautious driver to include a coverall or smock in his accessories in case he had to change a tire or "get out and get under."

Service stations (or filling stations as they were popularly called in the days of the snap side curtains, running board luggage carriers and a glass vase with artificial flowers for a more elegant interior) were not as plentiful at first as the average motorist would have liked. Many club bulletins listed "places to get gasoline or oil" on travel information folders. Usually, they were wayside stops which was really a general store with a single glass-domed pump outside under a canopy (the kind that are still occasionally seen today in out-of-the-way places, which inspire artists to set up an easel and capture a bit of Americana that has all but disappeared). Within the cities, it was another matter. Schenectady had several gas stations, some in combination with garages or auto sales rooms, which did a good business. One of the more popularly known stations was that run by Olney Redmond, ex-restaurateur, who built and later enlarged an attractive and well-patronized filling station in back of the Brown Furniture building (now Masonic Temple) along Dock Street which after 1925 became a most desirable location on Erie Boulevard just off State.

There were many stores and garages throughout the city and country which by 1922 sold parts and accessories for the roving motorist, things like adjustable luggage rack for the running board at $1.75, a sideview mirror at 50 cents and spare wheel cover at $1.25.

But of course the sale of tires and tubes were the biggest turnover items. Prices for tires ranged from an average of $6.95 for the fabric tire to $10.95 for cords, size 30x3.5. However, there were the "high-priced, super" tires which went as high at $58 for size 36x6.

Many of today's name brands were sold 70 years ago, such as

Goodyear, Goodrich, Fisk, Seiberling, Firestone and Kelly-Springfield. There were also Barney Oldfield tires, Converse, Salem, Howe, Norwalk, United States, Keystone, Leto, Empire and vacuum cup tires by Pennsylvania Rubber Co.

In the early days of motoring in America, log books were published and distributed by automobile clubs, manufactures and insurance companies.

These booklets usually contained maps which showed the "main roads" and "other roads" available to the daring motorist. Alongside were ads by hotels featuring "running water and electric lights," garages and gasoline stations hoping to lure some business on the "long trips" of 50 miles or more.

At hand is a 1916 hard cover edition of "The Log Book of a Motor Car," published by the Aetna Insurance Co. The car owner, who was a Schenectady man, made some of the following notations that year:

"Stalled at Stop 16, Troy Road. 9 p.m. Fouled plug."

"Trip to Saratoga Lake. Purchase five gallons gas for $1.25. Bad roads."

"Bought two gallons arctic oil for one dollar."

"Ended year's mileage at 2,240."

Probably the most interesting part of the log book — and amusing, too, from today's viewpoint — are the words of advice listed in the foreword. For example, it warns:

"Do not make the mistake of trying to drive the car and keep the log at the same time. Let the person beside you or someone in the tonneau keep it. It will relieve you and give them something to do. When you pass through a town, you can call off the odometer reading and let the other person jot it down, together with the name of the town and the time of day. The distances and time between towns and the totals can be figured out at lunch or dinner."

Then there is this observation:

"In making long tours of 100 miles or more a day, it is hardly necessary to note under 'towns passed through' the name of every small town or village. On the other hand, in making short local runs, particularly when off the beaten highway, it is interesting to put down every little hamlet or settlement."

In keeping the expense account in the log, it notes that under the heading of "Sundries" it would cover "your sins of extravagance in the way of lamps, horns, racks, tops, tools etc." It further advises to list under that category "your license fee, and in fact everything that the sport of motoring costs you except what is provided for in the other columns."

The author of the log warns the owner that "sometime trouble is going to overtake you" and then lists some of these possible trouble spots and what to do about them. The one we like best is this little gem:

"Some day your last inner tube will puncture. This always occurs when you have left your repair outfit home. Chewing gum can be made to serve as cement for a patch. If the chewing gum is lacking, too, then a stick surface can be formed on the rubber by soaking the spot to be patched with gasoline, and also the patch, and lighting the gasoline. The instant it has burned out, apply the patch. If carefully done, a patch can be made which will be tight enough to carry you 10 or 15 miles."

With the end of World War I and the country in a festive mood, the Schenectady Automobile Dealers' Association decided late in 1918 to help celebrate the return to peacetime living by putting on a show which would give the war-weary public a composite view of what a promising new industry had to offer in the way of both luxury and convenlence.

Schenectady's first auto show was set for the week starting Jan. 20, 1919.

It was sponsored by the association (which later was renamed the Schenectady New Car Dealers, Inc.) for the benefit of the Machine Gun Company and Companies E and F of Schenectady, hopefully that by the time of the show, the men would be home from France. As it turned out, although a few veterans had returned to this area, the troops of E and F would not be welcomed back to Schenectady until April, 1919.

The first auto show, as many succeeding ones, was staged in the old state armory at the top of Crescent Park. (The drill shed, bounded by Albany Street, Veeder Avenue and State Street, was torn down in 1947 and is now the site of Pulaski Plaza). Admission was set at 30 cents, including war tax.

It was a big success, as crowds flocked to the armory each of the five nights. There were the now traditional potted palms, placed in strategic spots to give the shiny new motor cars even morc of a touch of class and elegance. There was entertainment, too, provided by Pantin's orchestra and Miss Jeanette Ciermain and Miss Mildred Hewitt, vocal soloists.

James J. Callahan was manager of the show. Doors opened each night at 8.

W. L. Webster, first president of the auto dealers' association and later president of the Schenectady Automobile Club, had his Model T Fords on display.

Although auto production had not fully resumed its switch from the war effort, there were enough models to make Schenectady's first auto show interesting.

Reo was in prominence with both touring car and truck ("Oh, you'll get there all right... with that Reo!") Also, there were Dodge, Chevrolet, Buick, Franklin, Case, the Velie Six and Chalmers.

They were back, the next year, at the second annual show held the week of Jan. 19, 1920 — only there were newcomers to the automotive field and many more models for the auto enthusiasts to drool over.

These included the Chandler, Willys-Knight, Overland, Lexington, Paige, Packard, Studebaker, Hudson, Davis, Nash, Elcar, Dort, Oakland, Birch and the Kissel custom-built six.

The prices? Quite a variance, according to the demands for luxury, same as today. The Model T's went for $890 up, the Davis Fleetway for $1,695, the Studebaker from $975 to $2,750, Oakland roadster for $975, Buick from $1,435 to $1,895, Nash from $915 to $2,190, Hudson from $1,045 to $1,525, etc.

In Schenectady the week of January, 1919:

Stores were featuring new recordings for the Gramaphones and Victrolas, mainly on the Victor, Columbia and Pathe Labels. Among these were "Songs My Mother Taught Me" by vocalist Hulda Lashanska on

Columbia, "Danny Boy" by Madame Schumann-Heink, "The Rose of No Man's Land" by Charles Hart and Elliott Shaw, "Dreaming of Home Sweet Home" by Charles Harrison and "When You Come Back" by John McCormack, all on Victor.

The Literary Digest featured articles titled, "Why Italy Defied America's Peace Ideals" and "What Germany Must Pay."

Perfection stoves and Ideal fireless cook stoves were on sale. Napoleon "Larry" Lajoie, conceded to be one of the greatest infielders in the sport, announced his retirement from professional baseball after 20 years of active play.

Bill Shirley had just taken over management of the old Orpheum Theater at 409 State St., next to the Vendome Hotel, and had renamed it the Palace Theater. In a few more years, it would become known as the Strand. Playing at the Palace that January week of 1919 was William S. Hart in "The Tiger Man." Other local flickers had these offerings in silent movies: Theda Bari in "The She Devil" at both the Pearl and Happy Hour, Harry Morey in "Fighting Destiny" at the American, Charlie Chaplin in "Rival Masters" and Violet Mersereau in "The Native Girl" at the Rialto, Charlie Chaplin in "The Floorwalker" and "The Rink" at Proctor's (later to be renamed Erie), Norma Talmadge in "The Probation Wife" at the Lincoln, and Bessie Barriscale in "Hearts Asleep" at the Albany.

The Lincoln Theater, on Brandywine Avenue near Albany Street, advertised "automobiles parked and cared for free during showing of picture." It charged 25 cents with three cents war tax for both matinees and evening. Next week would be the movie, "Mickey" starring Mabel Normand.

All in all, it was a period of our history full of experiences and memories worth recalling for grandchildren who, having just adjusted the carburetor on the hot rod and ready for a trial run down the nearest freeway, might find the tales a little tall.

FORD CAR NOW PUT ON SKIS

The "Snowmobile" Which Travels 18 Miles an Hour Over Winter Roads Whether Cleared or Not.

They thought of doing everything with the model T, as shown in this 1924 advertisement.

204

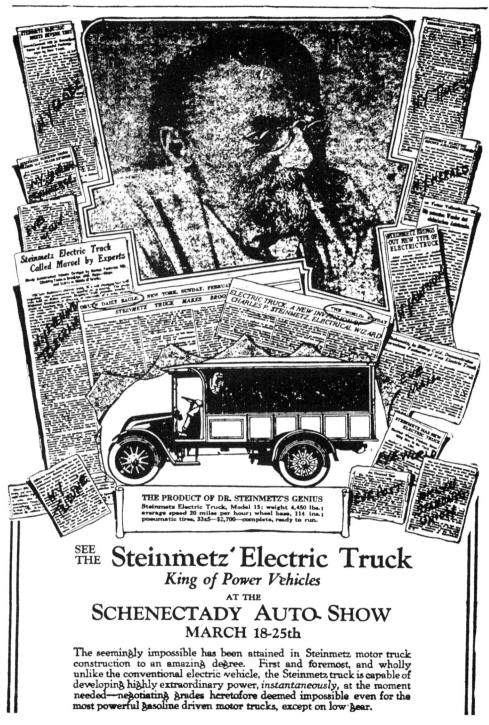

SEE THE **Steinmetz' Electric Truck**
King of Power Vehicles
AT THE
SCHENECTADY AUTO SHOW
MARCH 18-25th

The seemingly impossible has been attained in Steinmetz motor truck construction to an amazing degree. First and foremost, and wholly unlike the conventional electric vehicle, the Steinmetz truck is capable of developing highly extraordinary power, *instantaneously*, at the moment needed—negotiating grades heretofore deemed impossible even for the most powerful gasoline driven motor trucks, except on low gear.

The Schenectady Auto Show of March 18-25, 1922, featured the electric truck devised by Charles P. Steinmetz and associates. The group folded after Steinmetz died, but the battery-powered truck enjoyed some popularity through that decade.

26—Schenectady's Railroad Stations

A great change was taking place in the center of Schenectady's business district shortly after 1900. For the first time in its 70 years of existence, the railroad was raising its tracks above street level...but even more noteworthy to the average citizen, a new and modern passenger station was to be built.

There had been serious talk for years during the waning 19th century of eliminating the dangerous and time consuming grade crossings, but in 1903 the big project actually was started. The D.D. Streeter construction firm from Chicago was awarded the contract for erecting the series of bridges which would carry the trains over crossings at Maxon Road, Nott Street, Jay Street, Front Street, Green Street, Union Street, Liberty Street, State Street, Broadway, Edison Avenue (two), Weaver Street and Center Street.

Work on a large scale on the important State Street crossing began March 1,1905 and was concluded the latter part of 1907 when the entire project was at last finished. It was no easy matter to build this double bridge for both New York Central and Delaware & Hudson.

Involved were the tracks of the Schenectady Railway Co.'s electric trolley cars which crossed the railroad tracks at right angles on the trolley route along State Street. While the railroad tracks were being raised, the trolley tracks in turn were being lowered to accommodate the underpass for main street vehicles and overpass for the railroad.

This was to effect a vast change in the physical character of the city's "uptown" section of the shopping district, the area east of the Erie Canal (now Erie Boulevard). In years past, the city had learned to adapt to the freight and passenger trains which crossed the main thoroughfare, although it had become increasingly frustrating to pedestrians and business alike.

The city's records often record accidents at the grade level crossings, involving delivery wagons, impatient shoppers who chose to cross between stalled cars rather than wait and occasionally a trolley car which could not stop in time. Sometimes, in inclement weather, the watchman's bell was not heard and casualties resulted.

News of the project to raise the tracks received enthusiastic response by merchants and citizenry when it was announced about 1900. Quite naturally, there was a consuming curiosity as to how "the city would look" when it was completed.

Schenectady's first railroad station actually was a tiny one-story brick building built atop Crane Street hill soon after the pioneer locomotive DeWitt Clinton made its historic trip between Albany and Schenectady in 1831.

It was known as the western terminal for the Mohawk & Hudson Railroad and served the cars pulled up the incline tracks by pulley and ballast. For years, that part of Schenectady was known as "engine hill," even long after the terminal ceased operations within a decade.

The city's first station was later converted to a private dwelling and lasted until 1921 when it was demolished. It was located at 803 Crane St.

The city's first central passenger depot, however, was erected in

1842 between State and Liberty Streets but on the east side of the grade level tracks of the Utica & Schenectady and Mohawk & Hudson Railroads. The platform canopy for waiting passengers extended toward State Street from a wood-framed single story depot.

The trains pulled into the station alongside the Givens Hotel, built in 1843 by Resolve Givens at the intersection of State and Wall Streets. The old hotel was torn down in 1889 to make room for the Edison Hotel.

Schenectady's citizens were not too happy with the station built in 1842. It was found to be especially inadequate during the Civil War and the years following when canal and rail traffic increased. Therefore, there were happy citizens when final plans for its demise and replacement were announced in 1880.

Before the new railroad depot was constructed in 1882, the east side of Wall Street was not a pleasant sight. Clustered near the State Street crossing were a shabby little restaurant and saloon, weatherbeaten sheds and wood fences, grimy with soot. Isaac Banker's blacksmith shop was just across the Liberty Street canal bridge. The old Clute Foundry, whose Civil War marine building is historic, had fallen into decay on the opposite corner of Liberty and Wall Streets.

By 1890, however, the picture brightened. The foundry was replaced by a long brick building known as the Arcade (last occupied by IUE Local 301 and torn down in August, 1955.) The blacksmith shop and restaurant passed into memory. And, of course the Givens Hotel gave way to the new and modern Edison.

The station built in 1882 was a curious architectural creation. The one and one-half brick and stone building was topped by an odd-shaped slate roof and two mosque-like domes. A vaulted overhang on the Wall Street side accompanied the carriage trade and water nymph fountains added to the rather ostentatious scene. Still, there is little of record to indicate that the depot was anything but satisfactory in appearance or serviceability.

The building was now on the west side of the tracks on Wall Street and necessitated the closing of Liberty Street at that point. Pedestrians, however, could cross over the tracks on a steel-framed bridge. Schenectady's second central railroad station was in use for only 23 years, the wreckers moving in early in 1905 to prepare the site for the new Union Station — which was to be the last word in railroad passenger depots for its size and convenience.

While the railroad gangs elevated their tracks, construction crews worked on the new overhead crossings at 13 different locations from one end of Schenectady to the other starting in 1903.

It had been estimated to be a five-year job and perhaps was as accurate a target date as has ever been set by construction engineers. It was started March 1, 1903 and the new passenger station with the new level of tracks was opened March 1, 1908.

Sidewalk superintendents gaped as the work progressed, marveling at how a railroad could keep running while its rolling stock inched upwards to new levels day by day. It was a matter of teamwork, co-ordination and ingenuity.

Wooden trestles were erected at each crossing until concrete and

(1) Two-team hitch in front of Hathaway's Livery on Broadway near Smith Street. (2) An Alco touring car at the plant's Maxon Road employment office and restaurant, about 1915.

(1) Out "on the town" in their new roadster, at Pine Point Inn, 1917. (2) Hot rod driver in Reo runabout, 1912. (3) Motorcycles had to contend with rutted roads, too. Near Schenectady, 1912. (4) Schenectady Cycle Club poses front of 133 Nott Terrace, 1916.

(1) Usual busy scene at Olney Redmond's gas station, 1925. (2) Occupants had to "get out and get under" here to inspect trouble with Cadillac on road to Canajoharie, about 1912. (3) Redmond erected this global sign in 1925 to advertise the "World's Finest Gas Station" and Radio Station WGY.

(1) This Model T Ford, shown near Amsterdam in 1916, had just completed a month's cross-country trip from Los Angeles to New York. Millard Labrum (behind wheel) and brother Walter. They carried a tent and utensils aboard. (2) End of the Mohawk Avenue line at Toll Street, Scotia, 1916. (Photo courtesy Joe Dutcher).

(1) Splendor of the fountains in front of the 1882 railroad station that was replaced by Schenectady's new station in 1908. (2) Grazing cattle in field near Alpaus are startled by the passing of an Alco touring car, about 1912.

(1) State Street from the canal bridge, 1903. Edison Hotel is at left. (2) Engine steaming across State Street, about 1900. Opposite view, looking toward canal bridge in right background.

(1) First train to cross over new State Street overpass, March, 1906. (2) Construction of railroad overpass at Weaver Street, 1905, looking north toward canal, now Erie Boulevard.

(1) Gleaming interior of Schenectady's new railroad station shortly after it was opened in 1908. (2) The Wall Street side of the new station, with American Express Co. offices at left.

(1) A lonely looking figure, Charles A. Lindbergh strolls along Schenectady County Airport during unheralded visit here in February, 1928. (2) It was different when "Lindy" came here on July 28, 1927. A large crowd was on hand to greet him. He spoke briefly at a microphone. (3) His Spirit of St. Louis was guarded closely by security police.

(1) GE's first airplane quartered at Schenectady County Airport, 1931. From left, E. G. Haven, W. W. Miller and A. H. French. (2) Ford Pathfinder landed at the airport June 3, 1927 on a "Reliability Tour." (3) Airships of the day lined up in front of the airport's new hanger, June, 1928.

steel foundations were in place. New York Central freight was rerouted from Carman to Rotterdam Junction while the project was being carried out. However, passenger trains and Delaware & Hudson freight continued to pass slowly over the temporary trestles.

Meanwhile, the new passenger depot also was being constructed to accommodate trains at the upper level. A temporary passenger station was opened during the project between Green and Front Streets.

Liberty Street, which had been closed by the earlier station's location, was now being reopened — complete with overhead crossing.

What had been practically a still new passenger station, having been completed in 1884, was earmarked for destruction once final plans were made about 1900 for the raising of the railroad tracks throughout Schenectady.

It simply did not fit into the scheme of things, in which by 1908 it was hoped the 13 overpasses within the city would be completed and a new station built to accommodate the increasing rail traffic.

When the bridge work began in 1903 and the tracks were gradually raised, business at the central passenger station was phased out preparatory to its demolition early in 1905.

When the construction crews turned to the State Street overpass in March, 1905, the sizeable project of building the bridge and brick-faced arcade was coordinated with the erection of the new depot. At one point it was seriously considered to have a turnoff midway in the State Street overpass so that the electric streetcars might pass through the arcade and alongside the railroad station. It was soon discarded.

Schenectadians were openly excited over the railroad project, particularly the new passenger station. Architects drawings depicted it accurately and the imposing structure seemed to fit in with the city's image of a growing metropolis, bustling with new industry and increasing population.

It was named Union Station. In late February, 1908, an open house and public dance was held in the waiting room. Glowing editorials were written and praises reiterated from public and civic leaders.

Some interesting sidelights to the ball which signified the opening of the new station were provided in later years by friends of the author.

One of them was Philip H. Wertz, for many years managing editor of the old Union-Star when it held forth from the editorial and press building at 207-11 Clinton St. and which was torn down in April, 1971. Mr. Wertz related this tale concerning the "white tie and tails" ball staged in February, 1908, in the new depot:

"At that time there were several daily newspapers published in Schenectady and Albany and Bill Osborne worked on most, if not all of them. He said one, which will not be identified, had a somewhat arbitrary publisher who had among his sacred cows — things that must not appear in that paper — what amounted to a phobia against the word 'evening.' Reporters, editors, typesetters and proofreaders were under strict orders to change it to 'night' under all circumstances.

"The ball at the new station was reported in detail, even to listing the style and material of the dresses worn by the women. Both the reporters and the editors, printers, proofreaders, et al, did their jobs. The result was that next day readers of that newspaper were either startled or highly amused to read that Mrs. So-and-so wore such a 'night gown,' not 'evening gown.' Bill said from then on, the word 'evening' was used in that particular newspaper."

And this bit of recollection from Stephen St. John, long a plectrum instrument instructor and musical director in Schenectady:

"Not much has been written about the orchestra that furnished the music for that gala affair. It was the late, well known at the time, Rufus Zita of Albany and his 24-piece orchestra was made up of all expert musicians. Mr. Zita was at the time one of our outstanding violinists and who is still remembered by some of our local musicians. I well remember Rufus Zita as I later became a member of his orchestra that furnished the music which was enjoyed by those attending the ball which celebrated the opening of the depot.

"How well I remember that affair. It was attended by high officials of the New York Central and Delaware & Hudson Railroads, also by some state and local officials with white ties and long coats. How proud we Schenectadians were to have such a fine railroad station in our city."

It was, indeed, quite a remarkable building for the city at that period. The new track level was reached by stairway in the attractive interior. Gleaming marble walls supported by stone columns lent an atmosphere of grandeur. There was every convenience — lounges, newsstand, snack counter, rest rooms and an abundance of windows at the ticket counters. The big clocks at either end of the waiting room gave the time from inside and out. On the Wall Street side ample space was provided for parking of carriages and unloading of passengers' luggage.

The railway express took over the ground level warehouse sections on the north side, extending to the big sliding doors which opened on the Liberty Street Bridge's south wall. Many a Schenectadian will recall particularly the World War I dead arriving at this point.

Union Station was often the scene of political gatherings as presidential aspirants stopped through on the whistlestop tours and spoke from the station platform facing Wall and Liberty Streets. Many a local GI left in contingents during World War II from this station, more often as not bound for the first stop on his camp parade — Camp Upton.

It was not long after World War II, however, that the railroad passenger business began to decline. . .not too noticeably at first but taking a firm hold on the loss column in the mid-1950s. As the roads fought to keep the profit and loss figures at least constant, the upkeep of property such as Schenectady's passenger station became too much to bear.

Union Station, once proud and majestic in its setting near the new Erie Boulevard, was deteriorating into a drab monstrosity by 1960. Ten years later, the City of Schenectady was dickering for the purchase of the old depot, which had closed almost on its 60th anniversary.

Finally on Dec. 11, 1970, the sale of Union Station by Penn Central to the city for the sum of $20,000 was consummated.

When the men of SAS Equipment Co., of North Bergen, N.J., moved in early in 1971 to demolish the passenger station built 63 years earlier, they also took down portions of the railroad overpasses at Liberty and State Streets. These included about a 50-foot width of the State Street bridge and 65 feet of the Liberty Street bridge which once carried NYC trains through the center of town.

By August of 1972, the railroad station was leveled and, one by one, other buildings on the west side of Wall Street were down. By Labor Day of 1974, the whole area had been bulldozed and blacktopped for a parking lot along Erie Boulevard. For a time, railroad patrons used the small temporary passenger station out in Colonie. The Amtrak station in Schenectady, a tiny building erected on the site of the Union Station, opened in July 1979.

ALL ABOARD! - Edward J. Patten, train caller at Union Station in Schenectady announced arrivals night of Dec. 5, 1947 when the railroads were still busy with passengers.

27—Aviation...A New Age

THE AEROPLANE

The vacant land in the vicinity of McClellan Street and Rugby Road, popularly referred to as either the circus grounds or cricket field, had been carefully mowed and rolled a few days prior to July 4, 1912, in anticipation of an unusual holiday event.

Schenectady City Council had voted to appropriate the sum of $150 to guarantee a public demonstration of "aeroplaning," an awe-inspiring achievement which had come a long way since the Wright Brothers went aloft in the first heavier-than-air craft less than nine years before. The air show was billed as one of the features of that July Fourth and newspaper ads invited the people to come and see it, free of charge. Hundreds of people, some excited and others just curious, did show up well before the appointed hour of 2 p.m. J. Lansing Callan, an aviator assigned to the Curtiss Aircraft Corp., was there with his 8-cylinder, 60 horsepower Curtiss bi-plane (which was roped off to keep the public at a safe distance). However, the crowd was due for a disappointment. Callan decided, after a one-hour wait, that the air was "far too hot" for the machine to climb. Mayor George R. Lunn, who had been on hand early to mingle with the citizenry and kiss a few babies, had the sad duty to make the formal announcement of the air show's postponement.

Callan told newsmen covering the event that Curtiss aviators were instructed that they could not fly when "there is any unusual danger." Furthermore, Glenn H. Curtiss (already considered an aviation pioneer) would not employ men who were not likely to obey him and "this is one of the rules on which he is the most strict," Callan added.

Callan's contract with the city called for him to make a flight of at least 30 minutes within three days. So the next day, which was a late Friday afternoon, Callan again was at the uptown grounds with a crowd of about 3,000 — perhaps bigger than the previous day — to watch him take off. But the winds were too strong for Callan to remain aloft long so he circled about the boulevard area for roughly five minutes and called it a day.

There were still 25 minutes of flight time remaining so it was announced (again by Mayor Lunn) that the aviator would make another try at 3 p.m. the next day. The weather cooperated on the third attempt and Callan flew his red-and-cream craft around the city, finally circling over the Mohawk Golf Club and swinging back over the circus grounds where "it landed easily and gracefully."

Callan had at last earned his money and Schenectady had something to marvel over for days to come.

THE COUNTY AIRPORT

On the night of Feb. 9, 1927, the aviation committee of the Schenectady Chamber of Commerce had an important message for the people of the city: Land had been optioned for a municipal airport to be developed later that year.

The announcement was made at a dinner held at the new Hotel Van Curler honoring William P. MacCracken Jr., assistant secretary of commerce for aviation. John F. Horman, chamber president, said that 195 acres of East Glenville farm land had been optioned as the embryo of Port Schenectady. Furthermore, Mr. Horman told the enthusiastic gathering, the citizenry could feel it was their airport because they would be asked to finance the $100,000 purchase price!

The fund-raising drive began June 13 with a campaign dinner at the hotel. A huge sign was erected on one of the Erie Boulevard islands which proclaimed "Lindbergh made his goal . . . so can Schenectady" and marked the progress of "flight to finance" for the new airport. At the end of that week the final returns showed that $121,000 had been pledged to the civic enterprise.

When Charles A. Lindbergh flew his "Spirit of St. Louis" into the unfinished air base on July 28 to further the interests of commercial aviation, he was welcomed by a crowd of about 20,000. He was impressed by the fact that this was the first airport in the nation to be financed wholly by popular subscription. The "Lone Eagle," whose solo New York-to-Paris flight two months before had electrified the world, autographed a chamber photograph of the Erie Boulevard sign with a congratulatory note. The whereabouts of that artifact is unknown.

The Colonial Air Transport which operated the New York-Boston air mail route, leased land from the Schenectady Airport Co. to build a hangar in anticipation of making Schenectady the junction point of the Boston-Buffalo and New York-Montreal routes. Colonial was awarded the air mail contract from Albany to Buffalo on July 27.

Temporary dirt runways were used throughout that summer of 1927 which were found satisfactory for the 10-passenger planes as well as the light monos and bi-planes which came in.

Incidentally, the first ship to set down at Port Schenectady was a Waco two-seater (open cockpit) bi-plane piloted by Victor R. Rickard of Schenectady with A. J. Van Horn, chamber secretary, as passenger. The aircraft, which had been used for barn storming, landed precisely at 1:04 p.m., on June 1 after which Rickard joined in the official dedication ceremony.

On Aug. 30, contracts were awarded for the construction of a hangar and airport office, plus the grading and clearing for four runways. All was finished by December that same year.

When the Thomas Corners site was purchased, the level expanse of rural acreage consisted of apple groves, grain fields. As the work on the new runways progressed during the summer of 1927, there was a lot of sawing and burning of trees which stood along the southern portion of the field nearest Saratoga Road.

Even in its infancy, the Schenectady airport attracted many noted figures in the growing world of aviation. Lindbergh came back again in February, 1928, on his way to be honored by the State Legislature. Fraulein Thea Rasche, famous German aviatrix, flew in from Buffalo on Aug. 11, 1927, as a guest of the Schenectady chamber. She took off the following day in her snub-nosed bi-plane, waving lustily to a small party of Schenectady officials. A short while later, on her way to Floyd Bennett

Field, her craft developed engine trouble so she pan-caked into the Hudson near Poughkeepsie and managed to swim clear as the plane took an ignominious dive to the bottom of the river.

Other first year visitors to Schenectady's yet-unfinished airport were Major Herbert A. Dargue, Colonel H. H. Blee, Eddie Stinson, Harry Brooks, Berta Acosta and a team of three U.S. Marine aviators.

Amelia Earhart, one of the most renowned of America's women fliers, landed a trim monoplane at the local port the morning of March 27, 1929, and later did a broadcast at radio station WGY. In August, 1931, two months after they set a global flight record, Wiley Post and Harold Gatty put down in the "Winnie Mae" and later were feted as guests of General Electric.

Both Lindbergh's "Spirit of St. Louis" and Post's "Winnie Mae" are featured exhibits in the aeronautics section of the Smithsonian Institution as relics of the glorious past in early aviation.

It's been more than seven decades since the citizens of Schenectady responded eagerly and generously to the call for funds to build an airport. Port Schenectady flourished briefly with the dramatic fervor of commercial flying and individual exploits, but its prominence soon was overshadowed by the rapid growth of the Albany County Airport.

Still, it performs an important function as a civic air terminal and a national air guard base opened in 1948 since named the Stratton Air National Guard Base, home of the 109th Tactical Airlift Group. The annual Northeast Flight Airshow each August has drawn enormous attention by the public and air flight groups. An airport museum with its collection of flight material, aviation displays, and replicas of the past is a growing organization Flying instructions are available at a private aircraft school at the base. Without a doubt, the Saratoga Road facility retains its stake in the field of aviation along with an enviable history of pioneer flying.

WE MAY JUST AS WELL BE GETTING USED TO 'EM

Aviation was becoming a part of the scenery and very much in the public interest by the mid-1920s. Here is a cartoon that appeared on the Schenectady Gazette editorial page Sept. 3, 1926 which pretty much says it all.

Crowds watch with rapt attention as the British Airways SST comes in for a landing at the Northeast Flight Airshow at Schenectady County Airport in 1989.

PART SEVEN
Looking Back

This Feb. 3, 1922 advertisement of Flinn & Co. may recall for some the days of smaller stores and lower prices.

28—The Great Blizzard

$\mathcal{J}$ust mention the Blizzard of '88 and thoughts turn to a monstrous snowstorm which blanketed the northeastern U.S. There are not a great many people alive today who can say they "remember when" but still that great snowstorm has been used in succeeding years as a barometer of a winter storm's full potential and has long since been dubbed "the grand-daddy of them all."

All the ingredients were there on that Sunday, March 11, 1888 — a dull gray sky and a stillness which presaged bad weather. The storm began with a light snow that began falling just before noon, as people were leaving church services and heading home for the Sabbath dinner.

The storm intensified through the afternoon and evening, accompanied by gales of extreme velocity. By Monday morning, the shops in downtown Schenectady were sealed tight as several feet of snow had been whipped by the wind into drifts of 10 to 15 feet. And still it came, on through Tuesday and just after midnight Wednesday, March 14, until the snow finally subsided. The wind continued and the drifts grew deeper. Some of the piles of snow reached to second floor windows of homes in the area.

Along the streets, gangs of men shoveled the snow onto banks high above their heads. Some was carted away by horses and sleighs. Several days later, shopkeepers and their help were able to shovel walkways in front of their stores. The piles of snow by now were so high that pedestrians of that day for years afterward told their children and grandchildren about the big snow — so high "we couldn't even see the heads of horses in the street."

The fallen snow became compacted and, as a result, many people tunneled under the piles at curbside in order to reach their homes. Horses had difficulty ploughing through the drifted snow on the second day of the storm and there were many reports of people being snowbound in outlying districts. The 60-hour snowstorm deposited 46.7 inches of snow in this area.

Somehow, someone always managed to get through with provisions or medicine or whatever was needed in the midst of the blizzard. Milk and coal deliveries were postponed for nearly a week until roads were finally made passable. Rail traffic was halted Monday afternoon and did not resume until the next day.

In New York City, at the time of the great blizzard, the East River froze over for the first time within memory of living persons and it was feared the Brooklyn Bridge, then only five years old, might crumble when the ice broke up.

Stories about the Blizzard of 1888 have been passed down through the years by people who lived through it, many of whom are now gone.

The late Simon Schermerhorn of Rotterdam once told of an experience in connection with the storm when he (then 13 years old) and two other boys made their way down to River Road from the Campbell Road hillside above on the first morning of the storm. They started out with a sleigh and a team of horses but the heavy snow soon fatigued the animals. They were resting the horses near the old Two-Mile House when they heard Adam Maser, then proprietor of the inn, call to them from a second story window. The snow had drifted up against the front of the building, up over the front porch roof and was almost to the window sill from which Maser hailed the boys.

"Dig out my doorway to the water pump beyond and I'll repay you," he told the boys. "I've got to have water for my guests." The boys had come well prepared and after a time they managed to shovel out a tunnel from the hotel entry to the pump. They each earned a dollar, an exceedingly good wage considering grown men had to work a whole day to earn that much.

For almost four days after that, until the sun finally melted through the tunnel, the hotel staff drew water from the outside pump without being seen.

Up in the Rotterdam hills, far beyond the Cobblestone Reformed Church, an elderly man died peacefully in the home of his son and daughter-in-law. The storm was raging outside at the time. There was no need for a doctor, only a minister, but the family could not get out to summon one and reasoned that the prayers could wait until after the snow had abated. They wrapped the old man's body in a blanket and placed it in an enclosed back porch. Several days later, a funeral was held and the burial took place in Viewland Cemetery next to the Cobblestone Church.

Some men tried to make their way to work on Monday morning from long distances. Those who made it found that the works and other business places were closed; others grew fatigued and started back the way they came. Many were the stories of mothers and children who in later years described their anxious wait for father's return, watching him trudge wearily down the road with snow up to his armpits and finally arriving spent and gasping from his battle with the great blizzard.

During the storm, a train from Buffalo was stalled by giant drifts about four miles from Albany's Union Station. According to published reports, many of the passengers decided to leave the coaches and try to make their way into Albany on foot and some of them froze to death in the snow drifts.

The late Lewis McCue once recalled that as a boy of seven, he lived with his family at 31 Barrett St. when the big storm hit. On the first morning after the start of the blizzard, the house was dark when everyone thought it ought to be daylight. The family broke through the snow banked against the windows and discovered that it really was daylight. He said that he and some others burrowed tunnels under the deep snow on Barrett Street to carry pails of hot soup to some sick neighbors.

There was an attempt by a construction gang to walk from Niskayuna to Schenectady. They started at 7 a.m. encountered terrible drifts, stopped at a farmhouse for the night and reached Schenectady at noon the next day. Both ears of one of the men were frozen. The crew had been repairing a church in Niskayuna.

Those who remembered the storm generally agreed that in a few days the snow had miraculously all but disappeared.

29—Crescent Park Bandstand

*T*he weekly band concert at Crescent Park was one of the social highlights of the summer season in Schenectady for many years, dating back to about the early 1880s when the first bandstand was built in the upper section of the park.

These were the days when no self-respecting community could be without a porticoed bandstand on the green, a place to gather for an evening of family relaxation, entertainment and whatever music culture might be absorbed.

Schenectady was no different, as from the start people flocked to the park every Wednesday night to hear Rivette's Silver Cornet Band play their favorite marches, waltzes and overtures.

Prof. George Rivette, who taught music in his home on Lafayette Street opposite Chapel, played lead cornet and directed the dozen local bandsmen. His was the favorite concert group for many years, although occasionally a guest band such as Gartland's Military Band or the Scotia Band occasionally would play the Wednesday night outing.

The first bandstand in Crescent Park was not an imposing structure, but it was typical of the ones of its day. It was made principally of wood, painted green, with supporting pillars that lifted a reddish-orange canopy about 15 feet above the platform. For more than 30 years it was the focal point once a week for the hundreds who sat or stood or frolicked around it while the band played on.

In 1912, during Mayor George R. Lunn's first administration, the City Council decided Schenectady was in need of a more impressive bandstand, commensurate with the city's growing size. So down came the old canopied platform and in its place rose a $17,000 comfort station and bandstand, more than twice the size of its predecessor.

The lower part was built of brick and, like the earlier bandstand, was octagonal. The rest rooms in this section were maintained by the City Department of Parks and Recreation. Eight huge wood ionic columns supported a roof that was covered with corrugated metal tile. The platform itself was enclosed with a wrought iron railing.

The new bandstand, designed by City Engineer W. Thomas Wooley, was not popularly accepted by the public. Taxpayers cried it cost too much, that the old stand was good enough. However, the criticism died down within a year and in time the new bandstand became as much a park fixture, though not used nearly so often, as the old one.

The Schenectady Corps Band of the Salvation Army, which had built its citadel at 218 Layfayette St. in 1908, played most of the concerts from the new bandstand — only now the weekly musicale was a Saturday night attraction. Directed by Bandmaster Samuel Slater, the band drew large throngs until the summer of 1918.

By then the city was wholly concerned with the war effort. Instead of giving Saturday night concerts, the Salvation Army set up its canteen, or "doughnut hut," at the foot of Crescent Park on a full-time basis for servicemen. After the end of World War I, the bandstand never was used again regularly for concerts.

The Salvation Army later made Crescent Park the site of its Sunday night open air meetings. It had been the common practice for many years prior to the late 30s — particularly when buses began to replace the trolleys — for the men's band to play at open air services at State and Clinton Streets while the women's band went down to State and Broadway, in front of the Vendome hotel. Later in the evening, both bands would join at Broadway and march up State Street to the citadel for a service.

When Gen. Evengeline Booth, international commandant of the Salvation Army and daughter of its founder, visited Schenectady about 40 years ago she spoke at a large meeting in Crescent Park. The crowd overflowed into the streets as the diminutive blue-caped evangelist preached briefly from a small clearing near the bandstand.

During the intervening years, while the bandstand remained a useless luxury, its earlier critics occasionally harped on the folly of its ever been built. Perhaps the blame could be placed more directly upon a modification of social habits over those of the previous half century. The automobile, radio and movie theaters had done much to change family recreation.

The rest rooms remained open, although in later years the police had to keep a close check on the area when it became an habitual hangout for vagrants.

There was little surprise or regret on the part of the general public when the city announced in 1947 that the only building on the park premises was to be removed. The 35-year-old bandstand fell before a wrecking crew the following year and since then a circular flower bed has marked its site.

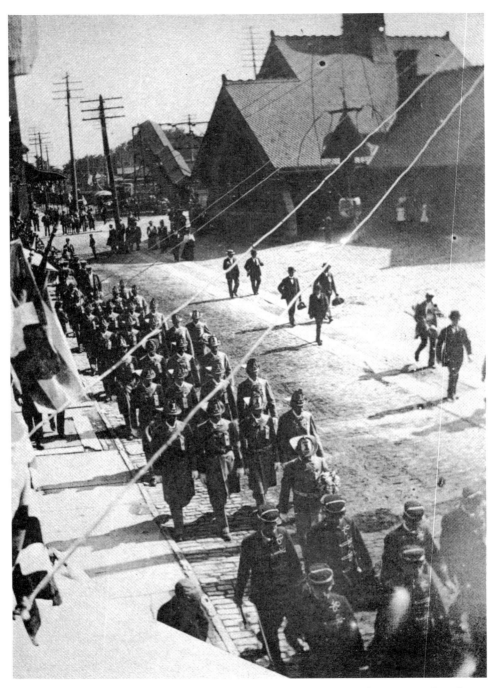

Out-of-town contingent arriving from Wall Street railroad station for firemen's convention in Schenectady, 1897.

30—A Busy Street

outh Center Street, renamed North Broadway after 1935, is that portion of Schenectady located between State and Union Street. You would scarcely know it today, but old "South Center" was a real lively thoroughfare not too many decades ago.

Let's take the era of the 1920s and early 30s, for example:

At the State Street entrance, to the right, was the venerable Hotel Vendome which for years stood as a sentinel to a commercial strip until it was razed in 1938 and replaced by the present Woolworth's store. Almost across the street was the old Henry Furman livery and warehouse building, later to be taken over by the Imperial for its annex and warehouse.

Next to that building was the "Happy Hour" theater which, from about 1915 to 1936, provided neighborhood theater entertainment for the poor families of the area—beginning, in fact, with D. W. Griffith's classic "Birth of a Nation." The theater even in later years charged 15 cents for adults and 10 cents for children. The Happy Hour, run by John J. Curry and Frank X. Shay, was sold in 1936 and was renovated and reopened that year as the Center Theater. Then it closed the following year and was made into a restaurant (The Coffee Pot) and barbershop (Center Barber Shop.) In the past decade, it was completely remodeled and is now Skype's Gallery.

Down that same side of the street were the Witbeck Co. warehouse (formerly the Gazette press building), Wilson & Co. meat packers, Peerless Barber Shop and the Dixie Lunch to the corner of Liberty Street. Today, all of the buildings north of the Gazette press to Liberty Street have been torn down to become a parking lot.

Between State and Liberty, from the Vendome Hotel were these establishments: Morris L. Johnson's men's clothing store, W. T. Hanson Co., Model Millinery, Kaufman Clieman's clothing store, S. Morris & Son household furnishings (at the corner of Franklin Street), Metropolitan Loan Co., Star Furniture Co. and Morris Schwartz the tailor.

Between Liberty and Union Streets, on the west side, businesses also dominated the scene along South Center. From the corner were: Wiencke's bar and restaurant (a popular place for Union College students, who sang a song which began, "Down to Wiencke's we shall go. . ." Swift & Co. meat packers, Kaufman S. Klayman clothier, Workingman's Lunch, and Schenectady Paper Co. At the very southwest corner of Center and Union once stood a three-story brick building (razed in the 1950s) which had been the site of the Schenectady Brewing Co., an early Schenectady industry.

On the corner of South Center and Liberty on the east side was Friedman & Co.'s meat market where inside, the floors covered with traditional sawdust, mounted heads of cattle and buffalo lined the walls. Next towards Union Street were: Ong Chong Wing Co.'s Chinese tea shop, James Priscilla grocer, Star Lunch, Joseph Massina grocer, Stanley Miller's second-hand furniture. Kaufman Clieman's drygoods store, the St. Clair Hotel (which had large plate-glass windows revealing a big lounge with old upholstered chairs and cuspidors), Strong's Express Co.

and the New Way Lunch run by Evangel Stathis and John Markos, where hot dogs and soda pop cost a nickel each.

At the southeast corner of South Center and Union was the ice cream store run by Mel Orphanitus (he was a Greek orphan), who made delicious candy under the name of Progress Confectionery Co. and served a specialty of chocolate ice cream with his own pineapple topping at the fancy wrought iron chairs and tables. Just around the corner was the Henry A. Kerste drug store.

One Saturday summer morning in 1929, there was a commotion on South Center near Union Street which drew a crowd of curious onlookers. It seemed the police were acting on orders to evict an eccentric old lady from her squalid flat at 5 Center St. which was on the upper floor of a small building which set in from the street at the end of an alleyway. She was known for her peculiarities and was considered entirely harmless, but now it was decided she should be committed to a mental institution for her own good.

The police did not figure the eviction would be difficult—but it was. Visably upset over the prospect of leaving her home, she slammed her apartment door shut and locked it, screaming invectives at the officers who tried to talk her into going peaceably. Finally, they had to break in the door and—lo and behold—a dozen or more cats and dogs came running out of the place. Later it was found that she had "adopted" these pets by luring them home with tid-bits, then keeping them locked in her house.

Well, anyway, the real climax to this incident came when she ran out on the street, wild-eyed and brandishing a meat cleaver. She also had an American flag wrapped around her, daring anyone to come near, even touch her. A policeman came up from behind, disarmed her and then she was taken away in a motorcycle sidecar.

Years ago, there was a proprietor of a South Center Street saloon between Liberty and Union Streets who took no sass from his customers. He especially abhorred those who bellied up to his bar, got drunk and argumentative. His method of prying them loose from his premises was to reach for a bullwhip and, if they did not leave promptly, let them feel the leather all the way out to the street.

As difficult as it is to believe today, two-way traffic was permitted on South Center until the early 1930s. But then the largest vehicles using it much before then were the American Express trucks with their raspy chain drive and solid rubber tires. A few moving company trucks, usually Model T's, often were parked along the street between Liberty and Union.

The second-hand furniture business was thriving up through the Depression Thirties and South Center was the place for it. Whenever the stock company of the old Hudson Theater wanted "period" furniture for its shows, it arranged a one-week rental deal with the Center Street stores.

31—Bobsledding

*T*he sport of bob-sledding, or "bobbing" as the old-timers called it, was popular in Schenectady among the more daring young men of the past century and their exploits provided many thrills not only for them but for community onlookers.

Bobbing, as it was practiced in the 1880s and early 1890s in many Northern states, is a lost sport. Few of our 20th century citizens have any understanding of the enthusiasm engendered by the bobbing championships as teams of from six to 36 men climbed aboard the wooden behemoths to vie for area championships.

Fortunately, the late City Historian William B. Efner Sr. in 1944 interviewed two Schenectady businessmen who were members of a bob team which figured prominently in one of the biggest bobbing carnivals ever held in Schenectady. And from them, Mr. Efner obtained and recorded their impressions of that great meet which gives some idea of how the bobbing captivated winter sports enthusiasts of that day.

He talked with Henry A. Kerste, who for 50 years after 1889 owned and operated his own pharmacy at 412 Union St., and James F. Burns, an electrical contractor who founded Burns Electrical Co. in 1890 here and was also in business 50 years. (Mr. Kerste died in 1955 at age 89 and Mr. Burns in 1964 at 95.)

Their story concerned the Schenectady carnival that night of Feb. 9, 1888 — a month before the great blizzard — when 47 sled teams from Schenectady and nearby cities competed for the championship trophy. All applications had to be received by one week before the races, so the community was well aware in advance of the contest which teams were entered and the statistics which were used to establish favorites.

As usual, the bobbing course for the championship was to be the Union Street hill from the head of "College Hill" (Nott Terrace and Union Street) down to the grade level tracks just below old Center Street. During the meet, hay bales were set up against barriers just east of the tracks in the event braking devices on the sleds failed after they crossed the finish line near Yates Street.

The Union Street hill was the favorite bobbing site and on any clear, cold wintry evening was the focal point of sledders just out for fun. A score or more teams usually were on the hill and hundreds would flock to the street to watch the evening's runs. Occasionally a bad spill would occur or a careless sleigh driver or pedestrian would fail to heed a guard's warning at a street intersection, with serious consequences. But considering the great length and weight of the bobs — some 30 feet or more and pulling about a half ton — casualties were comparatively few.

Mr. Efner once recalled that he was too young to participate in the sport of bobbing, but was permitted on wintry nights to "help sweep down the icy runway. . . and later in the evening to carry water in pails to flood the icy surface and make it slicker."

Back to the 1888 carnival which, in the estimation of both Mr. Kerste and Mr. Burns, was the year the sport reached its peak. . .

They were both members of the "Snow Queen" team which, along with the "Big Six" was most popular with local fans. By 1944, they were hazy about the names of others on the squad but managed these: Clarence Mead, Joseph B. Sothard (later a Ferry Street butcher), Harry Duryee, W. V. Steers and two whose surnames were Close and Donleavy.

Each team had its distinctive bobbing gear and costume, usually costly and elaborate. Early that carnival evening of 1888, the teams all paraded down State Street to the cheers of followers. Some pushed their bobsleds while others had hired teams of horses to pull them, the team seated majestically astride their gaily decorated vehicle. (The out-of-town bobbing teams had been arriving on afternoon trains and with them came hundreds of ardent rooters who augmented the thousands gathered that night along lower Union Street).

Grand marshal of the parade was George W. Marlette, while James H. Vedder was chief of staff. There were three divisions — the first headed by the 37th Separate Company's National Guard Band, the second by Shay's Fife and Drum Corps and the third by the Washington Continentals Fife and Drum Corps.

As the parade moved down State, the "Snow Queen's" paper decorations caught fire and caused a brief stir before it was extinguished. This did not perturb the men of the "Snow Queen," dressed that day in smart white wool coats and blue knit caps. They joked with the bystanders and said that "No one needed to light a fire under them to get them to win the race!"

In time, the bobbing teams were at the head of Union Street hill and then began a series of test runs as excitement among the bobbers and spectators mounted. With a roar, the monster sleds hurtled down the ice runway and within a minute approached Center Street, at which point the brakeman would release the heavy chains suspended beneath the bob. The chains, dropping under the iron runners, then threw off a mass of sparks as the bobs ground to a halt over the cobblestone pavement now devoid of ice.

The bob teams raced against time, not one another. Winning times often were only a fraction of a second from the runnerup. Length was considered the secret of speed — the longer the bob the more it could carry, the more team members the greater the overall weight and the greater the weight the greater the speed.

Captain Steers of the "Snow Queen" and Captain W. F. Lomasney of the "Big Six" were bobbing racers of long experience and they fully expected to be the leading contenders in the 1888 contest. However, it came to be noised about town that a new bob, "The Hurricane," might be the upset winner.

The outcome was a dead heat between the "Snow Queen" and the "Big Six," both negotiating the course in 45 seconds. "The Hurricane" finished fifth. On the run-off for first place and the championship, the "Big Six" won the honors by bettering its previous mark on the narrow ice trough by four seconds while the "Snow Queen" turned in a slightly slower time.

Mr. Efner wrote in his interview notes that he had asked Mr. Kerste what the "Snow Queen" team's reaction to the race were.

"Oh, we expected to win all right, so we were naturally disappointed," replied the former bobber.

Among the Albany bobs were "Tammany Hall," "Beverwyck" and "May Blossom." There were many from other communities but, to the best of Kerste's recollections, these were the other bobs and their captains from Schenectady and area:

"Ivanhoe," from Mohawkville (now 9th Ward), Captain Stephen Barrett Jr., five men; "Buffalo," Captain C. E. Butler, 20 men; "Pirate," Captain Myron Scrafford, 15 men; "Iroquois," Captain Herzog, nine men; "Clarondelet," Captain Nelson Dillenbeck, seven men; "Humpty-Dumpty," 12 men; "Mohawk Chief," Captain Frank Penny, 15 men; "Erminie," Captain Martin Swart, six men; "J. Elmer Ellie," Captain Harry Campbell, 15 men; "Liberty," Captain Frederick Paul Beattie, nine men; "Hibernian Student," 12 men; "Tornado," 12 men; "Hiawatha," Captain Chester Rowe, eight men; "Troubador," eight men and "Flying Dutchman," Captain Harman Peters, 15 men.

"See-a-See," Captain William F. Marsden, 10 men; "Iceberg," Captain Edward H. Reeves, 15 men; "Clingstore," Captain Edward Harbison, 12 men; "Not Left," Captain Hussong, 10 men; "U.S. Mail," Captain J. H. Vedder, 9 men; "We, Us and Company," Captain Simon Schermerhorn, 12 men; "Jay, Eye and See," Captain Charles Steinert, 15 men; "Osceola," Captain Earl Furman, 10 men; "Unknown," Captain Charles Wemple, 12 men; "Zephyr," Captain J. Wemple, 12 men; "Whirlwing," 12 men; "Oeonok," Captain W. Whitney, five men, and "Pride of Dorp," Captain William McInall, eight men.

This was the second bandstand in Crescent Park, built about 1913 during Mayor Lunn's first administration and lasting until the summer of 1948, the year this photo was made. It cost about $17,000 and was labeled "Lunn's Folly" by political critics, and yet was put to good use in the years preceding the mid-1930's. Today the site is marked by a circular flower bed near the top of the park (now called Veterans Park.)

(1) Schenectady's second state armory between State and Albany Streets at the top of Crescent Park. It was finished in 1899. (2) The State Street side of the state armory, a 1927 view. Crescent Park is in background. The armory was razed in 1947 and some of its stonework was used in the construction of St. Stephen's Episcopal Church that same year.

(1) The interior of Daniel Flinn's first store on lower State Street about 1908—when meat was a bargain. (2) A nostalgic scene, looking westerly down lower State Street about 1900. The facades may have changed, but many of these structures remain yet today.

(1) Joe Bones, a character about town in the late 19th century. (2) The countenance of Jim Cuff, the herb peddler. (3) Bartlett Jackson, the smiling bootblack of another era, as he approached old age in the 1920s. (4) The headstone of Jim Cuff in Vale Cemetery.

A familiar sight in Schenectady throughout most of the last century, the tall, gaunt figure of Jim Cuff stands in front of the one-room hut which was his home for many years. This photograph, from an original negative by W.J. Bevis, was taken a few years before Cuff's death in 1893.

(1) W. E. Underhill photo showing the "harbor" section of the Erie Canal in Schenectady about 1900. Dock Street is at left and the towpath at right. Today this is Erie Boulevard, looking towards GE. (2) The celebrated canal steamer, the Kittie West, on a cruise up the Erie Canal about 1905.

(1) The canal had been out of use for two years when this photo was made in 1917, showing the big ditch which had been cut through the city in 1825. Southerly view from State Street bridge. (2) The old canal was being filled in here in 1920, a view showing the buildings which had fronted on Wall Street in the canal days. The Ellis Building is at right.

(1) A July 10, 1924 photograph showing the completed boulevard from State Street to Washington Avenue. The northerly portion was completed the following year. (2) Winter of 1899. A delivery sleigh for Reeves-Luffman Co., forerunner of Wallace's, is parked in front of the Gazette office at 334 State Street.

(1) South Center Street (now Broadway between State and Union Streets) looking north from Liberty Street in 1915. It was a busy mercantile street in those days. (2) Decoration Day parade on State Street, Schenectady, 1913, with the surviving Civil War veterans (GAR) leading the way. Wallace's is in center background, and the cupolas of the Vendome and Edison Hotels can be seen in left background.

(1) The Snow Queen Coasting Club of Schenectady in full regalia when bobbing was a popular sport here. (2) Lower State Street, looking eastward toward the canal bridge, after the Blizzard of 1888.

32—Advent of the Chain Markets

THE FLINN STORES

$\mathcal{D}$aniel F. Flinn, having acquired some experience as a meat-cutter and grocery clerk in his native Albany, came to Schenectady in 1900 to establish his own grocery business, strictly on a "cash and carry" basis. The measure of success he enjoyed in subsequent years can perhaps be weighed by the fact that he was considered a pioneer in the development of chain grocery stores in this area.

Many today will recall a Flinn store in their neighborhood because the enterprising grocery executive branched out early in his career, growing from five stores in 1910 to 10 times that number by the time he retired and sold the business in 1937. "There's a Flinn Store Near" was the slogan used by Flinn & Co. throughout the last two decades of its existence.

Flinn, educated in Albany public schools and a private business school, formed a partnership with William J. Cassidy, then an Albany grocer. In 1900, Flinn & Co. acquired its first store when it bought out the grocery establishment of James J. Shea.

Shea's Market was well known, having operated for many years at 135 State St., four doors from the northwest corner of State and Ferry (the present site of Union Book Co.)

In 1903, they also started the Schenectady Public Market on Center Street just around the corner from State, and soon after that the market moved into the ground floor of the Vendome Hotel building — where it remained in business until 1936 when the hotel was being vacated preparatory to its being demolished. By 1938, the Woolworth Store had been built on the premises.

On the death of his partner in 1915, Flinn assumed full control of Flinn & Co. and was president of the Schenectady Public Market. This was the year that the company, now incorporated, really began to flourish.

For one thing, it was in 1915 that Flinn moved out of the original market on lower State Street and across the street into the building at the southwest corner of State and South Ferry St., listed at 142-44 State St. (the site where the former Stein's Clothes later was located).

This was the store where most Schenectadians recalled Flinn's stores beginning, even though Flinn had been at 135 State for nearly 15 years. This, incidentally, was the store where Louis Nicholaus' celebrated macaw, Loppa, often visited — a block down the street from his owner's restaurant — to bum a few handouts, such as soda crackers or dried peas.

Flinn launched on a program of expansion that ultimately saw him the head of more than 50 stores — some 20 of which were in Schenectady, an equal number in Albany and the remainder in outlying communities within a 50-mile radius.

In 1927, besides the original store still on lower State Street and the Schenectady Public market in the Vendome building, Flinn stores in

Schenectady were located at 1521 and 1338 State St., 816 Eastern Ave., 27 Van Vranken Ave., 1735 Union St., 423-1331-1701 Broadway, 795 and 1104 Albany St., 800 Hamilton St., 102 McClellan St., 102 Mohawk Ave. and 146 Vley Road.

When he started in business here, Flinn publicized the fact that he was operating strickly on a cash basis — buying his own goods for cash and retailing them for cash. These were the days, in the early 1900s, when customers had been accustomed to running up charge accounts for their weekly staples and paying off at least part of the bill at the end of the month. Flinn advertised that by conducting a "cash and carry" business he could regularly lower prices as the market fluctuated. His theory must have been widely accepted, considering the popularity of his stores, but it was relaxed considerably in the depth of the Depression 30s.

The early Flinn stores were typical of neighborhood groceries of the times. Several barrels near the door contained pickles, flour, beans and split peas; glass-covered bins atop one side of the grocery counter were filled with such edibles as ginger snaps and soda crackers (five pounds for a quarter); a huge red coffee grinder, often in operation, emitted that delectable aroma of fresh-ground coffee; bulk tea bins, all properly labeled, were on a shelf behind the counter; peanut butter (10 cents a pound) was stored in a lined wood box ready to be scooped out to order on heavy paper containers; the high and wide shelves on one side of the store were filled with such as canned preserves, oat meal and dried fruit; wheels of fresh creamery butter (22 cents a pound) and sharp cheese (15 cents a pound) glistened with a savory yellow glow beneath their glass covers; large fresh eggs in the dairy section went for 15 cents a dozen; potatoes, selling for 23 cents a peck, were in bushel baskets at the far end of the store, and granulated sugar (five cents a pound) was stored in wood bins alongside the counter.

However, the meat department for many years was the feature of the Flinn stores and as such commanded a large section of each establishment, usually one whole side and part of the back. In these days of inflationary prices and the furor over rising meat costs, the contrast of prices in 1910 with those of today might astound younger shoppers who have come to regard choice cuts as budgetary problems.

In 1910, for example, the meats displayed over crushed ice were tagged with these prices: Shoulder roast beef — 11 cents pound; pot roast — nine cents pound; dressed veal chops — 12 cents pound; fresh halibut steak 12 cents pound; stewing veal three pounds for a quarter; beef liver — three cents pound (generally for the family cat).

Although the former Shea store was the first owned by the Flinn concern, the Schenectady Public Market up at Broadway and State really formed the nucleus of Flinn's cash grocery store chain.

It was the impending loss of that site which may have convinced Dan Flinn that it was time to retire. He never looked for another location for Schenectady Public Market after 1936 and the following year he sold his grocery chain business. The stores then were sold individually, some to close in favor of another line of merchandising and the others to continue as privately-owned groceries.

On Tuesday, Dec. 2, 1941, Flinn became ill at his home at 12

North Church St. and he was rushed to Ellis Hospital. He died the following Thursday morning. A funeral mass was held in St. John the Evangelist Church on Saturday morning and burial was in St. Agnes Cemetery, Albany.

THE SCHAFFER STORES

In recent years, the affable Henry Schaffer had become known as a "collector of college libraries" because of his generous bequests to Union College and Union University for the construction of magnificent library complexes. But there was a time, for a span of nearly a half century, when he was a collector of grocery stores.

Schaffer, who came to this country shortly before the turn of this century with his parents and brothers as Jewish immigrants from Russia, was practically weaned on the grocery business in Schenectady, but he matured in the field as the head of a grocery chain which stretched in all directions throughout the Mohawk and Hudson Valleys.

Tall and lean, keen of mind and philosophical, Schaffer was still active in private business as of October, 1974, with an office on Wall Street in the northwest second story corner of what was formerly the Edison Hotel. He retired, however, from the grocery operation in 1958 when he sold the far-flung Empire Market chain to Grand Union in 1958. Ask anyone today who can remember past the mid-1930s and he will be almost certain to know of the Schaffer stores, because they were everywhere in this area.

Schaffer was the special guest of honor at ceremonies held the morning of Oct. 19, 1974, at the new adjunct to the Schaffer Library complex on Union College's campus. It was the third library he made possible through personal financing. The first was completed at Union in 1961, replacing the familiar domed Nott Memorial Library on that campus. He also financed construction of the Schaffer Library of Health Sciences at Union University's Albany Medical College in 1972.

Nearly 70 years ago, Schaffer helped direct and contributed financially to the building fund of the Schenectady YMCA when that organization sought a new building (and which was dedicated on lower State Street in 1927). The slogan then, as Schaffer recalls, was "Better to build boys than mend men." In more recent years, by his own admission, he had concentrated his philanthropic efforts toward building college libraries.

His reasoning was that the real young receive considerably more benefits today than a half century ago while post-high school youth need that extra boost upon entering the college level.

Schaffer, who never had the opportunity to go to college, said "education is our greatest commodity" and had decided that building good libraries is a way of fostering it.

While going to public school in Schenectady, Schaffer helped out in his spare time at his parent's small grocery shop on Center Street, just north of State Street. He left school at age 13 to work full time in Dan Flinn's markets and other grocery stores in the area, gaining the experience necessary to go into business for himself.

The young son learned a lesson from a sad experience suffered by his parents in 1911 when they finally had to fold the business after paying off all outstanding debts to wholesalers.

His parents had followed the example of many other merchants of that day by extending unlimited credit to their customers; some paid regularly, usually at the end of the week, but a lot didn't.

As he looked back on it, Schaffer saw the small-time independent grocer of those years as "nothing more than a welfare agency without recourse to the federal government for refund" in case the customers failed to pay. There was nothing left but to close up shop.

Schaffer opened his first store at the northeast corner of State and Furman Streets (a site now taken over by St. Luke's Church as part of its side lawn). For two years it was known as Standard Grocery, to differentiate it from his parents' credit operation.

He set a policy of cash and carry, in fact adopted the slogan, "Where cash is king." With quality merchandise and good service (including free delivery), Schaffer's initial attempt at retailing flourished.

In time, within only a few years, he began to open other stores and by 1913 changed the name of his operation to Schaffer Stores.

Older residents may recall that the stores were distinguishable not only by the variety of merchandise (meats, vegetables, canned goods, baked goods, etc.) but by their color—a bright orange. Schaffer explained how he hit upon the selection of the brilliant hue.

He had been considering the idea of painting his stores all one color especially after he began to form a chain of them. He had heard of the top executive of a competitive chain giving an order, "I don't care what color you paint my stores—as long as it's red."

So why not, Schaffer asked himself, an equally eye-catching color — orange.

By 1925, Schaffer Stores had amassed an impressive chain of 100 grocery stores and 25 meat markets scattered across the eastern half of the state. But that was only the halfway point in the firm's fantastic growth.

When the depressed Thirties rolled around, there were 158 Schaffer stores and it was then that the enterprising owner decided to try the self-service type market.

In 1934, he bought the building at 1108 State Street (just east of Brandywine Avenue) which had been the Fairlee Auto Sales headquarters of Leonard Fairlee. Schaffer decided not to listen to those who said the "super market" idea was foolhardy and opened a serve-yourself grocery in his newly acquired property under the name of Community Market. He operated it strictly as a pilot venture so that he could watch the public response to a new type of grocery merchandising.

As it turned out, the idea was popularly accepted and in a few years the new store became the Empire Community Market—the forerunner of bigger things to come. Schaffer then determined to make a bold move during a risky economic period. He closed the Schaffer stores and opened 41 super markets known as Empire Markets, a $50 million operation.

Although he pioneered the self-service market in this area,

Schaffer did not consider himself the progenitor of the idea.

"It was a typical American depression product which grew out of adversity. It was a good one, and the whole world copied it," he said. "As for me, I saw the Depression Thirties as a challenge and an opportunity — to change over from cash-and-carry, the darling of the time, to a new-fangled idea called self service."

Jackson's Gardens is a colorful part of Union College's campus, along with the rippling Hans Groot's Kill that runs through it.

33—The Old Armory

*F*ocal point of sporting events and community activities in Schenectady during the first third of this century was the old armory which once occupied the site above Veterans Park.

Actually, this was Schenectady's second armory. The first state armory was built in 1868 on the same spot, between Albany and State Streets and at the top of the wooded area once known as Crescent Park. That point of land then was the outskirts of the city.

Agitation for a new and larger armory in Schenectady began about 1890. When the 36th and 37th separate companies of the state guard left for service in the Spanish-American war in 1898, construction started on the second armory. It was completed the following year and was enthusiastically received by such glowing press accounts as:

"The new state armory at the head of Crescent Park is one of the finest in the state at the time. It is a building of magnificent proportion and a welcome addition to the important buildings of the city."

Built of red brick and stone, it was best described as "a mixture of old English castle and Romanesque architecture". Like its predecessor, it was three stories high but covered a wider area. There were offices and company rooms in the section facing the park to the west, while the high-arched drillshed was to the rear. The main entrance was on State Street, opposite Nott Terrace.

The 36th and 37th companies were succeeded in the guard by Company E, Company F and the machine gun company, who later took part in the Mexican border incident of 1916 and World War I.

The new armory soon came into popular use as a civic auditorium. Its big drillshed was the scene of many community dinners and rallies, and the Schenectady Boy Scout council held many Scout-o-ramas there.

Professional state league basketball held sway for a decade, while boxing and wrestling drew large crowds regularly. During the 1920s and 1930s, one of the top stars of the grappling world happened to be a local favorite. He was "Pink" Gardner, later to become Schenectady county's sheriff and still later its county clerk, but who was then world's middleweight and light heavyweight wrestling champ.

How the crowd roared when Gardner applied the "clincher," the airplane swing, to such topnotchers as Charlie "Midget" Fisher.

The 40-year-old building was sold to the county when Schenectady's third armory was built in 1938 on Washington Avenue. During World War II, General Electric used the abandoned building for a warehouse. Then, in the fall of 1945, it figured in the city's plans to streamline the section above Crescent Park to cope with the traffic bottleneck there.

The city council, which negotiated with the county board of supervisors for transfer of the armory site, included a capital budget item of about $250,000 in the 1946 budget for demolition of the armory and the widening of Veeder Avenue. Approximately $80,000 of this was needed for razing of the old drillshed and the development of a traffic dispersal area on armory place.

By the summer of 1947, wrecking crews had torn down the

armory. A portion of the lower part was used for the traffic crossover to Nott Terrace. The rest was developed by the Polish National Alliance into the picturesque Pulaski Plaza.

A view of old Dock Street along the Erie Canal in the 1880s, now Erie Boulevard south of State Street. Shops and warehouses prospered for many years along this route in Schenectady where the canal was so wide it was nicknamed the "harbor."

34—The Erie Canal

REXFORD

*I*t has been 60 years since the Erie Canal became outmoded with the opening of the larger Barge Canal, changing the self-sufficient canal town of Rexford into a residential community.

Since the building of the northern approach to the new Rexford bridge was started, even some of the vestiges of the glory and prosperity that once the hamlet of Rexford have disappeared.

Among these are the stone arches of the aqueduct which once shuttled the canal barges across the Mohawk River (a few of the piers have been preserved by the state to be maintained as a historic site), to the Cyrus W. Rexford store and McLane's Hotel.

There were two canal locks in Rexford, often referred to as the "upper" and "lower" locks, where business was brisk and the air rang with the shouts of "canawlers" fighting with one another to be the first through the locks.

There were four canal stores, two on the upper lock and two on the lower lock some 1,500 feet below.

Canal stores were a traditional part of Erie Canal life. They remained open 24 hours a day and seven days a week during the approximately eight months of the year the canal was open to traffic.

Store proprietors had cots in their establishments and did their sleeping on the premises. They were lucky to get an uninterrupted night's rest for the traffic didn't stop with sundown.

To facilitate the buying and handling of heavier merchandise, such as feed for the canal mules and horses, these items often were stacked on the porch of the store. It was also necessary for the stores to stock practically all household needs for the barges.

During the earlier days of the canal, the traffic consisted of single barges exclusively because the lock were long enough to accommodate one boat. In 1898, the locks were all lengthened to permit two boats at least on one side and "double headers" and even "triple headers" became common.

There were generally three types of boats — scows, lakers and bull-headers. The scows were the cheapest and were built in Tonowanda to sell for about $2,500. They were used exclusively to carry lumber from the mid-western states to Albany, which was a lumber center in the early days. There the lumber was shipped down the Hudson to New York and from there, even on to Europe.

The lakers were a more expensive type of barge and were used mainly for the transportation of wheat, corn, oats and barley. They cost between $4,000 and $5,000 and were known as Ithaca Lakers or Rochester Lakers, depending upon where they were built. The bullheaders cost considerably more, had paneled tops and were of fancier finish.

The division of canals maintained a residence at Rexford for a section superintendent and a large work building shed.

One of the jobs of the state canal employees was the removal each winter of the wooden sections of the aqueduct so that high water in the spring would not carry the structure away. The aqueduct of 1870 was the second one to be constructed at the site.

A toll bridge existed for many years on the upstream side of the aqueduct. This was washed out March 27, 1914, during one of the biggest floods of the Mohawk Valley.

For a few years thereafter a ferry was operated. A wooden span was built with the closing of the Erie Canal in 1916 and in 1922 a steel and concrete bridge was erected on the arches which once supported the aqueduct. This now has been replaced by the new steel bridge adjacent to the old canal crossing.

Rexford enjoyed further prosperity after 1901 when Jacob Ruppert, the New York City brewer, built the Grandview Hotel against the hill upstream from the canal. This began the development of a recreation park in anticipation of the opening of the Ballston-Saratoga line of the Schenectady Railway Company. Known by a variety of names, beginning with Luna Park and ending with Rexford Park, the facility drew thousands of people to the Rexford area each weekend from Memorial Day through Labor Day until the early 1930s.

Communities such as Rexford, rather than cities like Schenectady, received the most serious blow from the abandonment of the Erie Canal. The smaller towns had generally grown up around the canal locks because of the business that was available there.

ALONG THE CANAL

Interesting sidelights about a specific area of the Erie Canal in Schenectady have been preserved along with countless other reminiscences by the late William B. Efner Sr., former city historian.

His comments are filed at the Schenectady County Historical Society along with a photograph of the canal bridge at Jefferson Street, taken in 1920 preliminary to the filling in of the old canal bed and the creation of Erie Boulevard. The picture depicts the canal in a dismal state, having been abandoned four years before when the Barge Canal system was inaugurated. The old bridge is supported beneath by extra planking, the canal is only partly filled, debris is all about and the tow path at left is about twice its normal width.

But this photography is unique in that it shows the area untouched by wreckers and construction crews which moved in shortly after to build the modern boulevard.

These were Mr. Efner's comments about the picture in his own words:

"The bridge is typical of canal bridges throughout the city prior to the introduction of steel. The bridge was approached at either end by a sharp ascent from the normal street level.

"At the western end, south side, was Cornelius Anthony's two-story canallers store and a storekeeper's housing quarters on the second floor or street level and a wide entrance way from the tow path just north of the wagon which stands under the bay of the window above.

"Wide stairs led from the tow path to the store above. Canallers would run ahead of their approaching boar, make their purchases, dart from the store door on the Jefferson Street and be on the bridge by the time the boat passed under, ready to drop to the deck. The building in the foreground on the tow path level was a modern addition.

"The three-story building next west of the canallers store was owned by Cornelius Anthony, who occupied the ground floor. Two floors were rented. Next west of the three-story building was a two-story single family dwelling where a son, Charles L. Anthony, resided.

"At one time, the parents of W. B. Efner lived on the top floor, Mrs. J. DeWitt Efner being a daughter of Anthony. W. B. Efner was born on the top floor. As a boy, he lived on the second floor where windows looked out on the canal and the railroad beyond.

"The elm tree left of the bridge was planted by Anthony in the 1870s.

"On the easterly side of the bridge, where Jefferson Street intersected Pine Street, were large establishments and the railroad. Where the D & H railroad freight house stands, on the north side of Jefferson Street at Pine Street, was the towering Maxon elevator. Here grain was unloaded from canal boats, elevated to storage bins in the elevator building and later re-loaded into freight cars to be hauled to the coast cities.

"On the south side of Jefferson Street at Pine was the cavernous shell-like black frame coal shed of Cornelius Van Slyck. Coal came by boat and was unloaded by means of horse power and block and tackle to a miniature runway under the high ridge of the shed, being scooped up and later emptied into small wooden box-like trucks on small railroad wheels. The car with its load ran by momentum down the runway, being emptied by a trip over the proper bin. The shed would hold countless boat loads of coal — that was in the days of real wholesaling.

"South of the coal sheds were the broomcorn storehouse and broom shop of Van Slyck. The storehouse and shop burned in the late 1880s at which time the Anthony house and other nearby buildings caught fire but later saved by volunteer workers and firemen.

"W. B. Efner, a boy of 10, was working as a cash boy in Barney's store at the time, but arrived home while the fire was still a roaring hell. The broomcorn burned for days after the fire was under control.

"In the photo, the tow path is much wider than it was when the canal was in use. From the manhole cover in the foreground, it is probable that a sewer had been laid prior to the filling in of the canal.

"The litter along the tow path bank was typical of the scene each spring before cleaning time. Of course the water was let out of the canal each fall, except for six inches or so in the bottom left in for sanitary reasons.

"Spring time, May 1, brought the hordes of cleaners who came wallowing down the canal in the muck and filth of a year's accumulation. The men used wide spading forks, lifting the muck — now somewhat caked by the warm spring sun — and the litter of dead animals and waste material which had been thrown into the canal. This was thrown onto the tow path where it usually lay for days until water was let into the cleaned canal 'level' and a scow could be run through on which the filth was deposited and hauled away — but the stench remained for days afterward.

"This photo shows the marvelous masonry work of the canal period. It also shows the 'dry' stone walls along the tow path and berm bank.

"The wall along the tow path was slanting; the berm bank where the boats tied up were sharp upright. The tow path in this picture is as the canal was when partly filled in. At points along the tow path, planked grade from the bed of the canal to the path were met with, and had proper guard rails. At these points, horses were removed from the canal after tumbling from the path.

"At the extreme north, in the background, can be seen the Alpha Knitting Mill on the left, now the locomotive company laboratory lot, and the locomotive works on the right."

Horse racing on the canal during winter also was popular with those families who could afford the luxury of a spirited horse (or a matched team) fitted with special shoes having pointed cleats and also a light sleigh with glistening steel runners. Some of Schenectady's most affluent families indulged in the sport, adding a flair of family pride in choosing appropriate colored plumes that were attached to the horses' headgear.

These races depended largely on the weather. During weekends that the canal was frozen over but not covered with too much snow, the contestants would gather at the State Street bridge and race one mile along the canal to the north for a "friendly wager."

The ice skating, however, was for the common man and his family. The skating area south of the bridge often was crowded with the gliding, skimming enthusiasts. On certain weekends there would be a festival atmosphere — complete with hanging Japanese lanterns and, if warm enough, with live orchestral music.

Some years there would be canal boats and barges along the west bank, frozen in the ice where they were docked for the winter when a sudden freeze caught the canalers by surprise. Usually, the boatsmen would erect wooden barriers around the immobilized vessels in the hope that this would protect them from the elements and possible vandalism.

Ice skaters turned to Central Park's Iroquois Lake in full force anyway soon after the park opened in 1916. It has remained the city's popular skating spot through the years, offering a warm casino and outside "canned" music to add to the enjoyment of the sport.

Schenectady was becoming more than just a "canal town" after the dawn of the 20th century. It had awakened to the industrial era, and consequently to faster and more efficient commercial transportation.

Although the Erie Canal was not abandoned until 1915 and did not become the present Erie Boulevard until 1925, an editor of a local newspaper may have foreseen its doom as early as 1879 when he wrote:

"Business on the canal is very dull. Neither steam nor horseflesh is doing much in the way of propelling boats. Is the time coming when grass shall grow on the tow paths and the old ditch shall be pointed out as the relic of the slow progress of a slower age."

THE KITTIE WEST

The old Kittie West will cruise as long as there is a Schenectadian old enough to remember her. The colorful launch was a part of Schenectady's history and a symbol of the good life as for 30 years she plied her way up and down the Erie Canal on pleasure trips.

Powered by steam, she was 85 feet, six inches long; 14 feet, eight inches wide and licensed to carry a maximum of 134 passengers. A narrow promenade circled the launch between the gunnels and enclosed deck, while an observation platform topside afforded open air privileges. The wheel house was to the fore, directly behind the bow.

Schenectady became a canal town when the "big ditch" opened in October, 1825. It became involved with the bustling commerce which at the time helped to open the trade lanes between east and west (then midwest). However, the canal was also a means of public transportation, no matter how slow, and scenic cruises along the valley route were always popular.

There were pleasure boats before the Kittie West, but somehow none seemed to take to the public fancy as did Kittie. When she was docked alongside Brown's Furniture Store (later Masonic Temple) at State Street and Dock Street, it meant a Sunday afternoon's excursion perhaps to Aqueduct or a chartered trip upstream for a picnic or clambake.

The Kittie West was purchased in 1884 by James L. Foote, John Parker and Ed Joyner. Later Mr. Joyner died and Parker, then a well known restaurateur and political figure, sold his share to Foote. It was said the craft was built in 1867.

Usually the provisions that were stashed aboard the Kittie West for picnic or party cruises came from Louis Nicholaus' restaurant directly across from the ship's docking station. While the refreshments — lobsters, fish, chicken, hot dogs, watermelon, pop and beer — were checked aboard by Captain Foote, the passengers would be amused at the constant chatter of Nicholaus' parrot, "Loppa," perched as always on the exterior fire escape alongside the tow path.

On a summer's Sunday afternoon and evening, the Kittie West carried from 1,200 to 1,500 people to Aqueduct and back at a fare of 15 cents for a one-way trip and 25 cents round trip. In those days, Aqueduct (Rexford) was one of the big resort attractions in the area. The New York Central ran one train a day to and from Troy and the rest of the time, the "Kittie" plied her way back and forth.

Foote bought his coal for the launch from Bill Helmer for $3 a ton. Old Overhold whiskey sold for 90 cents a quart and Canadian Club for $1. John Parker served full-course roast beef dinners for 50 cents.

During the week, the Kittie West carried private parties to the picnics and clambakes scheduled in advance. Each July 4, the Chaldeans would charter her for a trip to Pattersonville. On another occasion, the Hibernians of Amsterdam would hire the boat for a trip to Fultonville and a clambake. Union College fraternities had special outings or initiations, the Red Men would go to Maxon's Grove for their annual outing and Chief of Detectives Ben Van Dusen arranged for use of the Kittie West for an outing for Masonic fellowcraft teams.

John Ellis, who operated a cigar store on the bank of the Erie Canal, was business agent for the ship's bookings. The average price for a full day's outing, including food, beer and the use of the Kittie West, was about $2 per person.

Conrad Snyder of Fonda bought the "Kittie" from Foote and shipped on her for two summers near Pattersonville before the Erie Canal was abandoned in 1915, replaced by the Barge Canal. Then he took the steamer Lobdell, with the intention of sailing the Barge Canal.

At Herkimer, Fred Ostrander of Little Falls bought the Kittie West, then in turn sold her for $300 to a man whose last name was Detine.

The new owner's cruise on the "Kittie" was her last. The famous boat sprang a leak one mile east of Herkimer and had to be beached.

The Kittie West, once the pride of canal, was left to the ravages of time, her engine stripped and windows broken.

THOSE WERE THE DAYS

Down at the Schenectady County Historical Society headquarters at 32 Washington Ave., daily visitors in 1974 were treated to a special exhibit on the Erie Canal and its relation to the Schenectady area.

It was a reminder that for about 85 years, until the waterway was abandoned in 1915 to be replaced by the Barge Canal system, "Clinton's Ditch" was very much a part of this city's physical and economic characteristics. It served as a commercial main street that was both cursed and blessed for the effects it had on the community.

It has been said that Schenectadians at first did not take kindly to the canal which curved out of the southwest from Pattersonville and sliced through the city toward the Rexford aqueduct. However, it did spur the growth of businesses in the area and its existence soon became something to live with. Years before the Civil War, Schenectady was properly dubbed a "canal town."

There are many today who can recall swimming in the canal, jumping from the Washington Avenue bridge near the General Electric Co. and even hitching a tow ride alongside the barges which plied the murky waters. There was ice skating in the winter along the canal too. In the general area between the Liberty Street bridge to just below the State Street span, the canal was kept clear of snow for public skating and on Saturday afternoons and evenings, ice carnivals would be held.

Nine city streets and a railroad crossed the Erie Canal here in a network of stone, wood and steel bridges. The busiest canal section in Schenectady was between Washington Avenue and State Street. It was twice the average 70-foot width of the regular canal and thrived with a conglomeration of feed and grain stores, harness shops and stables, coal and lumber yards and hardware shops. Little wonder it was called the city's "harbor."

Horses and wagons and people, not necessarily in that order, seemed to fall into the canal quite regularly once it was opened for navigation early in April. Usually the dunkings were by accident, but sometimes dock ruffians settled arguments by the "wet or dry method." The one wrestled into the water was wrong, the other right.

Items like these of 1859 appeared often in the local news columns:

"A horse and cart belonging to Brownell Coal Co. backed off their dock yesterday. The horse was saved from drowning after the harness was cut."

"A span of horses fell into the canal last night from the tow path opposite Dock Street. In falling, the horses drew a boy in with them. The lad was rescued at once by a man who jumped in after him. The horses also were saved."

"A canal driver between Schenectady and Freeman's Bridge was roped into the canal this morning. He floundered about in the water for awhile and finally regained the tow path."

The wind whipped vigorously up the canal lane on certain spring and fall days, just as it does today along Erie Boulevard. It caused no end of embarrassment to the ladies when, as they were crossing one of the street bridges, a sudden gust happened to blow their skirts upwards, exposing not only several fancy laced petticoats but a pair of trim ankles as well.

Hats often blew into the canal on these days. Once a dignified-looking woman paused on the State Street bridge to watch some activity below. Her portly bearing was reflected in her fine clothes — from her swishing brocaded skirt to her wide-brimmed blue velvet hat topped by a black ostrich feather. Beautiful auburn hair flowed from beneath it, caught at the back in a huge bun. Suddenly a blast of wind swept across the bridge and with it went the lady's fine velvet hat, sailing in the air and into the canal below. She hurried quickly from the scene, but for a moment she stood in shocked disbelief as she watched her hat, ostrich feather and auburn wig float slowly downstream. She was now a gray-haired woman.

Ice skating on the Erie Canal was a favorite winter pastime through most of the 19th century and up until the canal bed began to be filled in after 1915.

In Schenectady the area of the canal just south of the State Street bridge next to Nicholaus Restaurant was kept cleared of snow for those addicted to the art of skating.

This was before skiing became a popular winter sport in America and before adults did such things as ride snowmobiles over the countryside or sail ice boats across a frozen lake. The small fry relied chiefly on "belly-whopping" their sleds down hillsides, although some indulged in ice skating.

THE BOULEVARD

Just over a half century ago, in the year 1923, a marked change was taking place in mid-town Schenectady. That portion of the old and fabled Erie Canal which since 1825 had bisected the business district from Nott Street to Washington Avenue was being filled in and soon would become a wide and fashionable boulevard.

It was a sign of the times, the advent of the golden age of the internal combustion engine and its attendant promise of "a car in every garage" and travel horizons unlimited.

When the canal was being replaced by the broad sweep of pavement from the old American Locomotive Co. south to the General Electric plant, there were not many citizens around who were saddened at its passing. Since it abandoned operations in 1915, the Erie Canal became an unsightly spectacle.

The stagnant water, green with slime wherever it collected in the muddy canal bed, caused pedestrians to hold their noses while crossing the canal bridges during hot summer months. The big ditch also became a dumping ground for whatever anyone wanted to contribute — ashes, garbage, bed springs, dead animals and the like. A lot of people complained but the city administration kept putting off the street project with explanations to the effect that the cost estimates had not yet been obtained and that engineering plans were incomplete.

However, in 1923, through the urging of Mayor William W. Campbell, the city finally went after the boulevard project in dead earnest. Its construction was coordinated with the widening and paving of Washington Avenue from State Street across to the new boulevard. On Nov. 13, 1924, traffic was opened on the boulevard between Union and State. The whole project was completed and dedicated the following spring.

Most of the buildings along Dock Street (the eastern side of the old canal) were allowed to stand in 1923. J. B. White's big gasoline station (across from Olney Redmond's) was built in 1925 just before the city's new central fire station along what was once the tow path on the western side of the former canal route.

The sidewalks were paved in on both sides and the modern street lighting made the thoroughfare the "most brilliant boulevard in the world."

In more recent years, most of the canal-oriented buildings have been torn down — both north and south of the State Street crossing. The age of the automobile has gradually evolved into the age of the parking lots.

Schenectady's lower State Street, looking east from Ferry Street in the early 1880s toward the canal bridge (what is now the Erie Boulevard intersection). The cobblestone paving remained until 1895, when it was replaced by granite blocks. The Barney Co. store is third up from the left.

35—Way Back When

MEMORIES OF ANOTHER ERA

On the occasion of the renaming of Crescent Park as Veterans' Park in 1960, Walter J. Reagles of Schenectady was asked to design the granite memorial to be erected and dedicated on Nov. 11 that year.

Mr. Reagles — retired GE art director, former Schenectady postmaster, judge of Miss America contests, holder of the Silver Palm of the Academy of France, developer of the GE calendar, bonhomie, bon vivant, raconteur — at the time also penned these recollections of his boyhood days spent in the vicinity of the old park:

"When asked to make a sketch for a design for the memorial monument in Veterans' Park, I was most happy with the task because here, facing the park (then called Crescent Park) was my childhood home. Here I was born, here as a child I played, joyful and carefree.

"Facing the park was also the home of my grandfather and grandmother, born in Schenectady in 1800 and 1801. Below the park at the corner of State and Lafayette Streets and running through to Barrett Street was the wheelbarrow and wagon shop of my grandfather and his partner, 'Clute and Reagles.' The First Methodist Church stands at the corner of State and Lafayette, where my grandfather, who was a trustee of the church, and my grandmother worshipped and where I, as a boy, attended Sunday School.

"Our home was 611 State Street. The building yet stands, Breslaw's Outlet Store, but one can still see the upper floor and attic above the business storefront. Here I was born in 1885. My early recollections were the sound of sleigh bells, the snow softly falling as my parents would take me through the park in a child's sleigh.

"My grade school days were spent at old Nott Terrace School. Mrs. Morris taught the primary grades and I still remember how she put little shawls around our shoulders if the room was cold. For pure water, she would send two of us boys to the spring at Scott's sand bank (now the site of the Schenectady Museum) each day for a pail of water. The city water then carried the danger of typhoid.

"Next door to our home was Wiederhold's vacant lot where we played baseball. Next to the lot was the home of Isaac I. Yates, a retired navy officer, whose son was my chum. Our parents called us 'The Heavenly Twins.'

"I well remember the cobblestone pavement, the horse cars, the watering trough at the foot of the park, and the extra team of horses waiting in stormy weather to help pull the horse cars up the hill. I remember the gas lamps and the gas lamplighter as he made his rounds as dusk fell. I recall the fire alarm bell located in the steeple of the First Methodist Church. I remember Jim Cuff as he walked through the park from the Bowery woods with his bag of herbs. And the old State Armory I readily recall — headquarters of the 36th and 37th separate companies of the state guard.

"I remember old Christ Church (where the Plaza Theater was later built) facing the park and the band concerts in the evening with Rivette's Silver Concert Band. I remember when the one-ring circus raised their tents on what we called the Mynderse plot — State Street just above Close Street. Here I saw Signor Sawtelle and Pawnee Bill and his Wild West show.

"I remember the pitch men — medicine shows at their stand at the foot of the park that were the forerunner of the modern television commercials. However, I think they did it better and as a child I would look forward to these advertisers as they did not appear every 15 minutes but only five or six times a year for the summertime only.

"Yes, the park was, and is, a treasure land of youthful memories and happy recollections although much has changed. I feel, as expressed so beautifully by William Wadsworth:

"There was a time when meadow, grove and stream,
The earth, and every common sight
To me did seem apparell'd in celestial light,
The glory and the freshness of a dream
It is not now as it hath been of yore.
Turn wheresoe'er I may, by night or day,
The things which I have seen I now can see no more."

Walter J. Reagles died Aug. 21, 1983 at age 97.

SCHENECTADY IN 1891

A brief glimpse of Schenectady in 1891 as seen through the eyes of an "out-of towner" is contained within a yellowed letter written that year by a Pennsylvania man to his wife.

The letter was provided by Miss Ada C. Kirk of Malvern, Pa. It was penned by her grandfather, Wilmer Siter Kirk, on Aug. 23, 1891, who had been in Old Dorp for four weeks up to that time.

It has not been determined where he was employed but from his reference to the "shop" and "big drawings," it can be assumed that it was either the old Schenectady Locomotive Works or the very young General Electric Co.

His letter began:

"It is another Sunday. I find myself far from home. The church bells are ringing 12 o'clock. I have quite a round already today."

Wilmer Kirk then told how he and a fellow worker, Dick Healy, "looked up a place for table board" at $3 per week. The night before, they had obtained new lodging at a rooming house at 606 Smith Street (A "big front room with two windows and a side room for trunks, clothing etc. at $1.25 each.")

He continued:

"After breakfast, Kersey and I went to the State Street Bridge (now State Street and Erie Boulevard) and took the steam yacht on the Erie Canal, thence four miles to the Aqueduct — an immense bridge which conducts the canal over the Mohawk River. It is a very pretty ride. One can see fine farms on each side of the river and canal. They run parallel."

He mentioned a double fatality the night before, when a four-year-old girl apparently fell off the Aqueduct into the river and her father jumped in to try to save her. "A gloom is cast over the city today in consequence," Kirk wrote his wife.

He noted "This is the poorest town for a daily paper. Everybody speaks of it. Papers from New York, Albany and Troy are sold here."

"I think I will lie down right after dinner and toward evening walk on top of the hill (now Summit Avenue) to see the sunset," he continued in his letter.

"The most home-like place I have found here is a suburb called Mont Pleasant. It looks Jersey-like, country-like streets and houses all containing big lots. There are country schools. It is just over the line in Rotterdam township. Here they drop the 'ship' and say town only."

He mentioned two men from the shop, one from London and the other from New York City, who "think they are in the country here."

"More tall trees here than I ever saw. The streets are lined with them. It is dark in places, it is so shady."

At 2 p.m., Kirk came back to his letter-writing:

"Just returned from dinner. Veal, veal, veal. Last week the other table had lamb and veal numerous. The markets are full of young meats. High though.

"I saw 300 loaded freight cars standing on side tracks to start tonight. The D & H has 17 sidings and each will hold 70 cars. It is only a single track road, what must be the contents of side tracks of the four-track New York Central and Hudson.

"I have inquired for all the points of interest in the vicinity. Saratoga and Ballston are the attractions. And the men are continually talking Amsterdam and now I know why. It is a knitting and cotton and woolen manufacturing town. It is a town of several thousand and the majority are girls."

Kirk's letter to his wife back in Pennsylvania also contained these tid-bits:

"This house has no sewer, the closet is in the yard. I can't get a drink of water, only Saratoga water at drug stores on Sundays, five cents. The artesian at the shop fortunately agrees with me.

"I gathered goldenrod at the Aqueduct. It is on my bureau. . . Every indication of rain. I bought a $1.25 umbrella the first week."

According to his granddaughter, Wilmer Kirk was 34 years old when he was in Schenectady, stayed a short time and then went back to Pennsylvania. He worked to put himself through Drexel Institute of Technology and became a Philadelphia high school teacher of manual training at 40. He was a Quaker.

Kirk, whose father was a Civil War Veteran, died Dec. 12, 1937.

CHRISTMAS, 1899

Christmas Day in 1899 had a special significance for its celebrants. It was the last holy day of the 19th century and the year 1900 loomed around the corner.

It dawned with a sunny 34 degrees in Schenectady that Monday, Dec. 25, 1899. By the time the children had "played out" their toys by 2 p.m., the temperature reached the day's high of 40 degrees.

Featured story on the front page of the Gazette that morning was news of the Boer War in South Africa. The Capetown dateline said that "Christmas peace has stayed the hand of war" but that the Boers were busy extending their trenches in the continued battle against British troops.

Locally, a three-act comedy entitled "In Paradise" was playing matinee and evening performances at the Van Curler Opera House.

The complete railroad timetable was listed, as usual, for the New York Central and West Shore Railroads. In addition, the stage coach line advertised its holiday schedule.

The coaches pulled away from the Merchant's Hotel at 2:30 p.m. — one bound for Mariaville and Rynex Corners, and the other for Scotia, Charlton and West Charlton.

The Merchant's Hotel, known as a "farmer's hotel," was located on the north side of lower State Street between Ferry and Church Streets.

The Mohawk Gas Co., with offices in the Central Arcade building, Wall and Liberty Streets, advertised the Welsbach gas reading lamp "to make the room more pleasant and homelike, besides giving the only satisfactory light for reading, sewing etc."

There were several local arrests, principally on charges of intoxication, but otherwise the community passed a very normal and peaceful Christmas Day in 1899.

THANKSGIVING, 1914

Many years ago, on Thanksgiving, 1914, Schenectady as a city had much for which to be thankful. Times were good, as they say, and problems were mighty few.

The war which had been boiling in Europe since early summer, while it made most Americans apprehensive, still seemed "far off" and President Woodrow Wilson had promised to keep the country out of it.

Of course, everyone complained about taxes as they do now and have done through the centuries, but in the main people sat down to their Thanksgiving Day dinner with the hope that this way of life would not be changed too drastically.

Take the cost of food (it was not considered "rock bottom" then, by any means, but neither was it a topic of concern.) A frugal housewife could bring home a week's groceries for a five-spot, a sizeable but worthwhile dent in her husband's $20-per-week salary.

The Thanksgiving turkey cost 28 cents a pound in Schenectady (although the New York City price was down to 21 cents.) If the family preferred a prime rib roast, it could be had for 14 cents a pound. Sirloin steak went for 15 cents, chickens 20-28 cents, young ducks 30 cents and hams 18 cents.

These were the prices on other food items: Coffee, 19 cents a pound; bread, three cents a loaf; eggs, 27 cents a dozen; butter, 27 cents a pound; oranges, 15 for a quarter; potatoes, 14 cents a peck; sugar, 4 1/2 cents a pound (with a purchase of $1 or more of groceries) and cranberries, 10 cents a quart.

Before Dad stretched out on the sofa for his after-dinner nap, he probably would haul out his five-cent packet of Bull Durham tobacco which always advertised: "Enough to make 40 handmade cigarets." The popular machine-made brands were available at most tobacco shops but they were expensive: 10 cents for a pack of 20.

Schenectady as a city was the integral part of the county. The trend to suburban living had not even been thought of. The city population (according to the 1913 postal census) was 94,784. Though the city limits were not then as great as at present, this figure far exceeds the city's current population of 75,862 — all because the citizenry and mode of transportation were not ready 50 years ago for out-of-city life.

The American Locomotive Works and the General Electric Co. (which alone employed 15,000) were the lifeblood of the community. Schenectady was no longer the "canal town" of earlier days. Indeed, the 82-year Erie canal had just about expended its usefulness and plans were already made for its demise. The city fathers were discussing the filling-in of the canal route within the city limits, as soon as the state took final action in abandoning it, and foresaw an expansive boulevard in its place.

Motoring was fast becoming more of a convenience than a fad, and many families were investing hard-earned savings in an automobile.

Of course, they were expensive. The Hudson "Six" went for $1,750 while the Hudson "Four" cost $1,500. A Hupmobile also cost $1,500. Horses and liveries were plentiful in 1914, but the automotive era was closing in.

The Schenectady Railway Co. prospered as it had since the early days of the century. Interurban cars ran from the city to neighboring villages and cities. In fact a Schenectady-Pittsfield interurban line was then being studied. Trolley cars plied all sections of Schenectady and downtown was the gathering point. The McClellan street and Fuller street car barns were bulging with extra cars and traction equipment.

Local merchants found business on a high level and new products were selling fast. The Edison disc phonograph, in console and table models, was a popular seller in price ranges from $60 to $250. Parlor stoves brought $19 and up.

Men's suits sold for $10 up to $28.45. . .and a man who bought a suit with only one pair of pants to it was put down as a spendthrift. Men's and women's shoes cost on the average of from $1.50 to $2.

Schenectady in 1914 boasted eight "modern moving picture theaters." It had 23 public schools with 348 teachers and 12,240 pupils.

Union College had just formally opened its new gymnasium. The county courthouse and the trolley waiting room at Lafayette and State streets were only three years old. Ellis Hospital was conducting a $100,000 fund drive to support its new construction off upper Nott street.

A citizens' committee fusion ticket won control of both city and county government. The mayor was J. Teller Schoolcraft, while the chairman of the county board of supervisors was Charles W. Merriam, 11th ward supervisor.

The city's budget that year was $1,470,163 (the 1964 city budget was $9,087,759.) And in 1914, the county board of supervisors tried unsuccessfully to abolish the $1,200-a-year position of commissioner of jurors on the ground that the office was "considered unnecessary."

But now the coal bin had been filled, the Thanksgiving dinner amply provided. . .what were the problems besetting the world on Nov. 26, 1914?

The Pancho Villa insurrection had been put down by U.S. forces in the Mexican Border clash, but U.S. authorities were still looking anxiously for a responsible government to take over Mexico.

Prohibitionists were meeting in Schenectady and throughout the country in a movement to make this "a saloonless nation by 1920."

Boxing Commissioner James R. Price of New York City said boxing "is next to baseball in public popularity," and called on the state assembly to kill a bill which would repeal the boxing law.

President Wilson was so firmly entrenched in the public confidence that one political wag of 1914 wrote: "The Democratic smile increases with every name that has thus far been proposed for the Republican nomination for President in 1916."

But, of course the war in Europe — which Americans hoped would not become a world war — was of major concern. This, in part, was the editorial which appeared in the Gazette in 1914:

"Good fortune or the reverse is a matter of comparison. Look across the sea.

"There are ruined and blackened cities and villages with what were comfortable and handsome buildings a few months ago now heaps of ruins and piles of ashes.

"Homeless, moneyless, foodless in many cases, the condition of refugees in Europe is indeed pitiable. Families have been scattered, disease has stricken them, death has been on every hand. The black pall of war and its inevitable train of devastation and wreck and carnage... hangs over Europe.

"There is no such thing here. We are at peace...Surely in this one fact alone there is abundant cause for giving thanks, not only as a nation but for every individual family."

Patrolman Karl J. Peters is shown operating a signal apparatus at State and Broadway in Schenectady about 1924, the second type to be used at this intersection. Automotive traffic control was just becoming a concern. South Center Street, with the Hotel Vendome on the corner (former site of Woolworth Store), is in the background.

36—Tin, Bones and Herbs

SOME COLORFUL CHARACTERS

*N*icknames were commonplace not so long ago. They were usually colorful names which had a meaning far beyond the color of one's hair.

Funny thing the way odd nicknames stuck with a person in days gone by, and Schenectady had its share of them. "Alabama" Smith and "Red Eye" Van Slyck, for example, got their monikers from varied experiences with commisary whiskey during the Civil War.

Hallenbeck the Tin Peddler had that name and nothing else. No one seemed to know his first name, just Hallenbeck the Tin Peddler. He was a big Dutchman, wore a drooping mustache and was very close with the penny.

Hallenbeck was one of those old time peddlers who were welcomed by householders in outlying districts who found it difficult to get into town to shop. These were the late 1800s, and Hallenbeck, like so many of the peddlers of his day, made the rounds of the neighborhoods on different days. About every 10 days his big red and yellow wagon would come rumbling up the River Road heading west along the canal, then veer into Campbell Road toward the Rotterdam farms.

He would give out several loud blasts from a long silver horn to let the citizens know that Hallenbeck was on the way. This was always a signal for the youngsters to come running. They liked to chase alongside the bright wagon and shout at the burly peddler.

In between his visits, housewives would save up all old clothing beyond repair so they could "trade in" rags for tinware. White rags brought a higher premium than colored ones. Hallenbeck carefully weighed the rags, then allowed his customers about 30 or 40 cents toward the price of whatever she purchased — a dishpan, cooking kettle, pie tins, calico or flannel.

There were five doors on the side of his wagon, and at each stop, Hallenbeck would open all of them to display his goods. There were no white enamel pans in those days. Everything was tinware or blue agateware.

"Steamboat" Jake Van Patten was a Rotterdam man who got his nickname the hard way. He was tagged with that because one winter in the 1880's he worked hard to build a nice big boat to ride on the Erie Canal, and when spring came around Jake found it was just too big to get out of his cellar.

"Steamboat" Van Patten lived on a farm near where Schermerhorn Road today juts into Route 5-S. He operated a broom shop on what today is Broadway, near Weaver Street.

Another Van Patten, no relation to "Steamboat," lived along the canal above Schermerhorn Road near the Three Mile Store. He was John Van Patten and, surprisingly enough, he was never given a nickname. Not that he didn't deserve one.

John gave up growing broom corn in his fields, decided to enjoy the rest of his life on what he had saved. His hobby was inventing things.

One of his inventions was a small lantern that was adjusted to the top of a horse's head for "night driving." Only thing was, when he put it to a test, the bobbing light frightened the animal and it bolted up the River Road and never stopped running until the lantern went out.

Probably the most ambitious of John's ventures was the time he made an airplane. This, mind you, was in 1885 — about 18 years before Wilbur and Orville Wright actually flew a powered craft.

People were beginning to get the idea that it might be possible, though, when John assembled his 10-foot version of a flying machine.

There is no record of what materials were used in this early flying experiment, but the end result was that after coasting off the roof of a shed on his farm, John became lodged in an apple tree and had to be extricated.

After his "flight" of some 15 feet, John was far from discouraged. He even wrote a letter to Thomas A. Edison, also engaged in inventions at that time, and suggested that they collaborate on this flying idea.

The only drawback, John told Edison, was that his airplane was too quiet. People might be able to swoop down on other people and steal things from their farms. He had to find some way for the machines to make a noise, maybe like a bumblebee, so that those on the ground would know an airplane was around.

Powered flight, to give due credit to John, was still unheard of.

A man known as Joe Bones was best known among the bone gatherers of the Schenectady area in the last quarter of the 19th century. He wore a scraggly beard and a beatup short-brimmed hat as he strode through the streets, a knapsack slung over a shoulder as he called out, "Bones, bones, any old bones today." He used a cane but did not seem feeble in the least.

There was a man out Hoffman's way who caught rattle snakes for a living in that area of the Mohawk River where the venomous reptiles sunned themselves along the rocky shore. He wore stove pipe from just below his knees to heavy shoe tops as a precaution against surprise attacks and used a pronged stick to catch the rattlers, slinging them live into a leather bag he toted for that purpose. He sold the snake venom to local laboratories for anti-toxin serums.

Bartlett Jackson was an amiable bootblack who took all kinds of odd jobs about the railroad station, but his principal occupation was shining shoes and his regular spot was in front of the Ellis Building on State Street next to the stone steps which led down to Dock Street from the canal bridge. Day after day, he sat in the sun in front of the Ellis Building, giving up his stool whenever a prospective customer came by. Bartlett, who some said was a slave in his youth, was particularly well liked by the professional men in the vicinity because of his jovial nature — always flashing a wide grin whether at work or sitting alongside Johnny Ellis' cigar emporium.

They were all colorful characters of the Schenectady community a century ago. We have, however, purposely omitted the best known of them all, wishing to treat his story separately in the following section.

BIG JIM CUFF

There probably never has been, nor is there likely to be, another personality the likes of Jim Cuff the herb peddler who was very much a part of the Schenectady scene throughout a good part of the 19th century.

There are some persons living today who can recall the days when the strange angular man stopped at their homes with his basket of health remedies. Many others have heard countless stories of Cuff which have been passed down through the years. Some are true, but others, it is suspected, have been colored by fantasy.

Jim Cuff died in 1893, but no one knew his age. What is known about his early days is that he was born "sometime after 1800" on the farm of Hendrick Swits, on the south side of State Street opposite Jay Street. He took the name of James Hartley Swits but generally was referred to as Jim Cuff.

There have been conflicting statements as to whether his mother was a full-blooded Mohawk Indian and his father a Negro — or vice versa. It was his claim that his mother was an Indian squaw and his father a white man named James Hartley.

As long as anyone could remember, Cuff was a loner, living in a squalid one-room shack outside the city at a point near Albany Street and Brandywine Avenue. The hut was warmed by a small fire laid in Indian fashion in a depression in the earthen floor.

Cuffs features were predominantly those of a red man — a swarthy complexion, hooked nose and long, black hair. He carried his six-foot, seven-inch frame with the dignity of an ambassador but, because he always wore undersized castoff clothing, usually looked as though he were disjointed at the wrists and ankles. A neckerchief was fastened at the throat with a hollow bone.

Winter or summer, he had either galoshes or rubbers on his massive feet, and these he would scuffle ominously in response to any taunts children threw his way.

To adults, he was a hawkish oddity of the human race, a childlike giant who was to be both pitied and respected. In the eyes of the young, he was a freak to be gaped at from a safe distance even though their elders assured them the man was harmless and kindhearted.

It is not known how or when Jim Cuff made his debut as a "herb doctor." His livelihood was the sale of nature's cure for illnesses, in the days when people put more faith in a bottle of "Kikapoo Indian Saqua" than a doctor's advice.

Each morning, from early spring to the first frost, the giant half-breed roamed the Glenville and Rotterdam hills and parts of the bowery woods along the eastern summit of Schenectady. He ranged far and wide in his travels in this area and was known by one and all. Several times a week, he would cross the old Scotia Bridge and walk through the upper reaches of Glenville, collecting herbs on the way. He often stayed for a free lunch at one of the broom corn farms along the Mohawk Turnpike and then fished from the banks of the river before returning home for the night.

He also scoured the wooded areas in the Col. S.R. James' estate (now the site of Coldbrook and Stonegate Manor) and along the Rotterdam river flats of the Campbell Road section in search of roots, herbs and bark. Big Jim established a daily schedule for calling on customers. Many housewives compounded their own favorite home remedies (for coughs, colds, lumbago, arthritis, catarrh and whatever) from Cuffs basket collection.

Once a week he stopped at the home of Dr. Harman Swits at 218 State St. (replaced in 1921 by the Carl Co. building) to deliver a standing order of special herbs.

Later "Jim Cuff's Syrup of Tar and Wild Cherry" was manufactured and bottled by the Orisena Co. with offices at 209 State St. and laboratory at 105 South Ferry St. It was said that Cuff had no interest in the venture, but was pleased merely that the firm chose to use his name.

In those days, many people liked boiled milkweed which was prepared and eaten much the same as spinach. Cuff often picked huge bagsful of the tender common milkweek plants and delivered them regularly on order.

Because he had become a legendary figure years before his death, stories of Jim Cuff still live to enliven the otherwise dull facts of his existence.

His curiosity, like a child, was unbounded. The late Simon Schermerhorn told this story about Cuff which occurred about 1870:

One warm spring day, while gathering herbs in the southwest section of Rotterdam, Cuff walked up to the red schoolhouse (presently the location of the Schonowe School) and poked his head inside a window to see what was going on. He nearly scared the teacher and her charges half out of their wits. With a toothy grin, Cuff doffed his hat and went on his way.

And the late Harman D. Swits Jr. (son of the doctor) who perhaps knew of Cuff's mannerisms and personality better than most, once recalled an incident which combined the herb peddler's curiosity and constant search for respect by fellow citizens:

When Reeves and Luffman (later the Wallace Co.) opened their new store, Jim Cuff was the first to show up. Charles A. Luffman saw him standing in the chill morning air and offered to give him a personal tour through every floor of the building. When it was over, Cuff bowed majestically, shook hands with Luffman and departed.

Mr. Swits also recalled that Cuff often stopped by the county clerk's office, then at 13 Union St., and borrowed pen, ink and paper and solemnly seated himself to "write a letter." Although he was illiterate, Cuff would scribble and blot in thoughtful meditation, finally folding the "letter" and putting it in his pocket as he left the premises.

"How pathetic a figure. . .such fierce pride coupled with such superb dignity," Mr. Swits once remarked.

Cuff was a gentle, law-abiding citizen, probably having learned his lesson from a brush with the law on March 19, 1859. It was noted that day in an edition of the Evening Star:

"James Hartley, alias Jim Cuff, was arrested by a Duanesburg constable and brought to Schenectady bound with ropes today.

"Seems that his love of liquor started the trouble yesterday in a bar there. Big Jim, with his hand kept in a coat pocket as if he held a gun, threatened to 'blow off the head of the first man that touches me.' The constable came up to him and told him to shoot away if he dared.

"Jim sheepishly withdrew his hand from his pocket, his huge fist clenching a corn cob. He pointed it at the constable and then realized resistance was useless and surrendered.

"The constable got with him on the Schoharie stage for the trip to Schenectady and the jail. On the way, Big Jim leaped from the coach and started running as fast as his long legs would take him. However, the constable overtook him and bound Jim's legs this time."

As far as anyone knew, the herb collector was a stranger to any church in town. He often said he could not attend religious meetings because he didn't have fine clothes, adding "but I'll read the 14th and 15th chapters of St. John."

His belief in the hereafter was summed up in his one favorite remark, spoken tonefully in a deep, deliberate voice: "Someday we shall all be in equal skies."

As the years went by and the 19th century neared its close, Schenectady had become so accustomed to the sight of Jim Cuff's long and lean figure that he was as much a part of it as the downtown streets he frequented.

Those of the oldest generation were saying that he had been there when they were children. . . and "no doubt will still be here long after we are gone." Indeed he seemed ageless, some claiming he was at least 80, probably neared 90.

But on Feb. 26, 1893, this item appeared in the Gazette:

"Schenectady's big Indian, Jim Cuff, who has been ill of consumption and lung hemorrhages, was today removed from his hut to the county almshouse on Steuben Street."

He had complained of a "fleece in the heart." A week later, on March 4, Dr. William F. Clute signed a death certificate for "James Cuff Swits" listing pneumonia as the fatal illness. He made a conservative estimate of 72 for the age of the deceased.

Jim Cuff was buried in potters field in Vale Cemetery.

Tom Wallace, a stonecutter in that area and a lifelong friend, erected a small stone at the gravesite. On it he had inscribed a likeness of Cuff's profile and a simple, meaningful epitaph:

"Admitted to that equal sky."

PART EIGHT
On Through The Twenties

A 1918 postcard view showing a night view of State Street looking southward into old Center Street (now Broadway) and the Hotel Mohawk in background.

Quite unlike today's scene, this is the corner of Clinton and State Streets where Schenectady Savings Bank was built in 1905. The building shown here on the site just before it was demolished in 1904 was last used as a private residence by William Van Vranken. Before that it was a hotel, first the Munro House, then the Columbian Hotel.

278

37—Havens by the Wayside

$\mathcal{T}$he old inns, taverns and hotels are as much a part of Schenectady's past as its grist mills, broom factories and railway stations. They were an important segment of the growth factor of the old Dutch town, not to mention the social amenities they provided.

Since this volume deals with the period between 1880 and 1930, we will not go into detail here on the proliferation of taverns and wayside inns which occurred soon after the establishment of such as Douw Auke's Tavern just outside the stockade near where Mill Lane is now located or Robert Clench's "Sign of the Crossed Keys" which was about opposite the present downtown YMCA. Many proprietors simply opened their "drawing rooms" to the public for the convenience of turnpike travelers and, of course, to reap some profits from thirsty in-towners. Therefore, a long list of taverns with boarding accommodations has been handed down to us, a subject which perhaps can be dealt with later.

However, before taking into account those hotels which were established at or about the turn of this century, we would like to mention some of the more prominent spots which offered food, drink and bed to weary travelers passing through Schenectady during the mid-19th century and, in some cases, for some time after.

There was the Lottridge House on State Street, just above Nott Terrace. Formerly the William Van Vranken residence, the building became the Munro House, then the Columbian Hotel at the corner of State and Clinton Streets before in 1905 it became the Schenectady Savings Bank.

The Myer's House, formerly the Sharratt House, was in the Myer's Block on State Street just below the present State Arcade. The Temperance House, which catered to non-drinking railroad travelers, was located across the ground level tracks at the southwest corner of Liberty and Maiden Lane (now North Broadway.) Directly across from it was the Germania Hotel and later, run by Charles Wieneke, Wiencke's Tavern.

The Gilmore House was located on Washington Avenue near Water Street, close to the present armory site. Freeman's House was at the foot of State Street about where the entrance of the Western Gateway Bridge was constructed.

Just before and after the turn of this century, the Hotel Majestic was operated by P.J. Sullivan at 6-8 Water Street off lower State Street. It was a four-story brick building, containing 50 rooms, a cafe, a pool room and dining hall.

Today's impressive Masonic Temple building at State Street and Erie Boulevard was also a hotel site back in the days when the Erie Canal was in existence and that corner was known as State Street at Dock Street. Beginning with the opening of the canal in 1825, a wood frame building was erected as the Schuyler Inn, later to pass into other hands and successive name changes as the Putnam, Fuller and Germond Hotel. Finally, it was purchased by Isaac Ledyard who had it the longest as the City Hotel when it became a popular dining and meeting place until Arthur Brown purchased it in 1872 for his furniture store, where it ultimately became the present Masonic Temple building.

Some people today can still recall an old tavern up on the State Street hill between what is now Steuben and Martin Streets, the present site of the Viking's Restaurant. It was run by Louis Hildebrandt and for many years, until shortly after the turn of this century, provided a resting spot for the coach passengers on the old Albany Turnpike.

There are also many around today who will remember the Vendome Hotel, once located on the northeastern corner of State and Broadway (where Woolworth's store was situated and in business until 1994).

It was an impressive looking structure, its brick exterior painted white until sandblasted to a natural finish shortly before its demise in 1938. Basically, the old inn was three floors in both directions as it straddled the corner with a six-story clock tower at the apex. It was this ornamental cupola which made the Vendome a landmark for Schenectadians from the time it was remodeled from the Barhydt House in 1895.

That corner of State and Broadway (once called Center Street) occupied the ancient tavern site of Gilbert, Shields and other notable innkeepers dating back some 200 years. From 1878 to 1890, Andrew Devendorf operated the Carley House which he had built on that corner. John C. Myers' Ellis House was to the east of it on State Street. Then Charles Barhydt took over the Carley in 1891 and ran it until 1895 under the name Barhydt House.

H.A. Peck was the first proprietor of the Vendome and was succeeded by Edwin Clute in 1903. Clute, who had been proprietor of the Ellis House from 1900 to 1903, managed the Vendome until he left in 1907 to become proprietor of the Edison Hotel.

William Gleason later became manager of the Vendome and it was he who hired a string trio, directed by Stephen St. John, to play soft dinner music to the delight of the patrons.

Commercial establishments occupied the ground floor of the Vendome throughout its 42-year tenure in Schenectady. The first to move in when the renovated hotel opened in 1896 were William Sauter's drug store, Solomon's drygoods store and Herman's barbershop. In later years, up to the time it was razed, first floor shopkeepers were those of Edison Hats, Schenectady Public Market and Jay Jewelers.

When it became apparent in 1936 that the Vendome was to be torn down, there was considerable agitation to have the city consider widening Broadway from State to Union but it never materialized. The five-and-dime emporium replaced the Vendome in 1938.

The Columbus Hotel was at Union Street and Romeyn (now North Barrett) Street. The Millard Hotel, opposite the old station just west of the tracks, offered "meals and lodgings at 25 cents each" in the 1860s.

Samuel Wingate was proprietor of the popular Merchant's Hotel on the northern side of State Street between Ferry and Church Streets, its huge yard and row of stables making it an especially attractive stopover for farmers who drive into town with their produce to be sold in the early morning hours. (The old hotel building was razed in 1938.)

For years, up until 1904, the Wasson brothers ran the Park Hotel at the corner of State and Barrett Streets. It was a rambling two-story wood structure, complete with a saloon and lodging quarters.

Back around the time of the Civil War, and even a decade before, there was a cluster of hotels about the railroad crossing on State Street. We mentioned the Carley House earlier. That same building, from about 1850 to 1875, was once the Eagle Hotel. Just east of it was the Ellis House and then the American Hotel. To the west, next to the railroad tracks, was Drullard's Hotel run by Nathaniel Drullard. Before the crossings were raised after 1900, Drullard's Hotel had been taken over mainly by the railroad for offices. Across the street of the former Gazette Building, stood the Davis House at the time of the Civil War, run by Harvey Davis. Earlier, it was known as the Railroad House.

A popular tavern and hotel for many years was the Twoomey House, located on the point at Broadway and old Kruesi Avenue next to the railroad overpass. It was run by John Twoomey and later by his widow, Clara. The old building was taken down in the early 1960s.

The Curtis House, at Washington Avenue and Fuller Street, near the carbarn, later became known as the Roosevelt Hotel and it, too, was razed in the 1960's when the traffic interchange was being built in that vicinity.

In 1914, Isaac Hough (pronounced "Huff") a Schenectady realtor, took a gamble on rebuilding the property on the southeast corner of State Street and Broadway...and, as it turned out, he lost. Hough bought the old three-story commercial building and had it entirely remodeled inside and out, even adding a story. It was widely advertised that first year as "a hotel with most desirable accommodations, a lobby on the main street, 50 cozy furnished rooms with hot and cold water on every floor." The guests were asked to pay $4 to $6 weekly or $1 a day and up.

The two top floors remained unused for many years, the others gradually being rented as office and store space. And so it stands yet today, a rather attractive building of stylish architecture but not used to any great extent.

St. Clair's Hotel, a moderate-priced inn for men's lodgings, was located on old Center Street just below Liberty Street until those buildings on the northeast corner were razed in the late 1940s.

The Crown Hotel was built on Wall Street, corner of Liberty Street, on the site of the burned out Maxon Block in 1906. It was billed as "a commercial man's home" and hoped to capitalize on the business to be brought in by the new railroad depot across the street. Frank J. Khuen was its proprietor. However, it did not do as well as expected and in a short while its lower floor was leased out to businesses. By 1925, it had ceased operations altogether as a hotel. This was one of the buildings razed in 1970 on that block and the site is now part of the parking lot there.

Resolve Givens built a handsome three-story brick hotel building in 1843 facing the railroad tracks with side entrances on State and Wall Streets. The Givens Hotel enjoyed the reputation for many years of being the most popular eating and rooming house in town. It was in front of the Givens' porticoed front that President-elect Abraham Lincoln's Washington-bound train stopped on Feb.18, 1861, and where he addressed a large throng of people curious to see the man who was to face troublesome times. Here, too, was the hotel where Thomas A. Edison stayed for the night during his first visit to Schenectady in 1886 to see the property which was to become the Edison General Electric Co.

It was this spot—where the Givens Hotel was located—a hotel corporation chose for the proposed new Edison Hotel only two years after the inventor set up shop here. The Givens was torn down in 1889 and by the following year the brand new Edison took its place. It was four and one-half stories high and of red brick construction. It featured modern conveniences, even fire escapes and advertised "Every room an outside room." One of the rooms, more elaborately furnished than the others, was at first reserved for Edison's visits to Schenectady—which turned out to be infrequent. Edison's first stay at the new hotel was in October, 1890.

For several years, the curious domed cupola of the Edison and the peaked roof of the Vendome dominated the skyline of Schenectady's downtown area. Both were gone by the end of the 1930s.

Incidentally, the lower two floors of the old Edison Hotel were kept intact and remain today in that block, since called the Cushing Building, between the railroad trestle and Wall Street.

The Mohawk Hotel & Baths was constructed in 1907 a few doors in from State Street on what was then called Center Street, now Broadway. Several years later, the hotel was doubled in size and while it was well patronized it never quite enjoyed the popularity of the Edison Hotel. The Hotel Mohawk's ballroom was frequently used by civic groups for meetings and it was here, in 1917, that Schenectady Rotary Club held its first weekly meeting. In later years it was renamed Hotel Schenectady but most referred to it as Hotel Mohawk. It was closed in 1962 and, after several fires, was demolished in December 1977.

The Foster Hotel, one of the few still remaining, was built in 1910 next to the Schenectady Railway Company's new waiting room near the corner of Lafayette and State. Its primary objective was to corral as much business as possible from those interurban travelers who might have missed their trolley connections or were on business trips. Its main function today is as an apartment building.

It was the construction of the Hotel Van Curler in 1925 that caused the biggest stir in Schenectady. It was a hotel to be proud of, situated as it was next to what was to become the Great Western Gateway Bridge and on a newly widened Washington Avenue. A lot of private citizens bought stock in the hotel company, enthused over the future of Schenectady and all that was going on at the time.

The Van Curler came to be the focal point for most large civic gatherings, the huge ballroom and solarium being able to accommodate more people than was possible at any of the other hotel dining halls. Little wonder that shortly after the Van Curler began operations, the fortunes of the Edison Hotel and Hotel Mohawk began to dwindle.

The fates were kinder to the Van Curler Hotel. The influx of motels into the city spelled its doom fully 20 years ago, despite a brave attempt by the corporation to rekindle business by means of a huge addition. There was little surprise but a certain sadness within the city when, on the evening of Feb. 2, 1968, the Van Curler closed its doors as a hotel for all time.

However, it was rescued from obscurity, and possibly demolition, by the action of the Schenectady County Board of Supervisors. Looking ahead to making it the site of its proposed community college, the county purchased the bankrupt hotel four months later for $710,000. A few days later, on June ll, 1968, a public auction was held during which all of the hotel furnishings from the speaker's podium in the ballroom down to the last pot and pan from the kitchen were sold for $2,000.

The hotel was redesigned for use as a central college building (a major project which involved tearing out all room partitions of the floors above ground level for classroom construction) and opened in September, 1969, as Schenectady County Community College. The college facilities have been enlarged several times and the parking lots have spread outward over what was once the Binnekill and the Mohawk River's Van Slyck Island.

The Schenectady County Community College has come a long way since it opened in the fall of 1969 in what once was the Van Curler Hotel. Above new students entering the front entrance with vigor on "Orientation Day", Sept. 4, 1989.

38—The Noblest Calling of Them All

ELLIS HOSPITAL

*T*he history of Ellis Hospital goes back to Christmas Day, 1885, when the Schenectady Free Dispensary opened at 408 Union Street, just two doors above the Mercy Hospital (now the location of Spencer's Business Institute).

When Charles Ellis, president of the American Locomotive Works, died in 1890, it was found that his will bequeathed the sum of $25,000 to be used in establishing Ellis Hospital in memory of his father, John Ellis, the founder of Alco. So it was that on March 27, 1893, the hospital moved into an attractive three-story brick building on Jay Street adjacent to and north of the old City Hall which had been built in 1880. Both of these structures were razed in 1929 when that whole block was leveled to make way for the present City Hall building.

It wasn't long, however, before the hospital board of managers decided that the growing city needed more space and a modernly-equipped hospital. In April, 1903, the board sold the Jay Street building to the city (which later used it as a City Hall annex) and applied the proceeds toward a hospital building fund. After a thorough survey of available property, the board decided on a site at Nott Street and Rosa Road.

Contracts for the new hospital were let in December, 1904, and construction began in May the following year. The cost of the hospital complex — a main building and two wings — plus furnishings came to what was then a sizable sum of $165,000.

At the same time, a two-floor brick building also was constructed to house the nurses and trainees of the new hospital. Joseph W. Smitley (who married the widow of John C. Ellis and lived in the Ellis Mansion at Union Street and Nott Terrace which today is the St. John the Evangelist Church rectory) was then president of the hospital board of managers. He and his brother, John H. Smitley of Pittsburgh, provided the $15,000 to build and furnish the nurses' home in memory of their mother, Keziah Whitmore Smitley. She was born in Pittsburgh in 1814, married John Smitley in 1832 and died in Pittsburgh in 1893.

Thus the nurses' home became known as Whitmore Home and lasted until 1973 when it was deemed hazardous and no longer of use to the hospital. In its place is an employees' parking lot.

On Saturday, Oct. 10, 1906, the public was invited to tour the new Ellis Hospital from 1 to 6 and 7 to 9 p.m. The hospital and equipment were not complete in every detail but was ready for use. The following Monday morning, patients were moved from the old Jay Street building up to the new facility.

The Schenectady Railway Company's newly-completed street car lines made the hospital easily accessible to the public, a factor which convinced the board of managers that the decision to buy the spacious site was not at all unrealistic — even though people were saying at the time that the hospital was "way out of town."

For the next few years, the women's auxiliary of Ellis Hospital conducted "Red Tag Days" to assist the hospital building fund. They solicited funds each morning and night from the workers of GE and Alco and also from downtown shoppers. Each person who donated was given a red tag for his lapel. The women who collected wore red cross arm badges and carried red-sealed boxes.

Veeder and Yelverton's downtown drug store joined in the day's activities by offering a "Tag Day" sundae, a "delicious ice cream combination." For every one sold, five cents went to the Ellis Hospital building fund.

MERCY HOSPITAL

Even though Ellis Hospital was in operation, the physicians of Schenectady were all too aware that hospital services were far from adequate for a community whose population by 1910 had tripled that of 1880. Therefore, a group of doctors formed what was known in 1911 as Physicians' Hospital and leased the old Maxon House at 404 Union Street, next to Kerste's Drug Store, for the operation. Dr. E. MacDonald Stanton was named president of the group, Dr. J. H. Collins was secretary, Dr. J. J. O'Brian was treasurer and Julia A. Littlefield was hospital superintendent.

Tag Days were held throughout the city, much like the ones staged by Ellis Hospital in its drives for building funds, to help finance operation of Physicians' Hospital. In 1913, the project was incorporated and it then became known as Mercy Hospital, located at the same address. It was a well-run hospital, even though there was limited room space and an inadequate operating room. A horse-drawn ambulance was on call.

Ellis Hospital, however, grew to such proportions in medical and surgical efficiency and with greatly enlarged quarters by 1917 that Mercy Hospital decided to close that year.

GLENRIDGE HOSPITAL

Tuberculosis still was one of the nation's leading killers and treatment of the disease was in its clinical stages when ground was broken in the summer of 1911 for construction of the first permanent "TB" sanitarium in Schenectady County.

The County Board of Supervisors awarded a $35,472 contract for general construction of the buildings to James H. Johnson, low bidder. The hospital was to be built on the old Lamp farm between Hetcheltown and Glenridge Roads.

Opening ceremonies were held on Aug. 3, 1912. It was then called the Schenectady County Tuberculosis Hospital and was the exact site of the present Glenridge Hospital. The original sanitarium consisted of a wood frame administration building and several small "cure cottages" scattered about the grounds.

Within 15 years, however, the facilities were declared wholly inadequate for the increasing number of patients being treated. So, on June 14, 1927, the Board of Supervisors voted in favor of floating the first of six bond issues for the cost of construction and equipment of a new hospital.

The Glenridge Hospital building was completed and occupied in 1919. Its services were enhanced in 1938 by the construction of additional buildings, but it was the establishment of the diagnostic and treatment clinic in 1968 which propelled the hospital to an unusual type of medical service geared to the times. It definitely affected and reduced the need for extensive hospital care, for one thing. And it provided complete diagnostic examination and treatment at one sitting, for another.

It was set up in an attractive brick building once the nurses' quarters on the eastern portion of the well kept grounds. Largely through a generous endowment by the late John G. Smith, who had been a patient at Glenridge, the building was renovated throughout and modern equipment installed.

Actually, the treatment of tubercular patients was begun in Schenectady by the local American Red Cross chapter in 1907 when it established a summer day camp off Duane Avenue to provide some comfort to area residents afflicted by the dread disease. It was then considered a terminal illness. The "ozone" or open-air treatment was the only effective means known then to prolong the lives of those unlucky enough to have contracted tuberculosis. Death by tuberculosis was between 50 and 90 percent certain in those days, usually within a five-year span.

But then the county government stepped in to join the fight when in 1909 it leased a building in Aqueduct for the treatment of tuberculosis patients. The place burned down in 1911, however, and this set the stage for the permanent sanitarium on Glenridge Road.

It was when Dr. James M. Blake joined the Glenridge staff in 1934 and became its fourth medical director three years later that Glenridge became one of the leading sanitariums on the country. In 1976, as president of the American Medical Association, he was able to make the following statement in his annual report to the Board of Managers:

"This year, in reality, marks the accomplishment of that goal which some 20 years ago was only a hope and a dream; that is, the control of tuberculosis. We have now reached that point of time in history when tuberculosis in our community is no longer an endemic disease and can no longer be considered a significant public health problem. Tuberculosis is now only a sporadic disease taking its place among major diseases of the past such as typhoid fever, smallpox and poliomyelitis which have been conquered primarily through research and efforts of American medicine".

Dr. Blake's long career of 44 years at Glenridge Hospital and Diagnostic Center ended with the closing of the facility in 1978. The premises were taken over several years later by Conifer Park, mainly a drug and alcoholic addiction treatment center. One of its first tributes made to Dr. Blake once the facility was established was Conifer Park's dedication of one of the buildings to be known as The Blake Wing.

ST. CLARE'S HOSPITAL

St. Clare's Hospital does not fall within the category of the history of 1880 to 1930, having been built 1948-49, but we would be remiss in not giving it mention in this segment on general hospitals in Schenectady.

It has certainly played a significant part in local hospital service in the relatively brief time it has been on the scene, providing excellent hospital facilities and care at a time when there came a growing need for more institutions of mercy.

On June 13, 1948, in the hilly portion of McClellan Street which was one of the last bastions of the old pitch pine forest of this area, the late Bishop Edmund Gibbons presided over the cornerstone ceremonies of the new hospital. Twenty-five years later, on June 7, 1973, another cornerstone ceremony was held on the premises, this to be officiated by Bishop Edwin B. Broderick of the Albany Catholic Diocese, chairman of the hospital's board of trustees.

Already underway that year was a multi-million dollar addition which would more than double the size of the original institution. The people of Schenectady, as they had done a quarter of a century before, responded generously to the hospital's fund-raising campaign, in no small way recognizing the worth of a medical facility which since its inception cared for more than a several million persons.

The hospital has been enlarged several times over since its beginning...and is still growing with the most modern equipment, clinics, personnel, and patients.

Construction of St. Clare's Hospital off McClellan Street was under way when this photo was made in January 1947.

(1) The Vendome Hotel in 1932, four years before it was razed for construction of the Woolworth department store on that corner. (2) The old Twoomey House on Broadway at former Kruesi Avenue. It was a familiar fixture until removed in the early 1960s. (3) The Edison Hotel was built on site of the Givens Hotel in 1890 and for several years was Schenectady's leading hotel.

(1) An early view of Louie Hildebrandt's Hotel, located atop State Street hill until after turn of this century. (2) The Lorraine Block, in right background, is prominent in this 1907 view of State Street from Crescent Park. Wasson's Park House is this side of it, at Barrett Street corner. In far left background can be seen the new Parker Building.

(1) The Crown Hotel was built in 1906 at the corner of Liberty and Wall Streets opposite the railroad station but did not make the grade as a commercial hostelry. It was razed in 1971 with other buildings in that block. (2) The celebrated Hotel Van Curler on the night of Feb 2, 1968, when it closed its doors as a hotel after 43 years. (Photo courtesy Sid Brown).

(1) The Ellis Hospital used this building on Jay Street from 1893 until its Nott Street site was opened in 1906. Later it was used as the City Hall annex. (2) Mercy Hospital began operations in a two-story brick residence next to Kerste's Drug Store in 1911 but closed in 1917. (3) Schenectady was proud of the new Ellis Hospital when it was constructed "way out" on Nott Street by 1906.

(1) Tubercular patients receiving the "ozone treatment" on the porch of the tuberculosis sanitarium in Aqueduct in 1910. When the facility burned in 1911, Glenridge Hospital was built. (2) Long-skirted women shoppers on State Street near Ferry Street corner about 1900. Barney's is in right background. (3) The original Schenectady YMCA building, constructed by 1875, at the southeast corner of State and South Ferry Streets. Part of the building still remains.

(1) Crowds gathered along State Street to watch first contingent of Schenectady draftees leaving for camp early in summer of 1917. The scene is at Clinton Street opposite the Lorraine Block. (2) Scene at Edison Avenue freight yards as relatives bid goodbye to more draftees leaving for Fort Devens, Mass., the morning of Sept. 5, 1917.

(1) "Twenty thousand strong" at the third Liberty Loan rally at GE's main gate, spring of 1918. (2) Red Cross campaign meeting at foot of Crescent Park, summer of 1917. Note trolley waiting room at right.

(1) Exuberant parade still going on along lower State Street the afternoon of Nov. 11, 1918, celebrating the war's end. (2) Doughboys assigned to cantonment at end of Campbell Avenue crowd aboard bench car to reach their destination, 1918.

(1) Grim procession up State Street as first of World War I dead arrived in Schenectady, spring of 1920. (2) Fall of 1928 in downtown Schenectady with Al Smith campaign banner in full prominence. Former Union National Bank building is at left and Gazette building in center.

(1) Great Western Gateway Bridge under construction, Aug. 20, 1923. Binnekill is in foreground, while in left background can be seen the old Island Park. (2) "Dead Man's" curve being constructed in 1923. (Photo courtesy of Nick Dinardo). (3) The tragic bridge cave-in on Scotia end of bridge work, Sept. 17, 1923.

(1) Calvin Coolidge, symbolic of the "good times" period of the Roaring Twenties, is shown with his father and mother in this informal photograph made at the family home in Plymouth Notch, Vt., in 1918 when "Silent Cal" was elected governor of Massachusetts. Photo was presented to the late Surrogate William W. Campbell by Col. John Calvin Coolidge shortly after he administered the presidential oath to his son in 1923 upon the death of Warren G. Harding. The ceremony took place by kerosene lamplight in the sitting room of the Vermont homestead.

HOTEL HOUGH

WILLIAM MACHIN, Mgr.

RATE BY THE DAY, WEEK OR MONTH

Centrally Located One Minute from N. Y. C. Depot

Comfort and Cleanliness   European Plan   Elevator Service

Phones 1298 and 4357

Cor. State and Broadway   **SCHENECTADY, N. Y.**

Room by Day, Week or Month

HOTEL EDISON

JOHN H. MEEHAN, Manager

The Largest Rooms of Any Hotel in the City

With or Without Baths

Large Sample Rooms with Plenty of Sunshine

Every Room an Outside Room

313–315 State Street   **SCHENECTADY, N. Y.**

(1) Hotel advertising in the 1926 Schenectady city directory. By this time, the Hotel Van Curler had already established itself firmly as the premier hotel in town.

The first piece of steel to raise the superstructure of the St. Clare's Hospital $14 million expansion was swung into place on Dec. 7, 1972, marking the start of the building that more than doubled the community health care facility on McClellan Street. Msgr. Howard F. Manny (above), president of the board of trustees, tightened a special chrome-plated bolt to affix the girder in place at the easternmost corner of the one-story deep foundation to signal the completion of that phase in the rebuilding.

39—YMCA-YWCA in Schenectady

The first Young Men's Christian Association meetings were held in Schenectady in 1857 by a small group of citizens and the following year the YMCA was organized under the leadership of Professor John Newman of Union College. For a time, the group met in the Clute Building at 202 State St.

The project was abandoned during the Civil War years, but again took hold by 1867 when a constitution was adopted and a charter was granted by the state legislature. Nicholas Cain was elected president and rooms were rented in Van Horne Hall (now the site of the Schenectady Savings and Loan). Interest in the newly-formed group widened and by 1871, the sum of $40,000 was subscribed for the construction of a YMCA headquarters to be built at the southeastern corner of State and Ferry Streets (which site was purchased for $9,000). This was the building which in later years was occupied by S.R. James' crockery firm on the ground floor.

Through the years, Schenectady YMCA has grown steadily. Possibly its biggest year was 1925, when it was successful in raising $625,000 for construction of a modern association building at 13 State St. — the one standing today. It was completed by late 1927 and dedicated on Jan. 28, 1928.

It has spread out from its downtown headquarters. There are branches in Rotterdam, Mont Pleasant and Glenville; summer camps at Camp Chingachgook at Lake George, Tippecanoe in Rotterdam and the Bouquet River Lodge near Elizabethtown. The downtown building was renovated in 1969 at a cost of $800,000. Peter Pink is current executive director.

The Young Women's Christian Association was organized in Schenectady early in 1888 at a meeting of 44 women in the chapel of the First Presbyterian Church under the leadership of Mrs. Jay Westinghouse, Mrs. Frank Atwell and Mrs. John Westinghouse. Mrs. Maurice Perkins was the first president of Schenectady YWCA.

In July of that year, the YWCA rented rooms in the DeForest Building at 135 Jay St. It set up a program of classes in bookkeeping, stenography, Bible study, English, embroidery, China painting, physical culture and social evenings for employed girls. There was also a "noon rest hour" supervised by Mrs. Thomas Yelverton and Mrs. John Wiederhold.

The group was incorporated as the Young Women's Christian Association of Schenectady in 1892 and Miss E. L. Freeman was employed as general secretary with rented rooms at 242 State St.

The Schenectady YWCA purchased a building at 14 State St. in the Westinghouse block (now the park across from the YMCA building) in 1898. In 1926, it purchased the Washington Avenue property and on Jan. 28, 1931, dedicated the present Colonial style headquarters located at 44 Washington Avenue. William Dalton was chairman of the YWCA building committee.

Its current executive director is Mrs. Lola M. Weeks, who has held that post since January, 1969. She had been physical education director there since 1953.

Schenectady celebrants are shown whooping it up in the Monday morning of Nov. 11, 1918 after news of the World War I armistice was received here. This is a view of the paraders making their way up Dock Street toward State Street. The Erie Canal, now the boulevard, is at right.

40—The Big War

$\mathcal{T}$he people of Schenectady, like those of any other community in the United States, were hoping against hope that this nation would not be directly involved in the war which had been raging in Europe since 1914...but there was a general feeling that unless hostilities abated, it would in fact become a world war.

Woodrow Wilson had been reelected in 1916 on the conviction that "he kept us out of war" and yet the electorate understood that the patience of a president could be extended just so far. The German U-boat raids on shipping on the high seas at a cost of many American lives, the reported atrocities of the "Huns" against humanity in Europe and the spy cases uncovered in America in 1916 and early 1917 provoked an antipathy towards Kaiser Wilhelm and the Teutonic order.

By April, 1917, the war in Europe had come to an absolute stalement as England and France on the western front swapped lives on a mammoth scale with Germany on the other. President Wilson, finally exasperated by the admitted proposal by Germany to ally with Mexico in war against the U.S., went before Congress and was fully supported in his request for a declaration of war on Germany. The nation, which rallied behind his speech, was about to leave the complacent horse-and-buggy 19th century and emerge in the 20th, virtually against its will, as the most powerful country in the world.

From that time on, Schenectady changed too, shaken from the comfortable status of a fast-growing city involved in community progress to a new awareness that it was an important part of a national effort to help set aright a world that had gone beserk. It was called the World War with a slogan that its victory by the allies would "make the world safe for democracy." No matter that the country was not prepared to join in the horrible contest in Europe, the United States and its people nevertheless were now determined to wage it until the end.

What happened in Schenectady after the declaration of war until the dramatic armistice more than a year and a half later probably was typical of other cities across the nation, except that its war industry (General Electric, American Locomotive Co. and, later, the Army Supply Depot) placed its importance in a special category.

Aside from the wartime trauma of watching sons, husbands and fathers leave for the service, worrying about their welfare, waiting for their letters and keeping track of the daily war news with some trepidation, there was the need to do everything physically possible to help the war effort on the home front. And there was much to be asked of the citizenry, more than possibly had been anticipated by the most ardent patriot.

More and more women left the kitchens at home for jobs on the outside, including the factories, offices and even the streetcars where some of them took over as conductors to replace men who were now in the military. Overtime, on Sundays and holidays and weekdays, was now to be expected.

People were urged to do without butter, rather to use oleomargarine in order that animal fats could be diverted to glycerine needed for explosives. They were asked to practice "Hoover economy" (Herbert

Hoover was the wartime food administrator) and also cut down on the use of sugar and flour, even when it was available. The folks back home didn't mind this too much because they were told it was for "the boys overseas." There was later some grumbling, however, among those who received letters from their fighting doughboys to the effect that "we never see any of that stuff over here."

Coal was saved by regulating elevator service and, later in the war, by establishing "heatless Mondays" for all factories, businesses and public buildings. Pocketknife styles were reduced from 600 to 154 to save on steel. Baby carriages were standardized, also saving metal. The length of shoe uppers was cut down to save on leather and travelers were limited to one suitcase (salesmen to two trunks) in order to save on shipping space on the overburdened railroads. About 75,000 tons of tin a year was saved by eliminating its use in toys.

Schenectadians responded generously to the U.S. Navy's nationwide appeal for citizen donations of binoculars. More than 50 pairs were turned over within one week in January, 1918, for service in the war.

Special appeals were made for the purchase of Liberty Bonds—right up to the Fourth Victory Bond Drive in September, 1918, when Schenectady's quota was set at $5 million — and war saving stamps called Thrift Stamps at a quarter each. There were funds galore for the war effort, one of which was "Our Boys In France Tobacco Fund" to raise money to send cigarettes, cigars and pipe tobacco to the "Fighting Sammies" abroad. There was hardly a meeting, concert or theater performance without someone passing the hat for one of the war funds.

"Do Your Bit," exhorted a government ad in newspapers and magazines. "We've all got to get together and not just do our bit but every bit we can!"

Schenectady Mayor Charles A. Simon, early in 1918, appointed a committee to raise $500 for a group of Schenectady recruits whose personal belongings were destroyed in a New Year's night fire at Camp Devens, Mass. It was raised, and more, before the week was out.

The coal shortage became critical during the early months of 1918 and it resulted in an order by Dr. Harry A. Garfield, administrator of the national fuel office, for a general shutdown of industrial plants, offices and theaters east of the Mississippi for five days beginning Jan. 18 that year. This did not apply to war contract plants such as GE and Alco in Schenectady. All wholesale and retail stores dealing in food were closed Mondays at noon from Jan. 28 to March 25.

Even the Schenectady Railway Co. got into the fuel conservation program by rescheduling its stops up to but not more than 700 feet apart. Barrels were also placed at strategic spots along State Street with signs asking the public to save all peach stones and to place them in the barrels. They were to be used to make filters in gas masks.

Victory or "war" gardens brought out an army of amateur gardeners who sought to abide by the federal appeal for "a garden in every backyard" to lessen home consumption of staple foods needed for the troops and allies overseas. A city garden club was formed in Schenectady to advise greenhorn gardeners in the homegrown project.

The war songs played a part in bolstering patriotic fervor at home as well as in the cantonments and at the front. "Tipperary" was high on the list of favorites, along with Geoffrey O'Hara's stutterer, "K-K-K-Katy" and "There's a Long, Long Trail A-winding." Then there was "Roses of Picardy," "Goodbye Broadway, Hello France," "How're You Going to Keep Them Down on the Farm (after they've seen Paree)," "Over There," "Good Morning, Mr. Zip, Zip Zip," "Madamoiselle from Armentieres" and "Pack Up Your Troubles in Your Old Kit Bag."

The dawning of 1918 was not a happy time anywhere in America because there was the worry about the German counter-attacks and a fear that still enough was not being done on the homefront to bring victory to the allies. Even then, some war experts were predicting that the conflict might drag on another two or three years before the Kaiser could be brought to his knees.

Little wonder that the Gazette reported on the morning of Jan. 2, 1918, that "Schenectady had one of its quietest New Year's eves on record yesterday. There were a few on the street after midnight and little hilarity was visible at any time.

There was a patriotic spirit inherent in the graduation exercises of Schenectady High School held Jan. 29, 1918, in the Union College gymnasium. The interior was decorated in red, white and blue, with American flags everywhere, some school banners and potted palms on the raised platform. Rev. Eugene Noble, pastor of First Methodist Church, gave the invocation after the singing of the national anthem. Ralph Kingsley Chase won the speaking prize for boys with his oration of "The People of the U.S." by Grover Cleveland and Margaret Murphy won the prize for girls with "Spreading the News." Superintendent of Schools O.W. Kuolt presented the diplomas and noted that four of the graduates were in military service — Fred Elting, Paul Baumler, Daniel Campbell and John Osterberg. Their diplomas were given to members of the family. Principal E. R. Whitney, who would soon succeed Dr. Kuolt as school superintendent, presented the prizes.

The year 1918 wore on steadily, wearily and apprehensively as the news from the front fluctuated between good and bad. There seemed no hope during the first part of that year of the war ending soon because the German troops mounted several offensives after they had been beaten back. Both sides dug in for what seemed would be a long and costly war.

Schenectadians continued to work long hours at the factories and other places of business. They watched movies or played records for relaxation, contributed to war funds and supported the latest Liberty Bond drive. The various branches of the service did their bit to keep citizen patriotism at high level by bringing in bemedaled war heroes to speak at bond rallies and displaying such things as tanks, armament and captured German war relics in downtown Schenectady. After one bond rally in front of GE's main gate on a pleasant noon-day break in mid-June, a parade was formed (with appropriate banners and signs) and the workers marched along Dock Street up to the State Street canal bridge to show their unrestrained enthusiasm for supporting the war effort.

There were many evening orations, held in the various theaters and halls, by politicians, clergymen, civic leaders and military personnel. At one of these, Congressman George R. Lunn told his audience at the

Van Curler Opera House late in September, 1918, that the allies were slowly but surely edging the Germans closer to surrender. He called for absolute capitulation when the time came, saying "We will take the Kaiser's sword, but never his bloody hand."

Dr. Lunn was by now a staunch Democrat, having forsaken the Socialists in 1916, and it was thought he would remain in Washington for some time. In his first term of office, he had become an influential member of the House Military Affairs Committee and chairman of the sub-committee on barracks and cantonments. However, he was beaten in a close election on Nov. 5 by Republican Frank Crowther for the 30th congressional district. So Dr. Lunn returned to Schenectady and later won two more mayoral elections.

The people were still being asked to scrimp on certain foodstuffs, grow their victory gardens and save on fuel of all kinds. The government instituted "gasless Sundays" in the spring of 1918 to save gasoline for the war machines. Those who owned automobiles cooperated only half-heartedly with the order, however, since it carried no penalties and some of the motorists figured a Sunday afternoon was the only opportunity they had to take a drive into the country.

A public protest was made against the Schenectady Railway Co. in the fall of 1918 when that company sought to raise its fares for inner city travel from five to six cents. The reason given was that the War Labor Board had awarded SRC employees a raise so that they would now receive a minimum 48 cents an hour instead of 43 cents. Those who rode the trolleys to and from work—and there were many—complained that raising the fares was, in effect, against the war effort and many threatened to walk or ride bicycles if the company persisted in its "greedy ways." In the end, the request was withdrawn and city trolley fares would remain at a nickel for several years to come.

Then came the dreadful outbreak of Spanish influenza and pneumonia, which was at its worst in October, 1918, and lasted until just after Christmas. It was prevalent in the northeastern U.S. and New York State was one of the hardest hit. There were hundreds of cases of the flu in Schenectady and many died. Area schools were closed for two weeks in mid-October, theaters were closed to children and the local health officer warned against overcrowding of trolley cars. So, while the war news was getting better, the people back home were now fearful of an unseen enemy, a dread disease.

Pneumonia struck down the beloved pastor of Zion Lutheran Church on Oct. 12. Rev. Louis Schulze had been ill but a few days, and his death brought sadness to his congregation and the city. He had been with the church 38 years, coming to it when it was located on Jay Street just in from State and saw it move into the big new church building up on Nott Terrace. He had been active in civic affairs and was well liked by a wide segment of Schenectady. Because of the epidemic, a private funeral was held for Reverend Schulze at the parsonage, then located at 151 Nott Terrace.

On Thursday, Nov. 7, the premature announcement of an armistice in Europe brought forth some street frolicking and bell-ringing in Schenectady for a few hours before extra newspaper editions corrected the error which somehow had been flashed from Paris. (New York City went wild when the false news was first spread and did not subside for that day, even when the correction was made public.) The newspapers had been filled with news of an impending cease-fire for several days before the "fake" armistice, so there was every reason to believe it had taken place. Of course there was disappointment over the turn of events, but the feeling persisted that it was only a momentary delay, that the real end of the war was close at hand.

Then it came, and it literally caught the citizenry of Schenectady napping. The word was flashed over the wireless and received in the offices of the Schenectady Gazette at precisely 2:50 a.m. All hostilities were to cease at 6 a.m. Washington time (11 a.m. Paris time.)

The Gazette rushed the good news out to the streets just before 3:30 and extras soon followed to be rushed to the neighborhood sectors by those bearers of good tidings, the newspaperboys. Late shift workers bought them up and rushed home to tell their families, but there were countless "sleeping" citizens who heard the cries of "Extra . . . the war's over. . . read all about it!" and had rushed out in their nightclothes to buy the paper.

Within the hour, people in all stations of life joined in one of the wildest, most joyous celebrations downtown Schenectady has ever seen. They came down from the hills of Mont Pleasant and Bellevue, down from the upper reaches of State Street and Union Street, from the Goose Hill section of the Second Ward, from the stockade area and "flockie" district of the First Ward, from the GE and Alco works still attuned to the war effort and from townships outside the city. All of them—men, women and children—were bent on one thing: To make all the noise they could.

For the rest of that long day, the city wept, laughed with joy and hurrahed with unabashed emotions. This time, the news was real and there was no holding them back. Perhaps the general feeling of that day was summed up by John R. Magarvey, Alco manager, who said, "The news of the 11th is certainly much more gratifying than the disappointment of the 7th. We thank God it is all over and now our boys will be coming back home."

Everything on wheels that could move—autos, horsedrawn vehicles, motorcycles and bicycles—converged on a joyous downtown scene by 4 a.m. A parade had already started, beginning with a spontaneous delegation of cheering, whistling and screaming citizens led by the Newsboys' Association bugle, fife and drum corps. Big moving vans and trucks loaded with children, all shouting themselves hoarse, joined in the festivities. At first, there was no "line of march." The paraders just followed the leaders, up Dock Street and over Edison Avenue to Broadway and down State Street, where they regrouped for sorties into the nieghborhood streets. The city's fire department also decided to let off steam by taking joy rides through the streets in fire apparatus, with sirens and bells adding to the din of that early morning celebration. Church bells began pealing the good news and factory whistles shrieked in alternating long and staccato blasts. If there was a citizen still asleep in Schenectady by 5 a.m., that person had to be stone deaf.

By 7 a.m., the paraders stretched out for blocks. When they

marched down Dock Street again, many workers were heading into GE's main gate but were persuaded by the celebrants to take a one-day holiday (Nov. 11 fell on a Monday.) It is doubtful much work was done that day in the GE or anyplace else. Most of the stores and offices closed and the few pupils who showed up for classes soon were dismissed for the day.

By 9 a.m. there was a complete traffic jam in lower Schenectady. People crowded the sidewalks and milled in the streets amid stalled vehicles as cheer after cheer rent the frosty air and was lost in the clouds above. Over-exuberant horseplay caused a few slight injuries. Torpedo caps were placed on the streetcar tracks so that they would explode when the cars ran over them. A woman boarding a car at State and Ferry was struck by a hot fragment of a detonated cap and was later treated at Ellis Hospital for a burned lip. Somehow, many people got the idea of grabbing a turkey feather duster and a can of talcum powder to spice the occasion. There were many white faces and "dusted" coattails downtown that morning, but a few persons also suffered irritated eyes in the bargain.

In the early afternoon, soldiers from the Army Supply Dept and National Guard paraded, bearing their arms. They were soon joined by other groups who kept the parade going for several hours as most of the earlier celebrants, footsore and grateful just to stand still, watched from the curbsides. Red Cross nurses, in their crisp white uniforms and dark blue capes, carried a large American flag held parallel to the ground. A large picture of General "Blackjack" Pershing was mounted on an auto. The Red Men snake danced. Four men carried a black box resembling a coffin with a sign proclaiming, "The Kaiser is Dead!" Another man, somewhat inebriated but embued with the spirit of victory, goose-stepped in the parade with a sign on his back reading. "To Hell with the Kaiser."

The Schenectady Elks Club sponsored an impromptu patriotic concert at their clubhouse at 615 State St. in the late afternoon. During intermission, the guests sang "There'll Be a Hot Time in the Old Town Tonight," a song made popular during the Spanish-American War but quite appropriate for the occasion.

Throngs of people still walked the downtown streets until a late hour, as though they hated to see a glorious day end. They were, however, more subdued now—content to talk soberly of the real meaning of this day and the dawning of a new and exciting era.

There was, too, the subject that was on everyone's mind: The boys, God bless them, are finally safe and soon they will be coming home. Within a week, General Electric had rigged up a huge sign which was erected at the foot of Crescent Park, a sign with light bulbs that spelled out, "Schenectady Welcomes Its Warriors."

Hundreds of homecoming doughboys would see that sign in the coming months as they were greeted in parades and other festivities sponsored by the city and local organizations. But there were many who would not. The memory is all too clear to many people yet today of those flag-draped coffins which had arrived regularly at the American Railway Express depot beside the downtown railroad depot and which would continue to arrive long after the war had ended.

Schenectady welcomed back its warriors of World War I the afternoon of Wednesday, April 2, 1919, when about 225 men of Companies E and F of the 105th Regiment arrived at the railroad station and marched up State Street to the armory. It seemed the whole city had turned out, lining the sidewalks and part of the street, waving hats and flags, shouting and cheering.

The men had received their military discharges that morning at Camp Upton, after which they picked up their final army pay—plus a $60 bonus. It had been arranged for Mayor Charles A. Simon to receive a telephone call from the Albany station when the train carrying the Schenectady contingent arrived there. So this city was ready and waiting a half hour later when the "fighting Sammies" got into Schenectady Station. It set off a cacophony of bells, whistles and auto horns. The men assembled eight abreast in parade formation in the railroad station arcade at 1:45 p.m. and then marched up the main street, led by Col. James M. Andrews, commanding officer of the 105th.

There was a dinner-dance held in the armory that night in honor of the returning veterans. This included, of course, speeches by local dignitaries and military personnel—all paying glowing tribute to the men who left the city two years before and helped bring victory to the allies.

Bill Shirley, manager of the Palace Theater just above the Vendome Hotel, offered free admission to anyone in military uniform the rest of that week. Besides the main silent feature, William S. Hart in "Riddle Gawne," the theater advertised that movies of the homecoming parade in Schenectady the day before would be shown on the giant screen and invited the soldiers to "come see yourselves."

The Salvation Army hut, which had been set up in Crescent Park all during the war, continued to operate at that site for several months after. Free doughnuts and coffee were available to the servicemen, plus some entertainment such as the playing of phonograph records or piano with group singing. (The "hut" later was moved up to Guilderland Avenue for adjunct services of the Salvation Army.)

On Friday night of that same week, a young heavyweight by the name of Jack Dempsey gave a "sports-vaudeville" show at the armory under auspices of Companies E and F. Besides a few wrestling matches and acrobatic exhibitions, young Dempsey boxed three rounds with a black fighter, Lester Johnson, and told the crowd how he intended to fight "in close" to Jess Willard and dethrone the champion in their upcoming July 4 fight.

It had been announced through the press that an important caucus was to be held in St. Louis the following month to draft a preliminary organization of American veterans of the World War into a group to be known as the American Legion.

41—The Lorraine Block

*W*hen tenants began moving into its shiny new office space early in 1902, the five-story Lorraine Block had officially joined the ranks of the more impressive structures in downtown Schenectady—especially those located east of the Erie Canal bridge. It was looked upon as a symbol of the city's reawakening to an industrial and economic boom to begin the new century.

That was more than 90 years ago. By 1972, the Lorraine Block and other buildings which made up the block of State Street between Clinton and Barrett were demolished to make way for the new Albany Savings Bank building, a modern structure designed by the Schenectady architectural firm of Feibes & Schmitt. But, just for old time's sake, we might give a backward glimpse to the circumstances which surrounded construction of the Lorraine Block.

Welton Stanford, hardware store owner and real estate broker, bought up the State Street frontage at the northeast corner of State and old White (now Clinton) Street in 1899 and immediately had architects draw up plans for his "dream block." He envisaged a beautiful, modern building which would accommodate many kinds of business and turn a healthy profit. And he was right.

Welton had always known considerable wealth. He was the son of State Senator Charles Stanford and the nephew of Leland Stanford (who moved from Schenectady to California, became a U.S. senator and established Stanford University.) The Stanfords had lived at the old home, known as Locust Grove, at State and Balltown Road ever since Josiah Stanford bought it in 1859. Welton was the last Stanford to live in it as his widow moved to California after his death and the property later became the Ingersoll Memorial Home for Aged Men.

The Welton Stanfords had two sons, Welton Jr. and Grant, and a daughter, Lorraine. Thus when Stanford began dreaming of a beautiful office building, he thought also of naming it after his one and only daughter. This was done, and the name "Lorraine Block" was inscribed in the white stone facade over the fifth floor windows.

At the time of the building's completion, Lorraine Stanford was 14 years old. In 1910, she married Glen E. Huntsberger and immediately moved to California where she has lived ever since. Her husband was a graduate of both Stanford University and Harvard Law School.

Now a resident of Los Angeles, Mrs. Huntsberger wrote recently in answer to our query about any recollections she might have of the building which was named after her. She noted that "perhaps the one which remains most vivid was of Walker's Drug Store where they sold the most delicious ice cream sodas for only 10 cents."

(Walker's formerly Platt & Walker, moved up a few doors into the ground floor of the Lorraine Block shortly after it was built and was there for several decades).

It wasn't until 1906 that Schenectady could boast of a bigger and newer office building. That was the year the eight-story Parker Building was completed at 408 State St., named after attorney John R. Parker who held a major interest in it. Since it was purchased in 1964 by Raymond

Phillips, it has been called the Phillips Building.

Before he considered building the Lorraine Block, Welton Stanford had a real estate office at 145 Jay St. He owned the Stanford Hardware business, located in the Stanford Block on the northwest corner of Broadway (then Center Street) and State, which was a successor to Teller and Stanford Hardware. (After May, 1927, the late Abe Cohen, founder of The Imperial, bought the building and later expanded his store. When Imperial went out of business in the early 1980s it was taken over as an OTB center. Today, it occupies the whole property.) This was the building, incidentally, in which Charles Stanford established the old Schenectady Daily Union in 1865.

Teller and Stanford Hardware earlier was located across the street in what is known as the Dickhoff Building.

The corner property purchased by Welton Stanford for his proposed Lorraine Block consisted of a two-story brick building which housed several small businesses on the ground floor at the time, including Hebner & Sleeter's grocery store and Sam Lee's Chinese laundry, and apartments on the second floor.

Adjacent to the east, on the corner of Barrett Street, was the story-and-a-half wood-framed landmark known for years as the Park House and, later, as Wasson's Park House and Saloon. It was run by Andrew and Thomas Wasson and consisted of a huge barroom on the ground floor with rooms for men in the garret above. The long open porch in front, running the length of the building, usually was occupied by patrons who tilted their chairs back against the wall while they socialized or watched the passing traffic—which by 1900 was changing rapidly as the electric streetcars busily plied the city's main stem along with cyclists and horse-drawn vehicles.

The Park House was not around long after the Lorraine Block as finished in 1902. It was purchased by the Schenectady Illuminating Co. (forerunner of Niagara Mohawk Power Corp.) and replaced by a modern building for its headquarters (in later years to become Walker's Pharmacy.) The Wassons received $87,000 for the site.

One of the problems to be contended with, at the outset of the building of the Lorraine Block, was the Cowhorn Creek which flowed under the corner property. There was no intimation of any wrong-doing on the part of Welton Stanford, except that it was generally acknowledged that he used his influence and "pulled some wires" with both city and state authorities to get the creek flow diverted from his property.

(In 1939-41, the city made use of WPA funds to finally correct the Cowhorn Creek problem by constructing 96-inch concrete sewer mains to divert the flow from its Vale Cemetery source down Liberty Street, across Church Street and down to the Mohawk River discharge next to the Western Gateway Bridge ramp. The Cowhorn Creek is a derivative of the early Dutch name of Coehoorn's Kill, named after a man named Coehoorn who used its waters for mill purposes in the early 1700s. Its aboriginal name by the Indians was "Oronnowarrieguchrie.")

The Cowhorn Creek actually took its rise about a mile east of Schenectady, flowed down the McClellan Street-Eastern Avenue area through the cemetery, on over Liberty Street and through Clinton, westward across State to Dakota Street and on to the river. In the early 1800s in Schenectady, the creek and its several tributaries honeycombed the upper State Street area in the vicinity of Crescent Park and Nott Terrace. There was even a Cowhorn Creek plank bridge on State Street near Clinton in 1802 until years later (after the Civil War) the flow was covered by stone culverts a few feet below ground. Invariably, especially during spring runoffs, there were serious flooding conditions in the area as streets and cellars felt the impact of a choked Cowhorn Creek.

Once it was built, the Lorraine Block became Welton Stanford's business quarters. His was the first office to be opened. To the rear, Olney Redmond opened the first of his restaurants in Schenectady. (Later, in the early 1920s, Redmond built an ultra modern gas station just to the rear of the Masonic Temple on Erie Boulevard, one which he proudly proclaimed to be "The World's Finest Filling Station.")

In 1923, three floors were added to the rear portion of the Lorraine Block, in fact over that portion which had once housed Redmond's Restaurant. The building itself extended 102 feet along Clinton Street, with 53 feet of frontage on State Street. For many years, it was the only structure in the downtown area with two passenger elevators.

There have since been a lot of tenants in the Lorraine Block and rarely was it not filled to capacity. Its office space was a favorite of attorneys, especially, over the years. The ground floor business accommodations enjoyed some long-time occupants. One of these located at the corner of Clinton and State during the 1930s and early 1940s was the Farm Restaurant.

Between the fall of 1971 and the summer of 1972, a sweeping change took place in the State Street block between Clinton and Barrett Streets. First, the old Barcli (later Strand) Theater came down, the former illuminating company building at Barrett and State was next to go, followed by the Lorraine Block. The gaping space did not stay vacant long. Work was begun immediately on construction of the Albany Savings Bank, a modern brick and glass structure which was opened in 1973.

The Park House and Saloon, operated for many years by the Wasson brothers at State and Barrett Streets, was an early fixture of the city's main street east of the canal. Horse barns were in the rear. It was razed about 1905 and replaced by the Schenectady Illuminating Co. building.

This lone section was all that remained of the first Western Gateway Bridge near the Schenectady shore in January, 1974, a month after the new bridge was opened with a temporary ramp on the city side. The last to go, it was part of the first span's "Dead Man's Curve."

42—The Great Western Gateway Bridge

It was a great day for Schenectady on the mid-morning of Saturday, Dec. 19, 1925, when the Great Western Gateway Bridge was opened to public traffic. Square backed vehicles of the vintage of 1920 had lined up along Scotia's Mohawk Avenue and, at a signal, began streaming across the new bridge to the Schenectady side amid horn-honking and cheers of pedestrians standing along the bridge walks.

It seemed then that the "grand and glorious" Western Gateway fit in perfectly with the new look in Schenectady proper The Hotel Van Curler was newly built at the eastern extremity, the Schenectady YMCA would be completed shortly and the new Proctor's Theater was being constructed. What was perhaps more important — the old Erie Canal, which for 90 years had split the heart of downtown Schenectady, recently was filled in, repaved and opened that same year as Erie Boulevard, the best lighted boulevard in the country.

The bridge was three years in the making and was the outcome of pressure exerted in Albany after a flood of March, 1914, wrecked Freeman's Bridge and part of the Aqueduct crossing. The only remaining link, then, between Schenectady and Scotia was another flood-plagued span which crossed from Washington Avenue in Schenectady to Schonowe Avenue on the opposite shore. The last also was the trolley bridge, a steel structure built shortly after the old covered bridge was demolished about 1880. (Residents who can still recall crossing this steel bridge can attest to the "empty" feeling of seeing the river below through the gaps in the cross beams.)

Bids for the contract to build the superstructure were advertised in June, 1922, and the job was awarded a month later to the American Pipe and Construction Co. for $763,671. The work called for building all sections between two existing piers (having already been erected on both sides) but excluded the finishing of the roadway and sidewalks.

Thus began a long period of tedious work, which saw changes in engineering plans, bickering among companies doing sub-contract work, several flash floods which wrecked barges and equipment, and numerous accidents causing death, injury and delay.

The most disastrous mishap occurred the late afternoon of Monday, Sept. 17, 1923, as the last of the concrete was being poured for the 24th arch which connected the bridge to the Scotia shore. There was a sullen roar, accompanied by the sound of splintering timber as the whole framework gave way and dropped 450 tons of wet concrete into the channel. Men, some injured, were fished out of the water and rushed to Ellis Hospital and the GE Works Hospital.

All night long, gangs of water-soaked workmen sought the bodies of their missing comrades under the glare of floodlights. Derrick booms, operated from barges, lifted sections of the debris from out of the fast-setting concrete that was now a monstrous island in the channel.

It was found that a score were injured but four men lost their lives—Kenneth Davidson, Joseph Masseco, Joseph Miller and Vincent Polsinelli (who died later in Ellis Hospital.) There was a rumor that a fifth man was encased in the concrete, a rumor which persisted until 1960 when former Gazette Reporter Art Isabel dug deeper into the story and came up with an unusual story with a happy ending.

In checking back files on the mishap, Isabel noted that Clarence Rodenmacher was reported missing but that follow-up stories never mentioned Rodenmacher's name. As it turned out, Rodenmacher was very much alive and was now a machinist at General Electric Co. He told Isabel that during the confusion of the accident, he forgot to check out with the timekeeper and was put on the missing list. Only a youth at the time, Rodenmacher said his mother forced him to quit the job in favor of a safer one.

The abrupt 24-degree angle curve near the Schenectady end of the bridge was not long in being regarded as a hazard and soon was dubbed "Dead Man's Curve" for the serious and often fatal accidents it precipitated. In fact, only a few years after construction of the bridge, impartial bridge builders regarded it as "an engineering freak and curiosity" because of the curve.

The curve existed, according to the best recollections, because promoters of the bridge wanted its approach to Schenectady linked with State Street and the downtown shopping district. Engineers, who originally had plotted the course to extend in a straight line towards the new boulevard, decided the curve was the best answer. The State Department of Transportation has long since abandoned construction of such severe curves and aims now at keeping them closer to five degrees if a curve is at all necessary.

From the time enabling legislation was passed by the state legislature in April, 1922, to build the bridge until nearly a year after its completion, the Western Gateway was viewed as a "No Man's Land" as far as maintenance responsibility was concerned. Geographically, the span is an oddity because portions of it are located in the City of Schenectady, the Village of Scotia and the Towns of Rotterdam and Glenville. Finally, however, the state designated it as a special highway and therefore assumed responsibility for it.

In the original plans for the bridge construction was an alternate specification for a pair of trolley tracks to be laid in the center of the deck, with single lane auto traffic designated for either side. This was shelved, however, before the bridge surface was laid —even though steel ties were placed in the original surface in the event that tracks might be installed later (these ties were removed in 1960).

There also was a plan advanced by a state safety officer in 1950 for the construction of a center dividing mall on the bridge to slow traffic and cut down the accident rate. This, too, was aborted after some consideration.

The bridge may have been opened to the public in December, 1925, but the official dedication did not take place until the following June. This was the week set aside for the window dressing and all of Schenectady and neighboring communities joined in the festivities.

Gov. Alfred E. Smith, derby and all, arrived on Friday, June 11, 1926, to participate in the dedication ceremonies held at the Schenectady approach—which then contained a grass-plotted island in the center. The bands played, people cheered and politicians and civic leaders waxed eloquent as the bridge was duly acclaimed.

Schenectady Mayor A. T. Blessing called the new structure a "monument of cooperation, integrity, diligence and permanence to this city." Others referred to it as the "Bridge of Fame" and "the true gateway to the west." Upwards of 75,000 persons crowded along the banks on either side of the river that first night of the celebration to watch a fireworks display that began at 9:30. Police estimated that nearly 10,000 automobiles, the most anyone had recalled seeing in one place up to that time, were parked solidly on the bridge, lower State Street and six-deep along Washington Avenue to the boulevard.

Throughout the following week, the official opening of the Great Western Gateway Bridge was commemorated by special events — including a long tented avenue of exhibits set up along Erie Boulevard, Charleston dance contests and WGY sponsored broadcasts lauding "one of the engineering masterpieces of our time."

An hour-long parade from Scotia concluded the week's dedicatory celebration on Saturday night, June 19. The marchers assembled in the area of Reynolds Street and Glen Avenue at 7:30 p.m. for the parade down Mohawk Avenue and across the bridge. It was an impressive parade as more than 2,000 marchers and practically every rolling vehicle in Scotia took part.

About 600 members of the Independent Order of Red Men from throughout northeastern New York were in full costume, as was a tribe of Indians from the St. Regis Onondaga Reservation. Following close behind the bandsmen, floats and marchers was a solid brigade of autos. They came across the bridge four abreast, honking horns as people lining the walks cheered the sight of what eventually would become known as a traffic jam.

It was not more than a decade later that the warm glow began to pale as far as the Western Gateway was concerned.

The span had been the scene of countless accidents, particularly at the point of the curve, and as the fatalities mounted through the ensuing years there grew a clamor for bridge improvements—and even a replacement.

Although its bridge deck was completely overhauled in 1960, there persisted a dissatisfaction with the facility among the every-day users. The traffic tieups in the early morning and late afternoon hours persisted and commuters blamed most of it on the bridge.

State engineers in 1969 inspected the battered walls and decaying underpinnings, then declared the bridge unsound to the point of being hazardous. This prompted the state to enact a 20 mile-per-hour speed limit on the span for its last few years of life.

Finally, on Dec. 19, 1973—exactly 48 years after the first Western Gateway was opened—another ceremony was held in the shadows of the deteriorating span. Charles T. Male, who was a member of the State Assembly when the first bridge was built and was present at its opening, cut the symbolic ribbon which declared the new Western Gateway in operation and the old one closed for all time.

The new bridge was not as spectacular in appearance as the one built nearly a half century before. There was not as much concrete, but more steel, and it was built extensively on fill which had been hauled onto the river islands. There was a difference, too, in cost. The first bridge was erected at a total outlay of $2.5 million, but the second came to nearly $11.8 million.

OLD AND NEW - This view from Schenectady side shows progress of new Western Gateway Bridge in January 1974 as temporary entrance leads under the bridge about to be demolished.

It's An Awful Leak

By Albert T. Reid

The growing menace of bootleg whiskey in the midst of the Prohibition Era was characterized in this Schenectady Gazette cartoon of March 21, 1926.

43—The Roaring Twenties

The Roaring Twenties treated Schenectady little different from any other part of the country. Everyone was as relaxed as Cal Coolidge by the time 1925 rolled around and all the jitters and tensions of the Big War had passed. These were good times, raucus times, sensational times and all America was in tune with a new kind of delicious freedom that can come only with prosperity and a break with old traditions.

There almost was nothing new under the sun but it seemed an awful lot of people were trying to find it. Children went crazy for yo-yos while the adults staged dance marathons and Charleston contests. Flappers went around in short, beaded dresses with jazz bows peeking naughtily from just above the knees; in the winter they wore long, open coats and flopped around in unbuckled galoshes. The young men wore pork-pie hats and raccoon coats, usually complete with flasks of bootleg gin, and they sang 60 choruses or so of "It Ain't Gonna Rain No More" until three o'clock in the morning in jalopies painted gaudily with such messages as "Danger...Curves and Soft Shoulders."

While watching the dollars pile up, many folks were making whoopee— not only on the gin and hijinks but in nearly everything that smacked of frenzy or finance. Vaudeville died but the movies and radio took its place. Clara Bow had something known as "It" and women were becoming aware that dropped waistlines and flat silhouettes were out. It was the age of heroes. Babe Ruth was idolized in the world of baseball, Jack Dempsey became the darling of the fight crowd, Rudolph Valentino was the "Great Lover" of the silver screen until his dramatic exit in 1926, and Charles Lindbergh became the "Lone Eagle" after his famous solo flight to Paris in 1927. In a way, even the thugs and racketeers came in for their fair share of notoriety as such underworld figures as Al Capone, "Lucky" Luciano, "Pretty Boy" Floyd and Jack "Legs" Diamond hogged the headlines.

Phonograph records (Victor, Columbia and Vocalion) and player piano rolls were demonstrated upon request at most stores and furnished the latest song hits which the public snapped up and rushed home to hear. They came in a wide range of moods and tempo: "Where Do You Worka John?" "I Found a Million-Dollar Baby (In a Five and-Ten-Cent Store)," "Side by Side," "Alabamy Bound," "O How I Miss You Tonight," "Miss Annabelle Lee," "My Blue Heaven," "Sonny Boy," and yes, even "Jingle Bells."

Cluett & Sons at 203 State St. advertised widely that ukuleles were available for $2.25 and up.

In the Schenectady area, as elsewhere, the roadhouses and dance halls flourished amid the dancing craze of the Twenties. Every amusement park had its dance pavilion and frequently offered silver cups to "the prettiest girl" and "the handsomest man" or the couple who best danced the Charleston or Black Bottom. The FJ & G trolleys ran nightly during the summer months to Sacandaga Park while the Schenectady Railway cars were packed with evening revelers bound for Mid-City Park in Menands, Rexford Park or farther north to Forest Park at Ballston Lake. Up in Amsterdam, Healey's Park and Crescent Park (later Mohawk Mills

Park) also featured well known dance bands such as Symthe & Dunham's Georgians or the Arcadians for weekend dancing. There were dance halls at Poutre's Pond at the end of Broadway, at Mont Pleasant's Orchard Park on Second Avenue, at Central Park's pavilion. and at Firemen's Hall at Stop 7 Albany Road.

Some of the roadhouses which featured dance bands and contests were Rudd's Beach off Stop 12 Albany Road, the Birch Garden and Green Lantern on Saratoga Road, Blesser's Inn. the Orange Blossom Inn at Ballston Spa, the Mariaville Lake dance hall, Wenzel's Park at the end of Campbell Avenue and the White Swan cabaret at Hamburg Street and Curry Road.

One of the classiest establishments given over to ballroom dancing in Schenectady during the period following World War I was Cain's Dance Castle over the front portion of the Barcli Theater on Barrett Street. The entrance was on the left of the theater marquee. Francis M. Cain, proprietor, hired good orchestras and insisted on strict ballroom decorum, at all times. Any boisterous individuals were given a polite but firm heave-ho.

There were many local jazz bands which had no trouble finding work. The groups, usually comprising five or six musicians, played red hot music all night long for about two dollars per man. Some of them were McDermott's Orchestra, Meadowbrook's King Jazz, Blue Bozzi's Serenaders, Kalteaux' Kollegians and Zita's Blazers.

Because dancing was such a big part of the fast-paced decade, there naturally was great deal of publicity attached to it both in the types of dance steps and the way some dance halls ran their business. By 1924, there was hardly a community of any appreciable size in the nation where various civic groups or indignant clergymen failed to speak out against "the scandalous situation" in the terpsichorean phase of modern youth. Decency in dancing, it was asserted. could be accomplished by elimination of so-called indecent steps.

The "Black Bottom" and the "Shimmy" (actually borrowed from the burlesque shows) came in for a good share of criticism, along with the "hug-me-tight" version of the fox-trot.

The dime-a-dance palaces sprang up, mostly in the metropolitan areas, in which women were hired on a commission basis to dance with the men patrons. There was this report in New York City in November, 1924, critical of the "closed" dance halls which admitted only men:

"As a rule, no women except the hired girl dancers are admitted— or at least they are not welcome. The dance floor is partitioned off, and access to it is possible only through one or more gateways. Admission charges include six or eight dances. Thereafter each dance must be paid for at the rate of 10 cents; or in some instances, two dances for 25 cents. Dances are short, averaging from 40 to 60 seconds, and intermissions are from 30 to 60 seconds in length. Both patrons and the young women dance partners are exploited."

Of course the speakeasies were available during those Prohibition days to the "in" crowd. It added to the excitement of the times, or so many thought, to be directed secretly to a place selling illegal beverages and possibly even risking the chance of a police raid. Some of the "speaks" were private homes, mostly in downtown neighborhoods, which opened to "members and invited guests" on weekends.

There was a place on Jay Street, not far from the old city hall, known as the Altroon Club and it managed to survive the 14-year dry spell without serious difficulties with the authorities. ("It isn't what you know, it's who you know that counts these days," said those who wanted to see the speakeasies closed.)

Slim Conover ran a speak on Clinton Street near State. There was no slotted door to admit customers, but one was required to have a printed card before he was allowed to enter.

There was the Silhouette Club on lower Broadway and George Harris' place on Washington Avenue near where the state armory now stands. Dan Fredericks, who once tended bar at the new Hotel Van Curler, ran a speak on Liberty Street and later moved to Center Street.

One speakeasy, run by "Googie" R., flourished on Lafayette Street opposite the First Methodist Church. It was a second floor walk-up, and customers had to stand in a vestibule until a club employee let them in. This was their way of "screening" clientele and making as sure as could be that no federal men were admitted.

There was the Brass Rail on lower State, the Gold Star Restaurant near Duanesburg and a "private" club that operated in a small building on South Ferry street near the Boulevard. The Towpath Inn at Jefferson Street and the boulevard was a big favorite among speakeasies. Steve Crook had a place on Albany Street about six doors to the east of Brandywine Avenue and Andy Kay ran a speak on Congress Street between Third and Fourth Streets. About 20 speakeasies operated on Broadway between Edison Avenue and Kruesi Avenue (now Lower Broadway), most of them frequented by the city's black community. Hank Smith's place at 12th Street and Broadway was a popular Bellevue spot.

The late Paul Gay, a good-natured restaurateur who had his share of peaceable appearances in the local police station through the years because of periodic numbers and gambling raids, once discussed his Prohibition era experiences.

He ran afoul of the revenue men soon after the Prohibition Amendment took effect when he was caught drawing booze past the Canadian border. When he appeared before the magistrate, there followed a strange court proceeding in which the court finally allowed the act was still undefined, that merely possessing liquor constituted no breach of the law. He was fined $50 for illegal entry into the U.S. and for years later continued to drive up to Canada to get booze for his Schenectady speakeasies without getting into further trouble with the law. There would have been complications if he had been caught, however, because the law by this time had been clearly defined.

The 3.2 prohibition beer was generally frowned upon because it tasted "flat," so no respectable speak would have it on the premises (even in legitimate restaurants, if one knew the waiter or owner, he might order his beer "needled" with alcohol regularly sold at druggists). Good wine or liquor or something called "Pocono Moonshine" was served in the speakeasies or for take-outs. The price, of course, was pretty steep. A coke and a small bottle of corn liquor or alcohol also could be ordered, from a quarter up to a dollar.

Gay, incidentally, said he was quite a heavy drinker himself during the prohibition period but he "swore off when the good stuff finally came back in." His most popular speakeasy, according to his best recollection, was on Smith Street near Broadway opposite the Asia Restaurant.

The speakeasy problem was not a big concern to the local gendarmes, however. These were comparatively quiet "drinking clubs" and rarely were a public nuisance. The police concentrated on breaking up fights at the park dance halls and pinching speeders or drunk drivers—all of which kept them busy on any given weekend.

In the Schenectady area, there may not have been as much violence as was depicted in the televised series of Elliot Ness' "Untouchables," based primarily in Chicago and New York — and yet the rum runners, racketeers and highjackers were very real indeed. Police were called out sometimes, believe it or not, when a bootlegger was unfortunate enough to attract highjackers who simply relieved the bootlegger of his ill-gotten gains usually liquor brought from the Canadian border or from the New England coast "just off the boat."

Typical of such goings-on is the report in Schenectady police files in which a man, who later admitted he was a bootlegger, reported his car stolen by some "thugs" just outside Amsterdam at about 5 a.m. Nov. 7, 1924. When the car was found abandoned later on State Street, near the Ferry Street corner, Schenectady police extracted the story from the man.

He was transporting a load of Canadian-smuggled liquor when a high-powered car pulled alongside and another man jumped onto the running board, held a revolver against the bootleg driver's heart and ordered him to stop. They took over his cargo, valued at about $3,000, and drove him to the Rotterdam hills and told him to "start walking."

When found, the bootlegger's auto was given a good inspection by the police before it was released. It was a new roadster with a special body designed to carry heavy loads. The springs had several extra leaves, making them equal to light truck springs. Over the gasoline tank in the rear was a plate of armor steel, apparently meant to ward off bullets. The outstanding feature was the compartment which finished the lines of the special sports body. It was higher than the rear compartment of the ordinary roadster and rode directly on the heavy springs, adjusted so that it received a minimum of road shock.

The tragic death of Schenectady Police Capt. Albert L. "Bucky" Youmans was attributed to the racketeering element of the decade although the murderer or murderers were never found and no connection was established between Captain Youmans and any "lead" he might have been pursuing on unlawful characters.

Youmans and a partner, Patrolman John Flynn, were patrolling Edison Avenue the night of Nov. 28, 1924, when about 10 p.m. they fell victims of slugs and 12-gauge shot fired at them from a shotgun blast. The assailant, Flynn later said, had been crouched behind a tree. Flynn, who was hit in the ankle, managed to carry the mortally wounded Youmans to the nearest call box, about a block away, and summon help. Captain Youmans, hit in the head, stomach, left hand and right knee, died in Ellis Hospital the next day.

Especially popular with the swingers of the 1920s was the excursion each Saturday on the Hudson River Day Line down to Kingston Point

Park which had a large dance pavilion. For only $1.25 per person round trip, one of the line's three steamers (Alexander Hamilton, Hendrick Hudson or Washington Irving) offered a full day's fun beginning when the vessel left Albany at 9 a.m. and ending when it docked back at the Hudson River pier about 11 p.m. And there was drinking and dancing on board, both ways.

The restaurants, too, did a proverbial land-office business while people were on the go in the 1920s. Among the more popular eating places locally in those days were Nicholaus' Restaurant, Pelops, Daley's Lunch, Asia Restaurant, Canton Restaurant, Victoria Restaurant, Hotel Van Curler and, out in Colonie, Powell's Inn. The all-night diners were plentiful, catering to those who wanted to "eat and run."

The famous frankfurter sauce of the New Way Lunch was as popular years ago as it is today. It had two stores, one at 3 South Center (now Broadway near Union Street) and the other at 710 Albany St. where the main store still holds forth with hot dogs and the Stathis sauce yet the main attraction.

DeWitt's Lunch at 118 Jay St. was another popular lunch and late snack spot during the 1920s. Other enjoyable quick serve establishments were the 20th Century Restaurant at 145-47 Jay St., Waldorf's at 422 State St. and Frank C. Howenstein's Lincoln Lunch at 174 Jay St.

There seemed so much to do in those days that the older generation, besides wondering what the world was coming to, marveled at the young people's capacity for living life to the fullest — and with gusto. Theaters, dancing, amusement parks, house parties, swim parties, automobile rides, motorcycle rides, it went on and on like a carousel that would never run down.

Just as there were a lot of people who were having a ball with the carefree Twenties, there were also others who worried about the times. For one thing, the degree of drinking and the stuff that was being imbibed in the Prohibition era caused alarm among that segment of America which saw an evil in a slackening of the moral code they had been taught to abide by. Cheap liquor, whether bootleg or homemade, was in abundance and not many parties were complete without it.

In 1925, the New York State Department of Health issued a report that during May of that year there were 79 deaths in the state from alcoholism — or 11 times the number recorded for the corresponding month in 1920, a year when deaths from this cause reached a minimum following the advent of prohibition.

"The number of deaths from alcoholism has increased each year since 1920. If this indicated trend continues, it will not be long before the high annual levels of pre-prohibition days will be reached," the report stated. It decried the use among young people of "bad liquor" which not only was illegal but extremely harmful.

The older generation, especially, was upset with behavior of people who reacted to the pulsating beat of the 1920s. The so-called staid citizenry refused to go along with what they viewed as reckless, senseless and immoral behavior and feared for the future of the country if it persisted. They were brought up by standards of the Victorian age and therefore were puzzled and distressed by the goings-on of the younger set. They were aghast whenever they caught sight of a woman sneaking a puff on a cigarette, huddled in the seat of a passing auto—and right in plain sight in downtown Schenectady! The idea of women going into speakeasies, and sometimes even sitting at bars, was unbelievable even though it had become common knowledge. What was even worse, young men and women often stayed out together until the early morning hours. And the kind of dancing that was in vogue. . . outrageous!

Quite indicative of the viewpoint of those critical of the "new immorality" of the Roaring Twenties was this editorial which appeared in the Schenectady Gazette during the summer of 1925:

"Pleasure seeking and hard drinking by women and youngsters can mark but one thing—the decline of the present civilization. The world in which we live today is a mad, fast and wild place. Men rush to their offices, to their lunches and back to their offices as though time was the devil and forever after them.

'Women rush from this to that and even the children today must be taken here, there and everywhere in automobiles. The coming generation must have its pleasure and that pleasure must be fast and furious. The youth of today who does not carry a flask on his hip is scorned by beautiful young creatures with the bobbed heads that even the most staid and confirmed woman hater cannot refrain from now and then glancing at with pleasure.

"Today people are living too hard. All things entered into must apparently be accomplished within the shortest amount of time and with the maximum amount of hilarity and thrill if possible. Apparently the grave is but around the corner and we are rushing toward it with open arms and speeding feet.

"Would it not do us considerable good to stop for a moment now and then to look at our reflections in the mirror of life? Can we not take thought of where we are going in this mad haste? Surely, sober reason has not departed from all mankind. There must be some in this world who can take life calmly, wholesomely and wisely.

"Religion has commenced to squabble amongst itself. Empires are built one day and crash to earth the next. Men are successful today and tomorrow they are burdens on society; whether they retain their money or lose it, the result is the same. No sooner does a couple marry when shortly the daily press is filled with another scandal, another divorce.

"And last, but not least of all, it is the sad but truthful fact the friends we make to day last but in the sunlight. The light of another day sees them no more and the place where they were has become barren and bare.

"Friends, home and happiness are apparently things which civilization has forced us to forego in this mad foolish race forward. If it were forward it would be good, but it is not. We run in circles and know not where we are going."

But the whirling merry-go-round did finally run down. Some one pushed the "stop" button on what came to be known as "Black Thursday" in October, 1929. A few months later, young and old alike were facing the realities of a life with financial insecurity and a dreary future. The drabness of the Depression Thirties had set in with a most incongruous contrast to the gay abandon of the Roaring Twenties.

That, however, is another story. The world, and Schenectady, had just closed the chapter on some exciting times and entered into a new era — one of uncertainty and not quite as alluring as that which had just ended.

DY GAZETTE. SATURDAY MORNING. SEPTEMBER 18. 1928.

DRY ROT

The neighborhood movie houses helped spread entertainment around the city, as evidenced by this amusement section of the Gazette on Feb. 4, 1922.

APPENDICES

HOW SCHENECTADY GREW

In the early days of Schenectady's settlement, localities were left to take their own official count of the people within the local government's jurisdiction. It is estimated that about 300 persons were living in the stockade area at the time of the 1690 massacre. By 1765, about 2,000 were counted among Schenectady's population and about 2,400 a decade later.

Beginning in 1790, the federal government began to take a census throughout each of the states of the new nation, according to Article 1, Section 2 of the U.S. Constitution. The following table of the decennial census will give an indication of the growth of Schenectady and the effect of the economy on its population:

1790	2,520
1800	3,242
1810	3,939
1820	4,268
1830	5,120
1840	6,784
1850	8,921
1860	9,579
1870	11,026
1880	13,655
1890	19,902
1900	31,682
1904	56,096
1910	72,826
1920	88,723
1930	95,692
1940	87,549
1950	82,061
1960	81,682
1970	77,958
1970 county total	161,078
1980 city	67,972
1980 county total	149,766
1990 city	65,566
1990 county total	149,285

CENSUS DATA FOR SCHENECTADY

Persons

	1980	1990
Total	67,972	65,566

Race

	1980	1990
White	62,943	58,093
Black	4,132	5,597

American Indian, Eskimo or Aleut 130	191
Asian or Pacific Islander...........................364	696
Hispanic Origin 851	1,761
Other Race 403	889

MAYORS OF SCHENECTADY

Joseph C. Yates 1798-1808
John Yate 1808-1809
Abraham Oothout 1810-1811
John Yates 1811-1812
Maus Schermerhorn 1813-1817
Henry Yates Jr. 1817-1825
Isaac M, Schermerhorn 1825-
David Boyd 1826-1827
Isaac M. Schermerhorn 1828-1830
Archibald L. Linn 1831-
John I. DeGraff 1832-1834
Archibald L. Linn 1835-
John I. DeGraff 1836-
Samuel W. Jones 1837-1838
Archibald L. Linn 1839
Alexander C. Gibson 1840-1841
John I. DeGraff 1842
Alexander C. Gibson 1843-1844
John I. DeGraff 1845
Peter Rowe 1846-1847
James E. Van Horne 1848-1849
Peter Rowe 1850
Mordecai Myers 1851
A. A. Van Vorst 1852-1853
Mordecai Myers 1854
Casper Hoag 1855
Abel Smith 1855-1856
Benjamin V. S. Vedder 1857
Alexander M. Vedder 1858
David B. Forrest 1859
Benjamin F. Potter 1860
Arthur W. Hunter 1861-1864
Andrew McMullen 1865-1868
A. A. Van Vorst 1869-1870
William J. Van Horne 1871-1872
Arthur W. Hunter 1873-1874
Peter B. Yates 1875
William Howes Smith 1876-1878
Joseph B. Graham 1879-1880
A. A. Van Vorst 1881-1882
John Young 1883-1884
H. S. DeForest 1885-1886

T. Low Barhydt	1887-1888
H. S. DeForest	1888-1890
Everett Smith	1891-1892
Jacob W. Clute	1893-1897
Charles C. Duryee	1898-1899
John H. White	1900-1901
Horace S. Van Voast	1902-1903
F F. Eisenmenger	1904-1905
Jacob W. Clute	1906-1907
Horace S. Van Voast	1908-1909
Charles C. Duryee	1910-1911
George R. Lunn	1912-1913
J. Teller Schoolcraft	1914-1915
George R. Lunn	1916-1917
Charles A. Simon	1918-1919
George R. Lunn	1920-1921
George R. Lunn	1922
Clarence A. Whitmyer	1923
William W. Campbell	1924-1925
Alexander Blessing	1926-1927
Henry C. Fagal	1928-1931
J. Ward White	1932-1933
Henry C. Fagal	1934-1935
Robert W. Baxter	1936-1939
Mills Ten Eyck	1940-1947
Owen M. Begley	1948-1951
Archibald C. Wemple	1952-1955
Samuel S. Stratton	1956-1959
Kenneth S. Sheldon	1959-1960
Malcolm E. Ellis	1960-1971
Frank J. Duci	1972-1983
Karen B. Johnson	1984-1991
Frank J. Duci	1992-1995
Albert P. Jurcznski	1996-

SCHENECTADY CITY MANAGERS

LeRoy C. Purdy	1935-37
C.A. Harrell	1937-46
Arlen T. St. Louis	1946-49
Christian X. Kouray	1949-51
Morris Mandel Cohn	1951-54
Arthur Blessing	1954-62
Peter Roan	1962-67
Erwin Shapiro	1967-68
John L. Scott	1968-73
Peter Caputo	1973-76
Wayne Chapman	1977-79
Managerial system voted out	1978

SCHENECTADY COUNTY MANAGERS

Theodore Birbilis 1965-67
Robert W. Williams ....(acting) 1967-68
Carl F. Sanford 1968-77
Robert D. McEvoy 1978-

SCHENECTADY COUNTY JUDGES

A Court of Common Pleas and Oyer and Terminer was established in 1809 when Schenectady County was formed. Those who served as judges of this court on appointment by the Board of Supervisors were: Garret S. Vedder (1809-11), Gardner Cleveland (1812-22), David Boyd (1823-34), James V.S. Ryley (1828), Samuel W. Jones (1823-34), John Titus (1828-43), George McQueen (1833-48), Harmanus Peek (1835), Cornelius S. Conde (1838), Abraham Pearse (1839-49), Archibald L. Linn (1840-45), Abraham Warner (1843-48), Peter B. Noxon (1844-49) and Ira Amy (1846-51).

Steven B. Johnson 1851-54
John Sanders 1855-59
Stephen B. Johnson 1860-65
Judson S. Landon 1865-69
Walter T. L. Sanders 1870-73
Austin A. Yates 1874-78
David C. Beattie 1879-89
Edward D. Cutler 1889-96
Alonzo D. Strong 1896-02
Alexander M. Vedder 1903-08
Edward C. Whitmyer 1909-11
Daniel Naylon, Jr. 1912-18
John J. McMullen 1919-24
John Alexander 1925-31
James C. Cooper 1931-32
James W. Liddle 1933-55
Archibald C. Wemple 1956-75
George W. Stroebel 1976-84
Clifford T. Harrigan 1985-94
Michael C. Eidens 1995-

SURROGATES COURT

Wiliam J. Teller 1809-13
Robert Hudson 1813-15
Robert J. Teller 1815-16
John Yates 1816-21
Giles F. Yates 1821-40
John Sanders 1840-44
David Cady Smith 1844-48

Edward C. Whitmyer 1903-08
Alexander A. Vedder..1909-27
James C. Cooper 1927-28
William W. Campbell 1928-57
William F. Hahn, Jr..1958-73
George E. Severson 1974-86
Neil W. Moynihan..1985-92
Barry D. Kramer 1994-88

CHILDREN / FAMILY COURT JUDGES

Wiliam M. Nicoll...1951-62
Duncan S. McNab 1963-73
Howard A. Levine..1971-82
(left for Appellate Court judgeship)
Leonard J. Litz 1973-84
G. Douglas Griset 1981-66
L.J. Reilly Jr. 1985-88

RESIDENT SUPREME COURT JUSTICES

Joseph C. Yates 1808-1823
Alonzo C. Paige 1847-1871
Samuel Jackson...1871-1872
Platt Potter...1866-1879
Judson S. Landon 1874-1901
Edward C. Whitmyer 1912-1931
John Alexander 1932-1953
Charles M. Hughes 1954-1967
Morris M. Cohn 1955-1965
D. Vincent Cerrito 1967-1980
Guy A. Graves 1969-1982
William J. Quinn 1975-1988
Howard A. Levine...1981-1994
(Levine appointed to State Appellate Court)
Robert E. Lynch .1987-8888
Vito C. Caruso 1995-7777

POLICE JUSTICES

Elvin L. David 1836-1839
Jabes Ward 1831-1842
Joseph H. Vrooman 1842-1843
Albert B. Austin 1843-1857
David J. Tiebenor..1852-1856
Harman O. Felthousen...1856-1860
Marvin Strong 1860-1864
John F. Clute...1864-1868
A.J. Thomson...1868-1872
Charles Hastings 1872-1873

Madison Vedder 1873-1873
Abraham Gillespie 1873-1876
George W. Featherstonhaugh 1876-1883
Frederick F. Eisenmenser.....................................1883-1903
Andrew T. Wemple 1904-1907
Alvah Fairlee 1908-1913
John J. McMullen 1913-1918
John Alexander 1918-1924
Charles G. Fryer 1924-1949
Morris Marshall Cohn 1950-1955
(Cohn appointed Supreme Court Justice)
Mathias Poersch 1955-1956
Louis J. Rinaldi 1956-1961
James P. Houlihan...1961-1967
George W. Stroebel..1968-1975
(Stroebel became County Court Judge)
G. Douglas Griset 1975-1980
(Griset became Family Court Judge)
Clifford T. Harrigan 1981-1984
(Harrigan became County Court Judge)
Louise H. Smith 1984-

CHRONOLOGY OF HISTORIC EVENTS IN SCHENECTADY

1642—Arendt Van Curler toured Mohawk Valley, envisioned settlement on present site of Schenectady

1658—Alexander Lindsay Glen built home in Scotia

1661—Van Curler applied to governor for settlement permit

1662—Schenectady settled by Van Curler and 14 other patentees

1680—Jan Mabee house and inn built in Rotterdam Junction; First Reformed Church of Schenectady organized

1690—French and Indian war party attack and burn Schenectady settlement

1692—Schenectady settlement and stockade rebuilt

1696—French Indians killed a man and wounded another near Schenectady

1705—Queen's New Fort constructed within triple stockade

1711—Schenectady settlement alerted during "Queen Anne's War" with the French

1713—John Glen rebuilt Scotia mansion, later to be known as Glen Sanders Mansion

1714—Maalwyck House (now 511 Mohawk Avenue, Scotia) built before 1720

1715—Two military companies quartered in Schenectady

1735—Queen's Fort rebuilt in Schenectady stockade

1743—Schenectady and vicinity on alert during Old French War which lasted five years

1748—Battle of Beukendaal in Glenville

1750—Niskayuna Reformed Church founded

1753—Schenectady and vicinity alerted during Second French War which lasted seven years 1759; Work started on St. George's Episcopal Church

1760—First Presbyterian Church organized

1765—Duanesburg erected as a township by patent; Schenectady granted borough charter

1768—Ferry began operating from end of Ferry Street across to Scotia

1769—St. George's Episcopal Church completed

1770—Princetown Presbyterian Church organized

1771—Sons of Liberty raise Liberty Flag

1773—First Presbyterian Church completed

1774—Committee of Safety and Correspondence formed; St. George's Masonic Lodge in Schenectady organized; Sir William Johnson died

1775—Schenectady Committee voted to raise one company for service at Ticonderoga

1776—Three more companies of militia formed; Troop barracks and infirmary erected at Union and Lafayette Streets

1777—Gen. Washington visited and inspected Schenectady fortifications; all Schenectady militia ordered to Fort Edward to prepare for Burgoyne's attack on Ticonderoga

1778—Schenectady militia sent out when Cobleskill attacked by Joseph Brant party and later to Cherry Valley after attack by Walter Butler and Chief Brant raiding party; General Lafayette arrived on inspection tour of defenses; Schenectady chosen for concentration of supplies for Sullivan's campaign against the Indians in Mohawk Valley

1782—Gen. Washington paid city second visit

1784—First Reformed Church of Rotterdam (Woestina) founded

1786—Gen. Washington paid city third visit

1791—Joseph Shurtliff named Schenectady's first postmaster

1793—Moses Beal established stage line between Schenectady and Albany

1794—"Mohawk Mercury," Schenectady's first newspaper, founded

1795—Union College founded at Union and North Ferry Streets

1798—Schenectady chartered as a city; Joseph C. Yates became its first mayor;

1799—Schenectady mourned death of George Washington

1800—Duanesburg & Florida Baptist Chruch organized

1801—Schenectady adopted city seal

1804—Union College moved into new building, West College, at Union and College Streets; Dr. Eliphalet Nott began a 62-year administration as Union's president

1807—Mohawk Bank chartered; First Methodist Episcopal Church founded

1808—Mohawk River Bridge to Scotia from Schenectady built

1809—Schenectady County formed; Schenectady County Bar Association organized; present edifice of First Presbyterian Church completed

1810—Schenectady County Medical Society organized

1811—Albany Turnpike completed

1813—Glenville Reformed Church organized; Second Reformed Church of Rotterdam (Cobblestone) founded

1814—Union College moved "uptown" to present site

1816—Lancaster School founded on College Street

1817—Erie Canal construction started here

1818—First Reformed Church of Scotia organized

1819—First Reformed Church of Schenectady burned in waterfront fire, bateaux building facilities also wiped out

1820—Mohawk Bank moved across street into new building at Union and North Church Streets

1821—Princetown Reformed Church organized

1822—Joseph C. Yates of Schenectady became eighth New York State governor; First Baptist Church of Schenectady founded; eastern section of Erie Canal as far as Little Falls opened

1823—Jonathan Crane began flax and paint industry in mill at end of Crane Street in Rotterdam (that section called Mohawkville)

1824—Archibald Craig opened cotton factory in Pleasant Valley

1825—Erie Canal opened full length; Marquis de Lafayette visited city

1830—Work started on development off Jackson's Gardens at Union College

1831—Schenectady became west terminus of Mohawk & Hudson Railroad as the "DeWitt Clinton" engine and cars made first trip from Albany to Schenectady on Aug. 9; county courthouse under construction at 108 Union Street

1832—First railroad station in Schenectady built atop Crane Street hill; inclined plane was constructed on that hill as the Saratoga-Schenectady Railroad began operation; the Schenectady Bank was founded; a Cholera epidemic swept through this area

1833—New county courthouse at 108 Union Street completed; Howland S. Barney was 14 when he came to Schenectady from Minaville to begin employment as a drygoods clerk; Schenectady Female Academy founded at 43-45 Washington Avenue

1834—Schenectady Savings Bank founded

1835—Schenectady Lyceum began classes

1836—New railroad station built at State and Wall Streets; Smith Street development began; First Methodist Episcopal Church building erected on Liberty Street

1837—Nationwide financial panic affected local economy

1838—St. John the Baptist Church incorporated; Utica and Schenectady Railroad began operations; Albany Turnpike being constructed

1840—First Baptist Church of Scotia formed

1841—Railroad inclined plane abolished

1843—Downtown railroad station burned, another one built in its place

1844—Chester A. Arthur enrolled in Union College Class of 1848

1848—Schenectady Locomotive Engine Manufactory began operations; German Methodist Episcopal Church built at Union and Lafayette Streets

1849—Schenectady works delivered first engine, "The Lightning," to Utica and Schenectady Railroad

1850—Fort Hunter Plank Road opened

1851—Schenectady Gas Works began production; Hamilton Street opened; locomotive industry here became known as Schenectady Locomotive Works; Second Reformed Church founded

1852—Roy Shawl Works opened on South Church Street

1854—Schenectady Board of Education organized and West College building purchased for first public school; first synagogue in Schenectady founded on lower Liberty Street under the name Sha'are Shamayin; Christian Temple (German) Church organized on North College Street

1855—H.S. Barney Co. began business under that name

1856—First Baptist Church building constructed at 407 Union Street; Vale Cemetery developed; Westinghouse Farm Machinery Co. moved from Central Bridge

1857—Schenectady Evening Star founded; Vale Cemetery dedicated Oct. 21 and first burial held next month; Crescent Park developed on State Street hill; Mohawk Bank moved to new building on lower State Street; first YMCA meetings held in Schenectady; Lafayette Street extended from Liberty Street to Union Street; Schenectady Savings Bank moved to Levi Building opposite Wall Street

1860—"Wideawakes" formed to support Lincoln candidacy; Schenectady split on election

1861—Clute Machine Works at Wall and Liberty Streets built turret mechanism for USS Monitor; President-elect Abraham Lincoln stopped en route to Washington; First Reformed Church burned in Stockade area fire; war service recruiting began, most enlisting in 134th Regiment of New York Zouaves, later known as Co. A 18th Regiment, New York Volunteers organized by William Seward Gridley

1862—St. Joseph's Church founded; Sanitary Commission aided war effort by raising money at a fair in Van Horne's Hall

1863—Schenectady Locomotive Works delivered four engines to Union Army in a single order

1864—John Ellis, president of Schenectady Locomotive Works, died

1865—Schenectady Daily Union founded; Lincoln funeral train passed through Schenectady: Mohawk Bank became Mohawk National Bank

1866—Broom corn farms flourished and broom making became important industry in Schenectady and vicinity; Dr. Eliphalet Nott, Union College's president for 62 years, died; Volney Freeman built toll bridge across Mohawk River to Glenville off Maxon Road in Schenectady

1867—True Blue Society organized "True Blue" parade, held seven consecutive years; Schenectady Young Men's Christian Association organized as YMCA; Christ Church Episcopal incorporated

1868—First state armory built in Schenectady above Crescent Park; Christ Church built on State Street opposite Crescent Park

1869—State Street Presbyterian Church organized; Masonic Temple built on Church Street

1870—City police force organized with Isaac G. Lovett as chief; County Annex built at 13-15 Union Street; Union Hall opened

1871—Schenectady Water System developed; Schenectady YMCA purchased property at corner of State and South Ferry Streets for YMCA building; stockade foundation exposed during laying of water main along Ferry Street

1872—First Methodist Church building completed at State and Lafayette Streets; Union Classical Institute opened classes at Church and Union Streets; Nott Memorial Building at Union College constructed; Zion Lutheran Church founded

1873—St. John the Baptist Convent School opened on Liberty Street in former Methodist church building

1874—Mohawk River wooden (covered) bridge to Scotia removed and work began on a steel bridge using same piers

1875—Civil War Soldier's monument dedicated in Crescent Park

1876—Union College "Idol" placed on campus

1878—St. Joseph's Church completed

1879—Green Street Cemetery abolished, remains transferred to Vale Cemetery; Schenectady YMCA built four-story headquarters at corner of State and South Ferry Streets

1880—City Hall built at Jay and Franklin Streets

1881—Emmanuel Baptist Church organized; Washburn Hall built on Union's campus

1882—Work began on new railroad station

1883—Salvation Army began services in Schenectady

1884—New railroad station opened

1885—Schenectady Free Dispensary organized, forerunner of Ellis Hospital; city water system enlarged

1886—Thomas A. Edison founded Edison Electrical Machine Works in Schenectady

1887—Schenectady Street Railway Company began operation of horse-cars; Indian statue erected in Stockade area on Sept. 12; Zion Lutheran Church established on Nott Terrace; Maxon Block erected on Wall Street

1888—Four-day storm left record snowfall and drifts; Schenectady YWCA organized; Center Street Opera House opened; Zion Lutheran Church dedication took place May 18

1889—Givens Hotel torn down to make way for Edison Hotel named in honor of inventor Edison; Mohawk Gas Company and Schenectady Illuminating Company formed; Schenectady Building Loan & Savings Association founded on Wall Street

1890—Edison Hotel opened; typhoid fever epidemic broke out and lasted nearly one year; Albany Street Methodist Church constituted; new state armory completed on same site above Crescent Park; Edison General Electric Company established after mergers

1891—Schenectady Railway Company formed as streetcar lines were electrified; Louis Nicholaus opened German restaurant on State Street at canal; Union National Bank founded

1892—The name General Electric Company was established; Van Curler Opera House built; Congregation Temple Gates of Heaven moved to College Street; St. Mary's Church founded; Mont Pleasant Reformed Church founded

1893—Charles P. Steinmetz transferred by GE to Schenectady works from the Lynn plant; Ellis Hospital opened on Jay Street next to city hall; effects of national depression felt; St. Mary's Church built on Eastern Avenue; Bellevue Reformed Church founded

1894—City began installing granite block paving on State Street; Schenectady Gazette founded

1895—Louis Nicholaus remodeled restaurant on State Street; present Cobblestone Reformed Church (formally Second Reformed Church of Rotterdam) edifice completed

1898—Mohawk Golf Club was incorporated and shortly after built a nine-hole golf course along Rosa Road, complete with clubhouse

1899—Union Street School built at Union and North College Streets; Fuller Street trolley barns opened; Schenectady Elks Lodge 480 instituted

1900—Central Fire Station opposite Crescent Park opened on Aug. 9 as city's permanent fire department began operations; St. John the Evangelist Church cornerstone laid July 8; Bellevue Reformed Church cornerstone laid Aug. 12; GE Research Laboratory opened with Dr. Willis Whitney as director; Union Presbyterian Church organized; Parkview Cemetery established

1901—Albany interurban route of the Schenectady Railway cars began; Albany Street Methodist Church dedicated; Schenectady

Locomotive Works merged with seven other locomotive plants to become American Locomotive Company (Alco); First Unitarian Society founded in Schenectady; County Almshouse built on old fair grounds at Steuben Street; first mechanical voting machines ordered by city

1902—Lorraine Block opened at State and Clinton Streets; Scotia trolley route opened; Union Presbyterian Church constructed on Park Avenue; Schenectady Trust Company founded; Friedens Evangelical Lutheran Church cornerstone laid; Immanuel Lutheran Church founded at Congress and Fifth Streets

1903—North Building of Schenectady High School completed; Mohawk Club opened new quarters at Union and North Church Streets; Troy and Amsterdam trolley routes begun by FJ & G including runs to Schenectady; new public library at Union Street and Seward Place opened; Friedens Evangelical Lutheran Church constructed at Franklin and Clinton Streets; McClellan Street carbarn opened; St. Joseph's School built; Sacred Heart parish organized; Union Street Methodist Episcopal Church (later Eastern Parkway Methodist) organized; Police Chief William L. Campbell died at age 78

1904—St. John the Evangelist Church dedicated on Valentine's Day; Ballston and Saratoga trolley lines opened as Mohawk River trolley bridge had been completed; WCTU dedicated the drinking fountain at Crescent Park on June 14; Union Presbyterian Church building dedicated on June 19; contract let for raising of the trolley tracks throughout Schenectady to make way for overpasses; Luna Park at Rexford and Forest Park at Ballston Lake opened; Mohawk Golf Club moved to present Troy Road site; Scotia incorporated as a village; Mohawk (later Hudson) Theater opened; Brandywine School built

1905—Pleasant Valley trolley bridge built and formerly opened March 31 with greetings to Ninth Ward; Schenectady County Historical Society founded; Alco began auto and truck production; Elmer Avenue School built; Schenectady Savings Bank moved into new building at State and Clinton Streets; SRC began "Twilight Special" trips; work began March 1 on overhead railroad trestles

1906—Ellis Hospital formally opened Oct. 15; Parker Building completed; C.W. Carl opened a Carl Company store in Schenectady; Ernst F.W. Alexanderson of GE constructed first high frequency alternator used in long distance radio transmission: Crown Hotel built on Wall Street on site of Maxon Block; Citizens Trust Company founded

1907—Overhead railroad crossings throughout Schenectady completed; Empire Theater built at Albany Street and Germania Avenue; Mohawk Hotel constructed; financial panic in U.S. slowed economy; Franklin School built; Pilgrim Congregational Church built on upper State Street; St. Columba's Church parish organized; Maqua Company began operation

1908—New railroad station (Union Street) opened; Salvation Army citadel built on Lafayette Street; Fulton, McKinley, Lincoln, Horace Mann and Washington Irving Schools built; Schenectady classified as a second-class city; Edison Club established

1909—Wallace Company started as firm bought out Reeves & Luffman; Second Reformed Church building at Liberty and Jay Streets razed for site of new post office; Woodlawn Reformed Church formed; County centennial celebrated

1910—Barnum & Bailey circus fire at McClellan Street grounds; new Second Reformed Church building dedicated

1911—South Building of Schenectady High on Nott Terrace finished; Dr. George R. Lunn, Socialist, elected mayor; trolley strike during week of Oct. 21; GE announced 36,000 people on payroll; Wallace Company built new addition on west side; new post office (Federal Building) under construction; Henry Schaffer opened first store in Schenectady; Brown Furniture Company built five-floor building at State Street and the canal; Daily Union and Evening Star merged to become Schenectady Union-Star

1912—New Schenectady post office completed; First Glenridge Tuberculosis Sanatorium built; free text books provided for the first time in Schenectady public schools; the first Proctor's Theater (later to be named Wedgeway and Erie) opened Easter week; Odd Fellows Hall dedicated at State and Hawk Streets; Calvary Baptist Church cornerstone ceremony held; GE began pension system; Eugene V. Debbs, Socialist candidate for president, spoke in Schenectady; free trash pickup started in city

1913—New county courthouse opened; Schenectady Railway's new waiting room opened; Alco phased out auto and truck production; City Dept. of Education moved into 108 Union Street

1914—New county jail opened on Veeder Avenue; record river flooding in March caused much destruction; work was in progress for development of Central Park; Bevis Hill Reservoir in Niskayuna constructed; new Union College gymnasium opened; Hamilton, Van Corlaer, Yates and Excelsior (Woodlawn) Schools were built; Mica Insulator Company building opened

1915—Schenectady YMCA conducted its first summer camp at Lake George's Camp Chingachgook; new Christ Church building dedicated at State and Swan Streets

1916—Erie Barge Canal began operations; Morris Plan Company of Schenectady formed and located at 512 State Street; the Carl Company moved to its new store at 430 State Street

1917—Masonic Order purchased Brown Furniture Building for Masonic Temple; Erie Canal officially closed; first Schenectady contingent of draftees left for Fort Devens, Mass.; first of several Liberty Bond campaigns held; Ex-President William Howard Taft officiated at groundbreaking ceremony for All Souls Unitarian Church building at Union Street and Wendell Avenue

1918—Schenectady General Army Depot under construction in Rotterdam; All Souls Unitarian Church building dedicated; Spanish influenza epidemic hit Schenectady as it did nationally, lasting several months killing 404 of about 15,000 flu patients in this county; a month-long trolley strike resulted in five cents an hour more for SRC motormen and conductors; morning-long parade of happy citizens downtown when word was received early November 11 of armistice ending World War I

1919—Companies E and F welcomed home to Schenectady from France in parade up State Street to state armory; first automobile show held in Schenectady; Schenectady Trust Company opened new building at 316-318 State Street

1920—Congregation Temple Gates of Heaven moved to Rugby Road and Parkwood Boulevard; IGE Building 36 opened; Woestina High School built in Rotterdam Junction; Morris Plan moved to 131 Wall Street

1921—Hiker Monument unveiled in Central Park; Schenectady's first railroad depot, long used as a residence on Crane Street, was demolished

1922—Radio Station WGY went on the air from IGE Building 36 studios; George R. Lunn became lieutenant governor with Alfred E. Smith as governor of New York State; State Theater opened; Pleasant Valley School opened; Christian Assembly (Italian—English Pentecostal church) established; Schonowe Golf Course opened in Scotia; work on Van Curler Hotel construction started

1923—Charles P. Steinmetz died; Broadway Methodist Church dedicated; Werner Alexanderson, son of Dr. and Mrs. E.F.W. Alexanderson, kidnapped but he was found and his abductors arrested; Ingersoll Memorial Home for Aged Men opened; Glenville Bank (later First National Bank of Scotia) founded; Riverside, Oneida and Central Park Schools built; St. Columba's School opened; Schenectady Chamber of Commerce organized; work on construction of Great Western Gateway Bridge under way; Boston Store burned on Broadway

1924—Erie Boulevard partially completed; Capitol Trust Bank opened; Hudson Theater reopened with Harry Bond Players

1925—Hotel Van Curler opened in April, Great Western Gateway Bridge that December; original Euclid School burned; Scotia Masonic Temple cornerstone laid; Erie Boulevard formally opened; Morris Plan became Industrial Bank of Schenectady and moved into 224 State Street; Union College's Memorial Chapel was dedicated Oct. 25; Edison Golf Course opened; Asia Restaurant at Smith and Broadway opened March 17; GE Building 37 was built and the GE Monogram sign mounted on its roof

1926—Eagles' Home on Franklin Street opened; week-long dedication of Great Western Gateway Bridge held; new Euclid School opened; new Proctor's Theatre opened Dec. 27; Schenectady YWCA purchased property on Washington Avenue; Union-Star building opened on Clinton Street; Eastern Parkway Methodist basement rooms dedicated; Harry Bond and Tedd Brackett killed

1927—Schenectady Airport opened; Charles A. Lindbergh visited here July 28 on tour, two months after his Atlantic solo flight; Schenectady YMCA downtown building opened; first home television demonstration held in Schenectady by Dr. E.F.W. Alexanderson

1928—Air mail service inaugurated at "Port Schenectady"

1929—City Hall construction began as old buildings in that area were razed; Ritz Theater in Scotia opened; new Central Fire Station on Erie Boulevard opened May 1; Sears-Roebuck store opened on Erie Boulevard; new Glenridge Hospital buildings opened; Amelia Earhart visited city, spoke over WGY; Our Redeemer Lutheran Church in Scotia dedicated

1930—Jay and Liberty Streets widened at new City Hall block

1931—New City Hall opened; Mont Pleasant High School opened in fall as old Schenectady High became Nott Terrace High School; Plaza Theater opened; Rexford Park closed; Harold Gatty and Wiley Post, round-the-world fliers, visited city; new Schenectady YWCA building on Washington Avenue dedicated; Trinity Reformed Church founded; buses replaced trolley car in some sectors

1932—Capitol Trust Company failed as depression was taking its toll in all directions; the election of Franklin D. Roosevelt over incumbent President Herbert Hoover resulted in hopes of a change for the better

1933—Major addition to Schenectady Post Office started with Works Progress Administration (WPA) funds; likewise, federal funding counted for building of the giant-tiered Klondike ramp in Pleasant Valley; Rexford Park facilities were torn down

1934—Schenectady Museum founded; Hudson Theater burned Dec. 18

1935—Municipal Golf Course opened; City of Schenectady adopted Plan C (City Manager) form of government; Glendale Home constructed on Hetcheltown Road; top two floors of Edison Hotel razed; Schenectady Post Office project completed

1936—New State Armory on Washington Avenue under construction; Vendome Hotel building corner of State and North Broadway razed

1937—Schenectady Savings & Loan moved into new building at 267 State Street; old Westinghouse farm machinery office razed for construction of new WGY studios at Rice Road and Washington Avenue; Schonowe Apartments construction under way

1938—Woolworth store opened on Vendome site; new WGY studio building dedicated; Calvary Orthodox Presbyterian Church founded; Christian Temple Church disbanded; FJ & G trolleys ceased operation here; new armory completed April 25, first occupied by National Guard July 10

1939—Steel trolley bridge to Scotia closed; Television Station WRGB began operations in IGE Building 36 studios

1940—Identification badge system began at GE for security

1941—National Guard federalized, first Schenectady contingent left for Fort McClellan; Bellevue Maternity Hospital opened on Troy Road site; city and county draft boards organized

1942—First blackout held in Schenectady County; War Price and Rationing Board established; Alco began production of M-3 "General Grant" tanks

1943—Van Curler Opera House hall razed; Scotia Naval Supply Depot opened

1944—Alco began production of M-4 "General Sherman" tanks and M-36

"Sluggers"; Steinmetz home on Wendell Avenue torn down and a park in his honor established; Television Station WRGB moved into former Edison Club building on lower State Street

1945—First contingent of homecoming "G.I.s" welcomed; County Welfare Department established

1946—Lengthy strike at GE; Schenectady Railway Company removed last of electric streetcars from service

1947—Old state armory demolished; St. Stephen's Episcopal Church parish organized and church construction started; Steelworkers Local 2054 struck at Alco; old Crescent Park fountain removed; Lincoln Heights apartments project under way

1948—First Reformed Church burned in frigid night of Feb. 1; construction began on new St. Clare's Hospital; Air National Guard began operations at Schenectady County Airport; Crescent Park bandstand razed; County Public Library system established; President Harry S. Truman paid a campaign call

1949—Knolls Atomic Power Laboratory (KAPL) opened

1950—Mayor's Going-Away Committee formed to honor departing draftees

1951—Streetcar tracks removed from downtown State Street which was paved over with blacktop; American Legion Post 21 opened headquarters at 740 Union Street; Schenectady Railway Company filed bankruptcy; Eastern Parkway Methodist dedicated new sanctuary

1952—Nott Terrace widened; Schenectady Transportation Corporation founded

1953—Remainder of old Van Curler Opera House razed; Grout Park and Paige Schools built; Pulaski Plaza dedicated on site of old state armory; Dwight D. Eisenhower spoke in Schenectady on his presidential campaign trail

1954—Schenectady Little Leaguers won Little League World Championship at Williamsport, Pa.; New York State Thruway opened; city voters approved elected school board system, separating city and school administration

1955—Alco diversification created a new name: ALCO Products; Zoller School built; IUE Hall on Liberty Street torn down

1956—Temple Gates of Heaven congregation dedicated new synagogue on Ashmore Avenue and Eastern Parkway; Linton High School construction under way; Mohawk National Bank remodeled and enlarged State Street building

1957—Urban Renewal Project started east of City Hall; Senior Citizens Center founded with headquarters in former German Methodist Church at Union and Lafayette Streets; WGY-WRGB-WGFM moved into new Balltown Road studios; Senior Citizen's Center opened

1958—Linton High School completed and opened for classes in January; First Baptist Church moved to 1944 Union Street; Freihofer horse and wagon deliveries came to an end

1959—New Schenectady Savings & Loan Bank building constructed on site of Van Horne Hall

1960—Union College's Schaffer Library completed; John F. Kennedy and Richard M. Nixon visited Schenectady on campaign stopoffs; J.

Glen Sanders of Scotia died; tornado ripped through Schenectady County afternoon of July 24 causing extensive damage

1961—Glenridge Hospital observed 50th anniversary; Glen Sanders Mansion sold to private interest

1962—New County Office Building opened; South building of Nott Terrace High School demolished, North building remained for elementary classes; Hallmark Nursing Center opened

1963—Union College's Washburn Hall razed; Erie Theater likewise; County observance of Civil War Centennial held; Stanford Golf Course sold for mall development

1964—Remodeled County Judicial Building opened; Plaza Theater demolished; McLane's Hotel in Rexford razed; work started on widening of Route 146 through Rexford and construction of a new bridge at the aqueduct; ice storm starting night of December 3 caused by freezing rain, raising havoc with falling trees, loss of power lines and accidents

1965—Celebrated blackout occurred throughout northeast night of Nov. 9 lasting from 5:19 p.m. to 8:30 p.m., caused by power failure in grid system at Niagara Falls; Schenectady County adopted county manager (charter) form of government

1967—Civic efforts fail to purchase Glen Sanders Mansion as historic site

1968—ALCO doors closed by Studebaker-Worthington, ending the locomotive industry in Schenectady after 120 years; Hotel Van Curler closed but sold to Schenectady County for community college; Stanford Golf Course closed; Interstate 890 opened in Schenectady

1969—Schenectady County Public Library building opened on Liberty Street; Union Station closed; new Rexford Bridge opened on Route 146; Schenectady County Community College began first semester; Union-Star bought by Hearst Newspapers and moved to Albany as Knickerbocker Union-Star

1970—Mohawk Mall opened on Stanford Golf Course site; Glenville and Rotterdam observe town sesqui-centennials; county took over bus lines; Union College went co-educational

1971—Liberty Flag raising ceremony at First Reformed Church; Union-Star building on Clinton Street razed; historic GE Building 12 demolished

1972—Lorraine Block torn down; County Bicentennial Commission formed; downtown Grant's folded; Woodlawn Middle School built; Union Station razed; Strand Theater razed for construction of Albany Savings Bank building; Maqua closed; work began on major addition to St. Clare's Hospital

1971—New Western Gateway Bridge opened to public; Barney's, Wallace's and Kresge stores closed; new city police station opened; Off Track Betting operation started in former police station; Salvation Army dedicated new headquarters; crowds gathered about the Union College campus as cameramen were shooting scenes for the movie, "The Way We Were"

1974—FOCUS organized for downtown redevelopment; old Western Gateway Bridge demolished; St. Clare's Hospital addition opened;

Myer's Shop, Vinick's Clothing and Richardson Luggage closed shop

1975—City school offices moved to Brandywine School, vacating 108 Union Street that was later purchased by the Lawrence (Insurance) Group; Ellis Building corner of State and Erie Boulevard torn down; Nicholaus German Restaurant closed

1976—Bicentennial celebrations held in city and townships; Freedom Park in Scotia dedicated and opened in one-week festival July 18-24; Kerste's Drug Store closed; Nicholaus Building damaged by explosion and up for sale, later occupied by Maurice's Redi-Foods; Jimmy Carter, seeking nomination at the Democratic convention, stopped at Union College in April which he attended in the early 1950s as a young naval officer; Annie Schaffer Center opened June 14

1977—Huge paving lot covered northeast corner of State and Boulevard; the former R.C. Reynolds Building (later Breslaw Furniture) and former H.S. Barney warehouse were renovated as modern apartment complexes; Hotel Schenectady (former Mohawk Hotel) demolished

1978—The 400 Block on State Street from Broadway to Clinton, was being changed into storefronts with similar colors; Proctor's Theatre remained active in Broadway shows, movies and special events; Ellis Hospital parking garage opened

1979—Downtown Festival Day promoted by Chamber of Commerce and Downtown Merchants Association drew onlookers; Mohawk River regatta; downtown becoming noticeably in bad straits with fewer stores and shoppers along its main stem.

1980—New construction gives modern look to Ellis Hospital; Canal Square developed rear of 400 Block; Hulett Street bridge taken down

1981—Construction of modern four-lane Freeman's Bridge begun; new Cotton Factory Hollow Bridge opened Aug. 11, new central fire station opened on Veeder Avenue

1982—Warehouse on site of former Naval Depot outside Scotia in full swing

1983—City Hall clock tower burned; Karen B. Johnson elected as Schenectady's first woman mayor

1984—Downtown renovation project began between Broadway and Lafayette Street; Jay Street from Franklin Street developed as pedestrian mall; former Barney Company store remodeled as apartment building; new Freeman's Bridge opened June 26; Yates Village underwent extensive repairs

1985—Ellis Hospital celebrated its centennial; new City Hall tower and clock installation completed; State Theater demolished

1986—Wilmorite Corporation began construction of Rotterdam Square after old Campbell Mansion was demolished off Campbell Road; historic GE Building 10 razed

1987—Century-old Lawrence the Indian statue reinstated in Stockade after overhaul; efforts made to improve Hamilton Hill conditions; Sarnowksi home on Freeman's Bridge Road razed and Stewart's

Store erected

1988—Rotterdam Square Mall opened Sept.1; Bigsbee School razed

1989—Sears-Roebuck store on Erie Boulevard closed; new county jail on Veeder Avenue completed

1990—Schenectady County Community College campus underwent $11 million expansion; Daily Gazette moved from State Street to new facility on Maxon Road; First Baptist Church of Scotia celebrated its sesqui-centennial

1991—Broadway Center building on Broadway completed; old Hamburg Street Bridge in Carman demolished and new construction began; Carl Company stores closed

1992—Ten Eyck Apartments on Broadway undergoing reconstruction and renovation; Civil War soldier's monument given extensive cleaning

1993—New Hamburg Street Bridge opened

1994—The Polish National Alliance Hall and Marcella's Appliance store on Crane Street demolished and work begun on new Rite Aid pharmacy and a Marcella's store on that site. The PNA was opened in 1932, while Marcella's building was once the Pearl Theater; Woolworth's store at State and North Broadway closed after 56 years

1995—Renovation work on Union College's 123-year-old Nott Memorial building completed as college celebrated its bi-centennial; most buildings demolished in State Street block from Lafayette Street to Nott Terrace with plans for World Trade Center development; Schaffer Heights apartments beside Annie Schaffer Senior Center opened on Eastern Avenue; Liberty Park on lower State Street given facelift; Muncipal Golf Course's 60th birthday celebrated

ACKNOWLEDGMENTS

When the first edition of this book was published in 1974, it was intended as a story of what went on in the five decades between 1880 and 1930. There was no printing after the third edition in 1976, although local schools and libraries kept copies as more of a composite history of Schenectady's most memorable era. The chronology of historical events from the very start of its settlement up to the present, I've been told, was a useful feature for those interested in the total picture, dates included.

With this in mind, I have enlarged on some of the features and brought them up to date, including the chronological portion. In the first edition I acknowledged those of gave willingly of their time, talent and recollection. I shall do that herewith but solemnly, keeping in mind that in these 20 years many are deceased.

Those who shared their memories of various subjects contained within include Albert P. Bantham, Walter J. Reagles, Nicholas Dinardo, Miss Celia Rhein, Joseph S. Hayden, Emil J. Remscheid, Harry H. Hart Sr., Arthur Sausville, Paul Gay, Harold E. Blodgett, Harold "Doc" Clowe, William F. Eddy, Miss Cora Robinson, Mrs. Samuel Dickhoff, Ernest A. R. Cohen, Lewis B. Sebring Jr., Mrs. Earl W. Henion, David Washburn, Ralph M. Turner, Leslie and Cecile Brooks, and Oliver J. Lendrum.

Help on documentation of certain subjects was given by Bill Duffy, William Baird, Mrs. Lola M. Weeks, Charles Abba, Dr. James M. Blake, Joseph Spencer, Eugene Blesser, Barney Waldron, Judge Archibald C. Wemple, Miss Jane McCully, Stewart A. Vanda, Joseph A. Flora, Arthur D. Hilliard, Kenneth E. Buhrmaster, Joseph Dutcher, Herman Zamjohn and John Sauerborn.

Lastly, we would be remiss in failing to acknowledge the tremendous amount of historical research done by the late William B. Efner over the years, a city historian who was diligent in his job because he loved it. Without the groundwork he laid through persistence and hard work, we would not today be able to walk as easily down the pathways of time nor could we so thoroughly enjoy the sights along the way. That is why we are dedicating this volume to his memory.